MATH Trailblazers®

A BALANCED MATHEMATICS PROGRAM INTEGRATING SCIENCE AND LANGUAGE ARTS

Unit Resource Guide
Unit 2
Big Numbers

THIRD EDITION

KENDALL/HUNT PUBLISHING COMPANY
4050 Westmark Drive   Dubuque, Iowa   52002

A TIMS® Curriculum
University of Illinois at Chicago

UIC The University of Illinois
at Chicago

The original edition was based on work supported by the National Science Foundation under grant
No. MDR 9050226 and the University of Illinois at Chicago. Any opinions, findings, and conclusions
or recommendations expressed in this publication are those of the author(s) and do not necessarily
reflect the views of the granting agencies.

Letter Home

Big Numbers

Date: _____

Dear Family Member:

Big numbers occur every day in real life. Newspapers often report government spending in the billions. The population of the United States is in the hundred millions while that of China is more than a billion. The activities in this unit will help students better understand the size of numbers and how to work with them.

A major theme of this unit is computation. Students begin their review of multiplication and division facts. Paper-and-pencil methods of multiplication are reviewed, and estimation strategies are developed. You can help your child study multiplication and division fact families for the fives and tens with the *Triangle Flash Cards.*

Your child will end this unit by beginning a portfolio that will show his or her mathematical growth throughout the year.

Please contact me if you have any questions or comments.

Sincerely,

_____

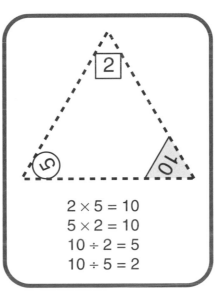

$2 \times 5 = 10$
$5 \times 2 = 10$
$10 \div 2 = 5$
$10 \div 5 = 2$

A fact family represented by a
Triangle Flash Card

Carta al hogar

Números Grandes

Fecha: _____

Estimado miembro de familia:

Los números grandes se usan todos los días en la vida real. Los periódicos a menudo informan acerca de gastos del gobierno que alcanzan los miles de millones. La población de los Estados Unidos es de cientos de millones, mientras que la de la China es de más de mil millones. Las actividades de esta unidad ayudarán a los estudiantes a entender mejor el tamaño de los números y cómo trabajar con ellos.

Uno de los temas principales de esta unidad son los cálculos. Los estudiantes empiezan a repasar las tablas de multiplicación y división. Se repasan métodos de multiplicación con lápiz y papel, y se desarrollan estrategias de estimación. Usted puede ayudar a su hijo/a a estudiar las tablas de multiplicación y división por cinco y diez con las *tarjetas triangulares*.

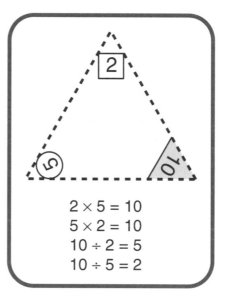

$2 \times 5 = 10$
$5 \times 2 = 10$
$10 \div 2 = 5$
$10 \div 5 = 2$

Los conceptos relacionados representados por una *tarjeta triangular*

Al terminar esta unidad, su hijo/a empezará un portafolio que se usará para mostrar su avance en las matemáticas durante el año.

Por favor comuníquese conmigo si tiene alguna pregunta o comentario.

Atentamente,

_____

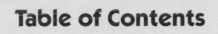

Table of Contents

Unit 2
Big Numbers

Unit 2

Outline

Big Numbers

Unit Summary

Students complete activities that involve reading and writing big numbers, using convenient numbers to estimate products, using paper and pencil to multiply, and reading scientific notation. This unit also provides opportunities to gather baseline data on students' mathematical abilities in these areas. Activities from fourth grade allow students to use base-ten pieces to review place value and addition and subtraction as needed. An Adventure Book, *Sand Reckoning,* tells the story of Archimedes and his estimate for the number of grains of sand needed to fill the universe. A short assessment problem, *Stack Up,* provides baseline data on students' abilities to solve multistep problems and communicate their solution strategies. The Student Rubrics: *Telling* and *Solving* are reintroduced and students begin collection folders to make portfolios. The yearlong review of the multiplication and division facts begins in this unit. Students use fact families to review the multiplication and division facts for the fives and tens.

Major Concept Focus

- addition and subtraction review
- place value
- multiplication with ending zeros
- big numbers
- paper-and-pencil multiplication
- estimation
- measuring length in centimeters
- exponents
- convenient numbers for computations
- scientific notation
- Student Rubrics: *Telling* and *Solving*
- using data to solve problems
- communicating solution strategies
- portfolios
- multiplication and division facts: 5s and 10s

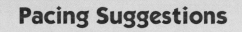

Pacing Suggestions

This unit is designed to be completed in 15 to 21 days. Students' knowledge of place value, familiarity with base-ten pieces, and computational skills will determine how quickly the class completes the unit.

- In Lesson 2, students assess their fluency with the multiplication and division facts and begin a systematic review of the facts they need to study. They continue their review in the Daily Practice and Problems in this and succeeding units. In this unit they review the multiplication and division facts for the 5s and 10s. All students should continue learning new concepts and skills while reviewing the facts. For more information, see the TIMS Tutor: *Math Facts* in the *Teacher Implementation Guide*. (This review of the facts is also available in the *Grade 5 Facts Resource Guide*.)

- **Use Lesson 3 or Lesson 4, but not both.** Both lessons review place value. Lesson 3 *The Base-Ten Number System* reviews place value, addition, and subtraction with base-ten pieces using material from fourth grade. Use Lesson 3 if students did not use *Math Trailblazers*® in previous grades. This will prepare them to use base-ten pieces in Grade 5 in lessons on multiplication and division. If students had *Math Trailblazers* in previous grades, use Lesson 4 *The Chinese Abacus* to review place value.

- For the remaining lessons, take advantage of the distributed practice and content spiral built into the curriculum. Move through the lessons using the minimum number of class sessions if students are familiar with *Math Trailblazers.* If they are not, use the maximum number of days as needed. Students will continue reviewing skills in the Daily Practice and Problems (in each *Unit Resource Guide*) and Home Practice (in the *Discovery Assignment Book*).

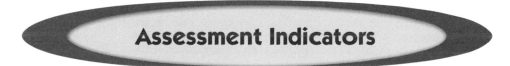

Assessment Indicators

Use the following Assessment Indicators and the *Observational Assessment Record* that follows the Background section in this unit to assess students on key ideas.

A1. Can students compare and order large numbers?

A2. Can students read and write large numbers?

A3. Can students multiply using paper and pencil?

A4. Can students multiply numbers with ending zeros mentally?

A5. Can students estimate products?

A6. Can students solve open-response problems and communicate solution strategies?

A7. Do students demonstrate fluency with the multiplication and division facts for the 5s and 10s?

Unit Planner

KEY: SG = Student Guide, DAB = Discovery Assignment Book, AB = Adventure Book, URG = Unit Resource Guide, DPP = Daily Practice and Problems, HP = Home Practice (found in Discovery Assignment Book), and TIG = Teacher Implementation Guide.

	Lesson Information	Supplies	Copies/Transparencies
Lesson 1 **Reading and Writing Big Numbers** URG Pages 32–48 SG Pages 26–34 DAB Pages 13–19 DPP A–D HP Part 2 *Estimated Class Sessions* **2-3**	**Activity** Students review reading and writing big numbers and use estimation skills to locate numbers on a number line. They play a game to practice reading large numbers. **Math Facts** Continue review of addition and subtraction facts as needed for individual students. **Homework** 1. Assign the Homework section in the *Student Guide.* 2. Assign the *Writing Big Numbers* Activity Page in the *Discovery Assignment Book.* 3. Assign the *Spin and Read Number Game.* 4. Assign Part 2 of the Home Practice. **Assessment** Use the Reading and Writing Big Numbers section of the *Student Guide* to assess writing numbers.	• 1 calculator per student • playing cards, optional • 1 clear plastic spinner or pencil and paper clip per student group	• 4 copies of *Digit Cards 0–9* URG Pages 43–44 per student group copied back to back • 1 transparency of *Population Lines* DAB Page 15, optional • 1 transparency of *Place Value Chart* DAB Page 19
Lesson 2 **Facts I Know** URG Pages 49–65 SG Pages 35–38 DAB Pages 21–24 DPP E–F HP Part 1 *Estimated Class Sessions* **1-2**	**Assessment Activity** This lesson launches the yearlong review of the multiplication and division facts that will continue in the DPP. **Homework** Assign Part 1 of the Home Practice that asks students to practice the math facts. **Assessment** 1. Students use flash cards and *Facts I Know* charts to assess themselves on the multiplication and division facts. 2. Record your observations on the *Observational Assessment Record.*	• 1 ruler per student • 1 pair of scissors per student and 1 pair for the teacher	• 1 copy of *Multiplication* and *Division Facts I Know* charts URG Pages 61–62 per student • 1 copy of *Information for Parents: Grade 5 Math Facts Philosophy* URG Pages 13–14 per student • 1 copy of *Centimeter Dot Paper* URG Page 63 per student • 1 transparency of *Triangle Flash Cards: 5s* DAB Page 21 • 1 transparency of *Triangle Flash Cards: 10s* DAB Page 23 • 1 transparency of *Centimeter Dot Paper* URG Page 63 • 1 copy of *Observational Assessment Record* URG Pages 15–16 to be used throughout this unit
Lesson 3 **The Base-Ten Number System** URG Pages 66–105 DPP G–J *Estimated Class Sessions* **2-3**	OPTIONAL LESSON DO EITHER LESSON 3 OR LESSON 4 **Optional Activity** This optional lesson reviews place value concepts using materials from fourth grade. This lesson is broken into three parts. In part 1, students represent numbers with base-ten pieces and review the Fewest Pieces Rule. In parts 2 and 3, students review the addition and subtraction algorithms by modeling these operations with the pieces. **Math Facts** Assign DPP item I.	• 1 set of base-ten pieces (2 packs, 14 flats, 30 skinnies, 50 bits) or 2 copies of bits and skinnies *Base-Ten Pieces Master* and 3 copies of flats and packs *Base-Ten Pieces Master* URG Pages 87–88 per student pair	• 1 copy of *The Base-Ten Number System* URG Pages 79–83 per student • 1 copy of *Addition with Base-Ten Pieces* URG Pages 89–91 per student • 1 copy of *Subtraction with Base-Ten Pieces* URG Pages 92–95 per student • 1 copy of *Recording Sheet* URG Page 86 per student

	Lesson Information	**Supplies**	**Copies/ Transparencies**
	Homework Assign the Homework sections in *The Base-Ten Number System, Addition with Base-Ten Pieces,* and *Subtraction with Base-Ten Pieces* Activity Pages.	• 40 connecting cubes per student group, optional • 1 pair of scissors per student group, optional • tape • overhead base-ten pieces, optional	• 1 copy of *Base-Ten Board Part 1* URG Page 84 per student group • 1 copy of *Base-Ten Board Part 2* URG Page 85 per student group • 1 transparency of *Recording Sheet* URG Page 86, optional • 1 transparency of *Base-Ten Board Part 1* URG Page 84, optional

Lesson 4

The Chinese Abacus

URG Pages 106–130
SG Pages 39–45
DPP G–J

Estimated Class Sessions
2-3

OPTIONAL LESSON
DO EITHER LESSON 3 OR LESSON 4

Optional Activity
Students construct and use an abacus to represent numbers. They compare place value on the abacus to our base-ten number system.

Math Facts
Assign DPP item I.

Homework
1. Assign **Question 1** in the Homework section of the *Student Guide.* Students need two copies of the *Abacus Pictures* Activity Page to complete the assignment.
2. Assign **Questions 2–13** in the Homework section of the *Student Guide.* Students may use their abacus to solve the problems.

Assessment
Use the *Number Changes* Assessment Pages to assess students' understanding of place value as modeled on the abacus.

• 1 piece of cardboard 14 cm by 24 cm per student
• 11 pieces of string 16 cm long per student
• 77 pony beads or ditali macaroni pieces per student
• 1 strip of half-inch masking tape 24 cm long per student
• 1 pair of scissors per student
• 1 cm ruler per student
• overhead abacus

• 1 copy of *Column Place Value Guides* URG Page 122 per student
• several copies of *Abacus Pictures* URG Page 123 per student
• 1 copy of *Number Changes* URG Pages 120–121 per student
• 1 transparency of *Column Place Value Guides* URG Page 122
• 1 transparency of *Abacus Pictures* URG Page 123

Lesson 5

Multiplication

URG Pages 131–156
SG Pages 46–55
DPP K–T
HP Part 3

Estimated Class Sessions
5

Activity
Students multiply large numbers with ending zeros and look for patterns. They then review the all-partials method of multiplication as well as the traditional multiplication algorithm (the compact method).

Math Facts
Assign items M, O, and Q and review the multiplication and division facts for the 5s and 10s.

Homework
Assign the Homework section in the *Student Guide.*

Assessment
Use the *Making Money* Assessment Pages as a quiz.

• 1 set of base-ten pieces per student group
• overhead base-ten pieces, optional

• 1 copy of *Making Money* URG Pages 147–149 per student
• 1 table from *Multiplication Table* URG Page 146 per student
• 1 copy of *Base-Ten Board Part 1* and *2* URG Pages 84–85 per student, optional
• 1 copy of *Recording Sheet* URG Page 86 per student, optional
• 1 transparency of *Base-Ten Board Part 1* URG Page 84, optional
• 1 transparency of *Recording Sheet* URG Page 86, optional

(Continued)

	Lesson Information	**Supplies**	**Copies/Transparencies**

Lesson 6

Estimating Products

URG Pages 157–166
SG Pages 56–59

DPP U–V
HP Part 4

Estimated Class Sessions
1-2

Activity
Students use convenient numbers to estimate products. Computational estimation is explored.

Math Facts
Assign item U and continue reviewing the multiplication and division facts for the 5s and 10s.

Homework
1. Assign *Questions 1–20* in the Homework section of the *Student Guide*.
2. Assign Part 4 of the Home Practice.

Assessment
1. Use some of the homework problems as assessments.
2. Use DPP item V to assess fluency with paper-and-pencil multiplication.

• 1 table from *Multiplication Table* URG Page 146 per student

---

Lesson 7

Sand Reckoning

URG Pages 167–171
AB Pages 13–20

DPP W–X

Estimated Class Sessions
1

Adventure Book
Using a story about the ancient mathematician Archimedes, students are prompted to think about large numbers.

Math Facts
Assign DPP items W and X for more practice with the multiplication and division facts for the 5s and 10s.

Lesson 8

Exponents and Large Numbers

URG Pages 172–181
SG Pages 60–63

DPP Y–Z

Estimated Class Sessions
1-2

Activity
Students review the use of exponents and then learn to read large numbers written in scientific notation. They read numbers on their calculator displays that are the result of calculations with large numbers.

Math Facts
Assign item Y.

Homework
1. Assign *Questions 1–20* in the Homework section of the *Student Guide*.
2. Assign DPP Task Z.

Assessment
Use the open-ended assessment problem in Lesson 9 *Stack Up*.

• 1 calculator per student

	Lesson Information	Supplies	Copies/Transparencies
Lesson 9 **Stack Up** URG Pages 182–198 DPP AA–BB *Estimated Class Sessions* **1-2**	**Assessment Activity** Students solve an open-response problem by estimating the number of pennies it will take to make a stack that reaches the moon. **Math Facts** Complete DPP item AA and continue reviewing the multiplication and division facts for the 5s and 10s.	• 1 calculator per student • 20 pennies per student group • 1 ruler per student	• 1 copy of *Stack Up* URG Pages 195–196 per student • 1 copy of *Centimeter Graph Paper* URG Page 197 per student, optional • 1 copy of *TIMS Multidimensional Rubric* TIG, Assessment section • 1 transparency or poster of Student Rubrics: *Solving* and *Telling* TIG, Assessment section, optional
Lesson 10 **Portfolios** URG Pages 199–206 SG Pages 64–65 DPP CC–DD *Estimated Class Sessions* **1**	**Assessment Activity** Students begin the process of putting together a portfolio. **Math Facts** Complete DPP item CC. **Assessment** 1. Begin student portfolios as a selection of best work. 2. Transfer appropriate documentation of the Unit 2 *Observational Assessment Record* to students' *Individual Assessment Record Sheets*.	• 1 folder per student • hanging rack or box for storing folders	• 1 copy of *Individual Assessment Record Sheet* TIG Assessment section per student, previously copied for use throughout the year

Preparing for Upcoming Lessons

If you plan to complete the optional Lesson 4 *The Chinese Abacus,* collect cardboard, string, and pony beads or ditali noodles to make the abacuses.

Students will need 20 pennies per group to complete Lesson 9 *Stack Up.*

Students will use *Triangle Flash Cards* to review the multiplication and division facts in Lesson 2 *Facts I Know.* You may want to laminate these cards or have students cut them out ahead of time to save class instruction time. The cards are in the *Discovery Assignment Book* following the Home Practice for this unit and in the *Grade 5 Facts Resource Guide.*

A current list of literature and software connections is available at *www.mathtrailblazers.com*. You can also find information on connections in the *Teacher Implementation Guide* Literature List and Software List sections.

Literature Connections

Suggested Titles

- Cole, Joanna. *The Magic School Bus: Lost in the Solar System.* Scholastic Inc., New York, 1990. (Lesson 9)
- Jenkins, Steve. *Hottest, Coldest, Highest, Deepest.* Houghton Mifflin Company, Boston, 1998.
- Sandburg, Carl. *Complete Poems.* Harcourt, Brace, Jovanovich, New York, 1970. (Lesson 10)
- Schwartz, David M. *How Much Is a Million?* Scholastic Inc., New York, 1985. (Lesson 8)
- Schwartz, David M. *If You Made a Million.* Scholastic Inc., New York, 1989. (Lesson 9)
- Schwartz, David M. *On Beyond a Million.* Dragonfly Books, Cambridgeshire, UK, 2001.
- Simon, Seymour. *Our Solar System.* Morrow Junior Books, New York, 1992.
- *The World Almanac and Book of Facts 2000.* St. Martin's Press, NY, 1999.

Software Connections

- *Ice Cream Truck* develops problem solving, money skills, and arithmetic operations.
- *Math Arena* is a collection of math activities that reinforces many math concepts.
- *Math Munchers Deluxe* provides practice in basic facts in an arcade-like game. (Lesson 5)
- *Math Mysteries: Advanced Whole Numbers* is a series of structured multistep word problems dealing with whole numbers.
- *Math Mysteries: Whole Numbers* is a series of structured word problems dealing with whole numbers.
- *Mighty Math Calculating Crew* poses short answer questions about number operations.
- *Mighty Math Number Heroes* poses short answer questions about fractions and number operations.
- *National Library of Virtual Manipulatives* website (http://matti.usu.edu) allows students to work with manipulatives including geoboards, base-ten pieces, the abacus, and many others.
- *Number Facts Fire Zapper* provides practice in number facts in an arcade-like game.
- *Number Sense and Problem Solving: Puzzle Tanks* develops logical thinking while practicing math facts.
- *Ten Tricky Tiles* provides practice with number facts through engaging puzzles.

Math Trailblazers lessons are designed for students with a wide range of abilities. The lessons are flexible and do not require significant adaptation for diverse learning styles or academic levels. However, when needed, lessons can be tailored to allow students to engage their abilities to the greatest extent possible while building knowledge and skills.

To assist you in meeting the needs of all students in your classroom, this section contains information about some of the features in the curriculum that allow all students access to mathematics. For additional information, see the Teaching the *Math Trailblazers* Student: Meeting Individual Needs section in the *Teacher Implementation Guide*.

Differentiation Opportunities in this Unit

Games

Use games to promote or extend understanding of math concepts and to practice skills with children who need more practice.

- *Spin and Read Number Game* from Lesson 1 *Reading and Writing Big Numbers*

Journal Prompts

Journal prompts provide opportunities for students to explain and reflect on mathematical problems. They can help both students who need practice explaining their ideas and students who benefit from answering higher order questions. Students with various learning styles can express themselves using pictures, words, and sentences. Teachers can alter journal prompts to suit students' ability levels. The following lessons contain a journal prompt:

- Lesson 1 *Reading and Writing Big Numbers*
- Lesson 4 *The Chinese Abacus*
- Lesson 5 *Multiplication*
- Lesson 7 *Sand Reckoning*
- Lesson 9 *Stack Up*

DPP Challenges

DPP Challenges are items from the Daily Practice and Problems that usually take more than fifteen minutes to complete. These problems are more thought-provoking and can be used to stretch students' problem-solving skills. The following lessons have DPP Challenges in them:

- DPP Challenge B from Lesson 1 *Reading and Writing Big Numbers*
- DPP Challenge J from Lesson 3 *The Base-Ten Number System* and Lesson 4 *The Chinese Abacus*
- DPP Challenges N and P from Lesson 5 *Multiplication*

Extensions

Use extensions to enrich lessons. Many extensions provide opportunities to further involve or challenge students of all abilities. Take a moment to review the extensions prior to beginning this unit. Some extensions may require additional preparation and planning. The following lessons contain extensions:

- Lesson 1 *Reading and Writing Big Numbers*
- Lesson 3 *The Base-Ten Number System*
- Lesson 4 *The Chinese Abacus*
- Lesson 5 *Multiplication*
- Lesson 10 *Portfolios*

Background
Big Numbers

The major focus of this unit is big numbers. You will also gather baseline assessment data on students' current mathematical knowledge and skills.

Students review place value concepts and computation. Estimation is emphasized. A yearlong, systematic review of the multiplication and division facts begins. Students' current abilities to solve open-ended problems and communicate their solutions are assessed. Finally, to provide evidence of the knowledge and skills students bring to fifth grade, important pieces of student work are placed in portfolios. This will help you assess students' progress throughout the year.

Big Numbers and Estimation

Big numbers occur every day in real life. The newspaper is filled with reports with numbers often in the billions. The population of the United States is in the hundreds of millions while that of China is more than a billion. How many more people are there in China? How many times would all the people in the United States fit into China? These are questions that children in the fifth grade can consider as they develop a sense of perspective of the world around them. The beginning activities focus on the magnitude of numbers in the millions and billions, so that students' work with large numbers is meaningful.

In this unit, children compare and estimate large numbers by identifying the closest thousand, ten thousand, and so on. Problems are formulated to discourage the often-observed practice of finding an exact answer and then rounding. Children are encouraged instead to use estimation to check whether their answers are reasonable. It is stressed that usually only estimates are needed when working with large numbers in real life.

Review of Place Value and Computation

Research shows that students who use manipulatives to construct large quantities develop a conceptual understanding of multiunits such as one hundred and one thousand (Fuson, 1992). It is useful to spend some time reviewing place value concepts and representing numbers and operations using different tools (e.g., base-ten pieces, base-ten shorthand, and place value charts).

The *Math Trailblazers* fourth-grade curriculum includes extensive work with the base-ten pieces to build understanding of number and operations. If your students did not work with base-ten pieces to develop place value, complete Lesson 3, an optional lesson that reviews these concepts. In Lesson 5 children use the pieces to review the concept of multiplication. In Unit 4, division is discussed in the context of the base-ten pieces.

Base-ten pieces. In previous grades, the base-ten pieces were given nicknames: the **bit** (1 cm × 1 cm × 1 cm), the **skinny** (1 cm × 1 cm × 10 cm), the **flat** (1 cm × 10 cm × 10 cm), and the **pack** (10 cm × 10 cm × 10 cm). Teachers and students used a common shorthand to depict each base-ten piece when communicating their methods for solving problems. The nicknames distinguish the pieces from the quantities they represent. By using nicknames, the blocks can also represent decimals. When modeling whole numbers, the bit has a value of one unit, the skinny is ten, the flat is 100, and the pack is 1000. Figure 1 shows the pieces, their value when the smallest piece has a value of one unit, and the corresponding shorthand for each piece. When modeling decimals, other pieces besides the bit can represent one whole. For example, if the flat is designated as one whole, the skinny is one-tenth and the bit is one-hundredth.

Nickname	Standard Name	Value	Picture	Shorthand
bit	one	1	⬚	•
skinny	ten	10	▭	/
flat	hundred	100	▱	⬭
pack	thousand	1000	◻	⬭

Figure 1: *Base-ten pieces*

Paper-and-pencil methods. Children first review multiplication with base-ten pieces. This unit also reviews two paper and pencil methods for multiplication—the **all-partials method** and the more traditional **compact method** as shown in Figure 2.

All-partials method   Compact method

$$
\begin{array}{r}
186 \\
\times 3 \\
\hline
18 \\
240 \\
300 \\
\hline
558
\end{array}
$$

$$
\begin{array}{r}
{}^{2\,1}186 \\
\times 3 \\
\hline
558
\end{array}
$$

Figure 2: *Two methods of multiplication*

You may choose to have students concentrate on the all-partials method and not discuss the compact method. Because all intermediate computations are recorded, the all-partials method is easier to understand than the compact method. It also promotes estimation skills.

Whether or not you choose to do both algorithms, it is not essential to spend too long on learning computation methods here. There will be plenty of opportunity for students to practice and refine their skills throughout the year.

NCTM's *Principles and Standards for School Mathematics* calls for students to multiply and divide whole numbers fluently. Students are also expected to select appropriate methods and tools for computing from among mental computation, estimation, paper and pencil, and calculators. As stated in the NCTM document, "Although the expectation is that students develop fluency in computing with whole numbers, frequently they should use calculators to solve complex computations involving large numbers or as part of an extended problem." (p. 155).

The *Math Trailblazers* curriculum reflects that view. By the end of fifth grade, students using *Math Trailblazers* are expected to demonstrate fluency with paper-and-pencil procedures for multiplying and dividing relatively small whole numbers (2-digit factors and divisors). They also develop facility with mental calculations and estimation involving multiplication and division of larger numbers. These skills, in combination with a strong problem-solving strand, allow students to select appropriate methods and tools for computing. In most cases, a good estimate is all we need when working with large numbers. When an exact answer is required for a product or quotient of two large numbers, a calculator is the tool of choice.

Computational Estimation

When computing with large numbers, it may be necessary or more appropriate to estimate, rather than find an exact answer. Computational estimation involves replacing the original number or numbers in a problem with more "convenient" numbers and then computing (usually mentally) with these numbers. For example, one apple costs 37 cents. To estimate the cost of 4 apples we might round 37 cents to 40 cents then multiply 4 × 40 cents mentally. The convenient number we chose here was 40 cents. This type of estimating is an important life skill. When discussing estimation, it is important to emphasize that different estimates may be reasonable. For more information about computational estimation as well as other types of estimation, see the TIMS Tutor: *Estimation, Accuracy, and Error* in the *Teacher Implementation Guide.*

Multiplication and Division Facts

In Unit 1, students reviewed the addition and subtraction facts through items in the Daily Practice and Problems. Lesson 2 of this unit begins a systematic, strategies-based approach to reviewing the multiplication and division facts. This builds on multiplication and division work in previous grades. The formal review of the math facts will continue in the Daily Practice and Problems and Home Practice in each succeeding unit. For more information on the distribution of math fact practice, assessment, and descriptions of strategies, see the *Grade 5 Facts Resource Guide.* Information is also in the TIMS Tutor: *Math Facts* in the *Teacher Implementation Guide* and the DPP guide in this unit. To inform parents about the curriculum's goals and philosophy of learning and assessing the math facts, send home a copy of the *Math Facts Philosophy: Information for Parents,* which immediately follows the Unit Background.

Baseline Assessment and Portfolios

Each student is valued for the knowledge and skills he or she brings to the mathematics classroom, and each student is expected to make significant gains throughout the year. To provide an ongoing record of this growth, it is useful to collect examples of student work now and as the year progresses. In Unit 1 students placed their completed labs in their collection folders in preparation for beginning formal portfolios. In this unit, the problem *Stack Up* in Lesson 9 can be added to collection folders as a record of students' current problem-solving and communication skills. In Lesson 10, students organize their portfolios by choosing items from their collection folders, create a Table of Contents, and write about the pieces they include. By including these early attempts in their portfolios, any improvement in work on similar problems solved later in the year can provide evidence of mathematical growth.

Resources

- *Assessment Standards for School Mathematics.* National Council of Teachers of Mathematics, Reston, VA, 1989.
- Fuson, Karen. "Research on Whole Number Addition and Subtraction." In *Handbook of Research on Mathematics Teaching and Learning,* ed. D.A. Grouws, pp. 243–275. Macmillan Publishing Company, New York, 1992.
- Hiebert, J., T. Carpenter, E. Fennema, K. Fuson, D. Wearne, H. Murray, A. Olivier, and H. Piet. *Making Sense: Teaching and Learning Mathematics with Understanding.* Heinemann, Portsmouth, 1997.
- Isaacs, A.C., and W.M. Carroll. "Strategies for Basic-Facts Instruction." *Teaching Children Mathematics,* 5 (9), pp. 508–515, 1999.
- Kilpatrick, J., J. Swafford, and B. Findell (Eds.) *Adding It Up: Helping Children Learn Mathematics.* National Academy Press, Washington, DC, 2001.
- Payne, J.N. (Ed.) *Mathematics for the Young Child.* National Council of Teachers of Mathematics, Reston, VA, 1990.
- *Principles and Standards for School Mathematics.* National Council of Teachers of Mathematics, Reston, VA, 2000.
- Sowder, Judith. *Estimation and Number Sense.* In *Handbook of Research on Mathematics Teaching and Learning,* ed. D.A. Grouws, pp. 371–389. Macmillan Publishing Company, New York, 1992.
- Stenmark, J.K. (Ed.) *Mathematics Assessment: Myths, Models, Good Questions, and Practical Suggestions.* National Council of Teachers of Mathematics, Reston, VA, 1991.
- Stigler, J.W., S.Y. Lee, and H.W. Stevenson. *The Mathematical Knowledge of Japanese, Chinese, and American Elementary School Children.* National Council of Teachers of Mathematics, Reston, VA, 1990.

Information for Parents

Grade 5 Math Facts Philosophy

The goal of the math facts strand in *Math Trailblazers* is for students to learn the basic facts efficiently, gain fluency with their use, and retain that fluency over time. In fifth grade, students review the multiplication and division facts.

A large body of research supports an approach in which students develop strategies for figuring out the facts rather than relying solely on rote memorization. This not only leads to more effective learning and better retention, but also to development of mental math skills useful throughout life. Therefore, the teaching and assessment of the basic facts in *Math Trailblazers* is characterized by the following elements:

Use of Strategies. In earlier grades, students first approached the basic facts as problems to be solved rather than as facts to be memorized. In all grades we encourage the use of strategies to find facts and de-emphasize rote memorization. Thus students become confident they can find answers to fact problems they do not immediately recall. In this way, students learn that math is more than memorizing facts and rules which "you either get or you don't."

Distributed Review of the Facts. Students study small groups of facts that can be found using similar strategies. In fifth grade, the multiplication and division facts are divided into five groups. During the first semester students review these facts, one group at a time. They practice both the multiplication and division facts in each group. Students use flash cards to review groups of facts at home. Using this systematic approach, they build upon the fluency with the multiplication and the division facts gained in fourth grade.

Practice in Context. Students also review the facts as they use them to solve problems in the labs, activities, and games.

Appropriate Assessment. Students are regularly assessed to determine whether they can find answers to fact problems quickly and accurately and whether they can retain this skill over time. A short quiz follows the study and review of each group of facts. Each student records his or her progress on "Facts I Know" charts and determines the facts he or she still needs to study.

Facts Will Not Act as Gatekeepers. Students are not prevented from learning more complex mathematics because they cannot perform well on fact tests. Use of strategies, calculators, and printed multiplication tables allows students to continue to work on interesting problems and experiments while they are learning the facts.

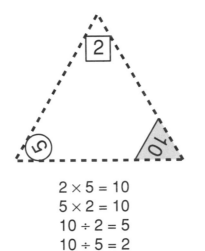

A fact family represented by a
Triangle Flash Card

$2 \times 5 = 10$
$5 \times 2 = 10$
$10 \div 2 = 5$
$10 \div 5 = 2$

Información para los padres

El objetivo de enseñanza de los conceptos matemáticos básicos en Math Trailblazers es que los estudiantes aprendan los conceptos básicos eficazmente, logren el dominio de estos conceptos y mantengan ese dominio con el paso del tiempo. En 5to grado, los estudiantes repasan las tablas de multiplicación y división.

La investigación realizada respalda la aplicación de un enfoque en el que los estudiantes desarrollan estrategias para resolver los problemas de conceptos básicos en lugar de aprenderlas de memoria. Esto no sólo permite un aprendizaje más eficaz y una mejor retención, sino que también desarrolla habilidades matemáticas mentales que serán útiles durante toda la vida. Por lo tanto, la enseñanza y la evaluación de los conceptos básicos en *Math Trailblazers* se caracteriza por los siguientes elementos:

El uso de estrategias. Los estudiantes enfocan primero a los conceptos básicos como problemas para resolver en lugar de tablas para memorizar. En todos los grados, alentamos el uso de estrategias para hallar soluciones y damos menos énfasis en aprender de memoria. De este modo, los estudiantes tienen más confianza de poder hallar las soluciones de problemas de cuales no se acuerdan. De esta manera, los estudiantes aprenden que las matemáticas son más que tablas y reglas memorizadas que un estudiante "sabe o no sabe".

Repaso gradual de los conceptos básicos. Los estudiantes estudian pequeños grupos de conceptos básicos que pueden hallarse usando estrategias similares. En quinto grado, las tablas de multiplicación y división se dividen en cinco grupos. Durante el primer semestre, los estudiantes repasan estos conceptos básicos, un grupo por vez. Los estudiantes practican tanto las tablas de multiplicación como las divisiones relacionadas en cada grupo. Los estudiantes usan tarjetas para practicar los grupos de conceptos básicos en casa. Usando este enfoque sistemático, se refuerza el dominio de las tablas de multiplicación y división adquirido en cuarto grado.

Práctica en contexto. Los estudiantes también repasan los conceptos básicos cuando los usan en experiencias de laboratorio, actividades y juegos.

Evaluación apropiada. Evaluamos a los estudiantes habitualmente para determinar si pueden hallar respuestas rápidas y correctas a problemas que involucran los conceptos básicos, y para determinar si pueden retener esta habilidad con el paso del tiempo. Los estudiantes deben completar un examen corto después de estudiar y repasar cada grupo de conceptos básicos. Cada estudiante registra su progreso en tablas tituladas "Las tablas las conozco" y determina qué tablas necesita estudiar todavía.

El nivel de dominio de los conceptos básicos no impedirá el aprendizaje. Los estudiantes seguirán aprendiendo conceptos matemáticos más complejos aunque no les vaya bien en los exámenes sobre los conceptos básicos. El uso de estrategias, calculadoras y tablas de multiplicación impresas les permite continuar trabajando en problemas y experimentos interesantes mientras aprenden los conceptos básicos.

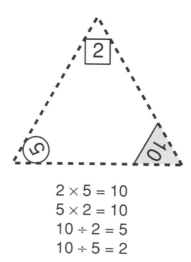

$$2 \times 5 = 10$$
$$5 \times 2 = 10$$
$$10 \div 2 = 5$$
$$10 \div 5 = 2$$

Los conceptos relacionados representados por una tarjeta triangular.

Observational Assessment Record

(A1) Can students compare and order large numbers?

(A2) Can students read and write large numbers?

(A3) Can students multiply using paper and pencil?

(A4) Can students multiply numbers with ending zeros mentally?

(A5) Can students estimate products?

(A6) Can students solve open-response problems and communicate solution strategies?

(A7) Do students demonstrate fluency with the multiplication and division facts for the 5s and 10s?

(A8) _____

Name	A1	A2	A3	A4	A5	A6	A7	A8	Comments
1.									
2.									
3.									
4.									
5.									
6.									
7.									
8.									
9.									
10.									
11.									
12.									
13.									

Name	A1	A2	A3	A4	A5	A6	A7	A8	Comments
14.									
15.									
16.									
17.									
18.									
19.									
20.									
21.									
22.									
23.									
24.									
25.									
26.									
27.									
28.									
29.									
30.									
31.									
32.									

Unit 2

Daily Practice and Problems
Big Numbers

A DPP Menu for Unit 2

Two Daily Practice and Problems (DPP) items are included for each class session listed in the Unit Outline. A scope and sequence chart for the DPP is in the *Teacher Implementation Guide*.

Icons in the Teacher Notes column designate the subject matter of each DPP item. The first item in each class session is always a Bit and the second is either a Task or Challenge. Each item falls into one or more of the categories listed below. A menu of the DPP items for Unit 2 follows.

N Number Sense	✖ Computation	🕐 Time	🔷 Geometry
C, G, H, J–L, N–P, R–Z, BB, DD	A, B, D, E, N, O, R, T, V, W, Y, BB, DD	C, D	

$\frac{5}{\times 7}$ Math Facts	$ Money	🎵 Measurement	📈 Data
I, M, O, Q, U, W–Y, AA, CC	B, E	F	C, F

Refer to the *Daily Practice and Problems and Home Practice Guide* in the *Teacher Implementation Guide* for further information on the DPP. This guide includes information on how and when to use the DPP.

Note that Lessons 3 and 4 are labeled as optional. The Unit Outline recommends using Lesson 3 or 4, but not both. Do not skip the DPP items for these optional lessons (DPP items G–J). Note also that Challenge item N will not be appropriate if your class does not complete Lesson 4 *The Chinese Abacus.*

Review and Assessment of the Math Facts in Units 2–8

By the end of fourth grade, students in *Math Trailblazers* are expected to demonstrate fluency with all math facts. Lesson 2 of this unit and the DPP begin a systematic approach to reviewing the multiplication and division facts. Work with the facts continues throughout the DPP in fifth grade.

The multiplication and division facts are divided into five groups. In Lesson 2, through the use of *Triangle Flash Cards,* students review the first group of facts, the 5s and 10s. The following table lists the five groups of facts and indicates when they occur.

For a detailed explanation of our approach to learning and assessing the facts, see the *Grade 5 Facts Resource Guide.* Information is also in the TIMS Tutor: *Math Facts* in the *Teacher Implementation Guide.* Also, see the *Information for Parents: Grade 5 Math Facts Philosophy,* which immediately follows the Unit 2 Background.

Unit	Math Fact Group
2	Group 1: 5s and 10s
3	Group 2: 2s and 3s
4	Group 3: squares
5	Group 4: 9s
6	Group 5: The last six facts: 4×6, 4×7, 4×8, 6×7, 6×8, 7×8
7	Review all five groups.
8	Assess all five groups.

Unit 2 Lesson 2 and the DPP

In Lesson 2 of this unit, students begin to review the first group of facts, the 5s and 10s.
In Part 1 of Lesson 2:

- Students quiz each other on the multiplication facts in the first group—the 5s and 10s. They use *Triangle Flash Cards* to assess themselves on the facts. They sort the cards into three piles: those they know and can answer quickly, those they can figure out with a strategy, and those they need to learn.

- They begin a record of their fluency with the multiplication facts for the 5s and 10s by using a self-assessment page called the *Multiplication Facts I Know* chart. They circle the multiplication facts they know and can answer quickly. This chart is updated throughout Units 3–8.

In Part 2 of Lesson 2:

- Students review the division facts for the 5s and 10s using fact families (e.g., $5 \times 3 = 15$, $3 \times 5 = 15$, $15 \div 3 = 5$, and $15 \div 5 = 3$).

- They practice the multiplication and division facts for the 5s and 10s.

In Part 3 of Lesson 2:

- Students again sort the flash cards for the 5s and 10s, this time focusing on the division facts.

- They circle the division facts they know and can answer quickly on a *Division Facts I Know* chart, which they will update throughout Units 3–8.

After completing Lesson 2, students continue to practice the facts for the 5s and 10s during the unit by completing DPP items I, M, O, Q, U, W, X, Y, AA, and CC. DPP item CC is a quiz on the multiplication and division facts for the 5s and 10s. (See Lesson Guide 2 for specific instructions on how to use *Triangle Flash Cards* and the *Multiplication* and *Division Facts I Know* charts.)

Math Facts in the DPP for Units 3–8

Throughout the year students review the multiplication and division facts as they use them in labs, activities, and games. However, the systematic review and practice of the facts take place primarily in the DPP.

The math fact items in the DPP for Units 3–6 parallels what takes place in Lesson 2 and the DPP in this unit:

1. A DPP item instructs students to quiz each other on a group of facts using the *Triangle Flash Cards*. Students sort the cards into three piles as described earlier. The DPP item reminds students to update their *Multiplication* and *Division Facts I Know* charts.

2. Several DPP items help students practice a particular group of facts.

3. A final DPP item assesses students on a mixture of multiplication and division facts. Students update both their *Multiplication* and *Division Facts I Know* charts.

(Note: Part 1 of the Home Practice in the *Discovery Assignment Book* reminds students to take home their flash cards to practice the facts with a family member.)

The DPP for Units 7 and 8 reviews all five groups of facts. Students sort the cards for all the groups and update their *Facts I Know* charts. In Unit 8, a final DPP item contains an inventory test on all five groups of facts. The test helps teachers and students assess the facts they know and those they still need to learn. During the second semester, students can use their *Triangle Flash Cards* to practice the multiplication and division facts they have not circled. The second semester's DPP includes additional math fact review, especially of the division facts. These provide opportunities for students to strengthen their fluency with the math facts.

Content Note

The math facts program is closely linked to the recommended schedule for teaching lessons. Thus classrooms that deviate significantly from the suggested pacing will need to make special accommodations to ensure students receive a consistent program of math facts practice and assessment throughout the year. The *Grade 5 Facts Resource Guide* outlines a schedule for math facts practice and assessment in classrooms that are moving much more slowly through lessons than recommended in the Lesson Guides.

Daily Practice and Problems

Students may solve the items individually, in groups, or as a class. The items may also be assigned for homework. The DPPs are also available on the Teacher Resource CD.

Student Questions	Teacher Notes

A Addition and Subtraction Practice

Solve the following problems using paper and pencil. Estimate to check if your answer is reasonable.

A. $356 + 76 =$ B. $1037 - 763 =$

C. $484 + 158 =$ D. $4656 - 2937 =$

TIMS Bit

A. 432

B. 274

C. 642

D. 1719

B Nickels and Dimes

There are some nickels and dimes on the kitchen table. The total is 65 cents.

1. How many nickels and how many dimes might there be? (Give several answers to this problem.)

2. What is the fewest number of dimes that might be on the counter? Then, how many nickels would there be?

3. What is the fewest number of nickels that might be on the counter? Then, how many dimes would there be?

4. There are 9 coins on the counter. How many nickels and how many dimes are on the counter?

TIMS Challenge

1. 1 nickel 6 dimes
   3 nickels 5 dimes
   5 nickels 4 dimes
   7 nickels 3 dimes
   9 nickels 2 dimes
   11 nickels 1 dime
2. 1 dime 11 nickels
3. 1 nickel 6 dimes
4. 5 nickels and 4 dimes

Student Questions	Teacher Notes

C. Median Time

Michael's father takes the train to work. He arrives on the platform every morning at 6:20 A.M. On Monday, he waited 15 minutes for the train. On Tuesday he waited 8 minutes. On Wednesday he waited 7 minutes. On Thursday he waited 10 minutes and on Friday, 13 minutes. What is the median number of minutes Michael's father waited for the train?

TIMS Bit

10 minutes

D. Adding Time

Felicia's skating practice lasted for 2 hours 45 minutes on Tuesday and 3 hours 35 minutes on Thursday. She found the total amount of time she practiced on these two days.

        2 hours 45 minutes
     +3 hours 35 minutes
        5 hours 80 minutes = 5 hours + 1 hour +
                                      20 minutes

Felicia practiced 6 hours and 20 minutes.

Solve these problems.

A. 1 hour 35 minutes + 4 hours and 15 minutes

B. 4 hours 16 minutes + 3 hours and 37 minutes

C. 2 hours 28 minutes + 6 hours 54 minutes

D. 6 minutes 52 seconds + 3 minutes 43 seconds

TIMS Task

A. 5 hr 50 min

B. 7 hr 53 min

C. 8 hr 82 min =
   8 hr + 1 hr + 22 min =
   9 hr 22 min

D. 9 min 95 sec =
   9 min + 1 min + 35 sec =
   10 min 35 sec

Student Questions	Teacher Notes

E Making Change

David buys a CD that costs $14.49 with tax. He gives the sales clerk a $20 bill. How much change will he receive? Name the least number of coins and bills he can receive.

TIMS Bit $ ✖

$5.51—one $5 bill, two quarters (or 1 half dollar), and one penny

F Measuring Pencils

Measure the length of four classmates' pencils to the nearest centimeter. Record the information in a data table. Then find the median length of the pencils.

TIMS Task ◩ ⚖

You can distribute a copy of the *Two-column Data Table* Blackline Master or you can have students create their own data tables. The column headings could be: Owner's Name and Length of Pencil in centimeters.

G Write the Number

Write a number that has:

A. 6 tens and 3 ones

B. 91 hundreds and 6 tens

C. 73 tens

D. 8 hundreds and 14 ones

E. 50 tens and 8 ones

TIMS Bit N

A. 63 (Examples of other appropriate answers: 463; 25,763)

Answers will vary. One possible answer is given for each.

B. 9160

C. 730

D. 814

E. 508

H Smallest and Largest

1. Rearrange the digits in 1997 to make the smallest possible number.

2. Rearrange the digits in 1997 to make the largest possible number.

For Questions 3 and 4, you may use a digit more than once; however, the number should begin with a nonzero digit.

3. Write the smallest four-digit number possible using the digits 0 through 9.

4. Write the largest four-digit number possible using the digits 0 through 9.

TIMS Task N

1. 1799

2. 9971

3. 1000

4. 9999

I Multiplication and Division Sentences

Lin has 15 flowers to place in 3 vases. How many flowers go in each vase if she divides them evenly?

A. Draw a picture to illustrate this problem.

B. Write a multiplication sentence and a division sentence that describe this problem.

TIMS Bit $\frac{5}{\times 7}$

A. Pictures will vary, but the important idea here is that division can be used to arrange a group of objects into smaller, equal-sized groups.

B. 3 vases × 5 flowers in each vase = 15 flowers; 15 flowers ÷ 3 vases = 5 flowers in each vase

J Leaves on a Tree

Find a tree. Estimate the number of leaves on your tree. Explain how you made your estimate.

TIMS Challenge N

Answers will vary. One way to determine an answer to this type of question is to take a sample from a smaller area of the tree and then multiply.

(K) Rounding

1. Round the following to the nearest hundred:

   A. 381   B. 829   C. 705

   D. 2323   E. 4881   F. 8975

2. Round the following to the nearest thousand:

   A. 2323   B. 4881   C. 8975

   D. 4097   E. 1446   F. 19,488

TIMS Bit   N

1. A. 400   B. 800
   C. 700   D. 2300
   E. 4900   F. 9000

2. A. 2000   B. 5000
   C. 9000   D. 4000
   E. 1000   F. 19,000

(L) Big Numbers

1. Write the following numbers in order from smallest to largest.

2. Then, write the numbers in words.

   6,549,920   4,954,020
      945,209   456,299

TIMS Task   N

1. 456,299; 945,209; 4,954,020; 6,549,920

2. four hundred fifty-six thousand, two hundred ninety-nine;

   nine hundred forty-five thousand, two hundred nine;

   four million, nine hundred fifty-four thousand, twenty;

   six million, five hundred forty-nine thousand, nine hundred twenty

---

(M) More Multiplication and Division Sentences

There are 20 students in gym class. They divide into pairs to practice sit-ups. How many pairs of students will practice sit-ups?

A. Draw a picture to illustrate this problem.

B. Write a multiplication sentence and a division sentence to describe this problem.

TIMS Bit $\frac{5}{\times 7}$

A. Pictures will vary.

B. 2 students per pair ×
    10 pairs = 20 students;
    20 students ÷ 2 students per pair = 10 pairs

N **Using the Chinese Abacus**

Explore multiplication on the Chinese abacus. Explain how you can solve the following problems on the abacus. Use pictures of the abacus and label your work.

A. 21 × 5

B. 38 × 10

TIMS Challenge **N** **✳**

A. Input 21. Remember each bead in the sky section is 5 times greater than a bead in the same column but in the earth section. Therefore, exchange each bead in the earth section for a bead in the sky section. Then, exchange the two beads in the sky section of the tens' column for an earth bead in the hundreds' column. 105 is the answer.

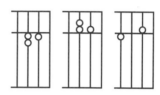

B. Each column to the left has a place value 10 times greater than the value of the column to the right. Exchange the 3 beads in the tens' column for 3 beads in the hundreds' column. Trade the beads in the ones' column for corresponding beads in the tens' column. The answer is 380.

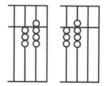

Student Questions	Teacher Notes

◉ A Juicy Problem

Two shipments of fruit were delivered to the school cafeteria. One shipment contained 8 sacks of oranges, 50 pounds to a sack. In the other shipment, there were 7 sacks, also 50 pounds to a sack. How many pounds of fruit were delivered to the cafeteria in all?

TIMS Bit

First shipment = 400 pounds

Second shipment = 350 pounds

750 pounds of fruit were delivered in all.

or

15 sacks × 50 pounds per sack = 750 pounds

℗ Place Value and Product Size

Copy the following diagram onto your paper:

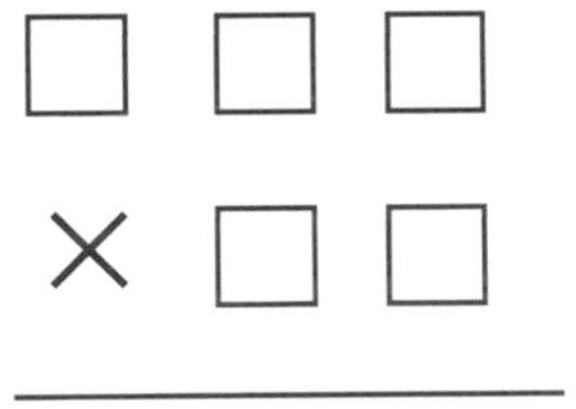

☐ ☐ ☐

× ☐ ☐
_____

Choose any 5 digits 1 through 9 to solve these problems. (You can use the same digit more than once.) Use the same 5 digits to answer Questions 1–3.

1. Arrange the digits to produce the largest product possible.

2. Arrange the digits to produce the smallest product possible.

3. How many different products are possible using your 5 digits?

4. Choose 5 new digits and answer the questions again.

TIMS Challenge

Students should be allowed to use calculators to work these problems. There are a variety of solutions. Discuss answers as a class.

Student Questions	Teacher Notes

Q Facts for 5s and 10s

A. $10 \times 3 =$ B. $35 \div 5 =$

C. $80 \div 10 =$ D. $9 \times 5 =$

E. $5 \times 10 =$ F. $25 \div 5 =$

G. $10 \times 10 =$

TIMS Bit

A. 30   B. 7

C. 8   D. 45

E. 50   F. 5

G. 100

R Partial Products

Irma solved a multiplication problem using the all-partials method of multiplication. Look carefully at her work below. What multiplication problem did she solve?

$$
\begin{array}{r}
\times \\
\hline
27 \quad = 3 \times 9 \\
60 \quad = 3 \times 20 \\
720 \quad = 80 \times 9 \\
\underline{1600} \quad = 80 \times 20 \\
2407
\end{array}
$$

TIMS Task

83×29 or 29×83

S Changing Numbers

Always begin with the number: 7,382,491.

Change it to:

A. 3 hundred more

B. 9 thousand more

C. 12 million more

D. 70 thousand less

TIMS Bit

Remind students to use the original number each time. No calculators.

A. 7,382,791

B. 7,391,491

C. 19,382,491

D. 7,312,491

Student Questions	Teacher Notes

T Multiplication Practice

Solve the following problems using paper and pencil. Estimate to make sure your answer makes sense.

A. $516 \times 7 =$

B. $7083 \times 3 =$

C. $97 \times 33 =$

D. $72 \times 8 =$

E. $20 \times 47 =$

F. $23{,}488 \times 5 =$

TIMS Task

A. 3612

B. 21,249

C. 3201

D. 576

E. 940

F. 117,440

U Patterns with Zeros

Do these problems in your head.

A. $5 \times 3 =$

B. $5 \times 30 =$

C. $5 \times 300 =$

D. $5 \times 3000 =$

E. $5 \times 30{,}000 =$

What is the pattern when you multiply numbers that end in zero?

TIMS Bit

A. 15

B. 150

C. 1500

D. 15,000

E. 150,000

Students should see that in these problems the number of zeros in each product is equal to the number of zeros in the problem.

Student Questions	Teacher Notes
V Multiplication Practice Solve the following problems using paper and pencil. Estimate to make sure your answer makes sense. A. $46 \times 7 =$ B. $77 \times 16 =$ C. $54 \times 35 =$ D. $38 \times 30 =$ E. $62 \times 40 =$ F. $7134 \times 5 =$	**TIMS Task** N A. 322 B. 1232 C. 1890 D. 1140 E. 2480 F. 35,670
W Multiplying by Numbers Ending in Zeros A. $50 \times 7 =$ B. $600 \times 50 =$ C. $60 \times 10 =$ D. $800 \times 100 =$ E. $500 \times 9 =$ F. $200 \times 5000 =$	**TIMS Bit** N A. 350 B. 30,000 C. 600 D. 80,000 E. 4500 F. 1,000,000

X Related Facts

Solve each problem. Then name a related division sentence for each.

A. $500 \times 5 = ?$

B. $10 \times 30 = ?$

C. $1000 \times 5 = ?$

D. $400 \times 50 = ?$

TIMS Task   N $\frac{5}{\times 7}$

A. 2500; $2500 \div 5 = 500$ or $2500 \div 500 = 5$

B. 300; $300 \div 10 = 30$ or $300 \div 30 = 10$

C. 5000; $5000 \div 5 = 1000$ or $5000 \div 1000 = 5$

D. 20,000; $20,000 \div 50 = 400$ or $20,000 \div 400 = 50$

Y More Multiplication with Numbers Ending in Zero

Find the missing number, n, in each sentence to make that sentence true.

A. $100 \times n = 5000$

B. $50 \times n = 25{,}000$

C. $500 \times n = 35{,}000$

D. $n \times 100 = 10{,}000$

E. $500 \times 40 = n$

F. $n \times 80 = 4000$

TIMS Bit   N $\frac{5}{\times 7}$ �҉

A. 50

B. 500

C. 70

D. 100

E. 20,000

F. 50

| Student Questions | Teacher Notes |

Z Making Comparisons

Compare the expressions on each side of the line. Without calculating, decide if $<$, $=$, or $>$ goes on the line to complete each number sentence. Then explain how you decided.

A. $43 + 42 + 44$ ___ 43×3

B. $231 + 232 + 231 + 230$ ___ 5×231

C. $624 + 468 + 211$ ___ $468 + 210 + 625$

D. 3080×70 ___ 3008×70

TIMS Task Ⓝ

A. $=$; 43×3 is the same as $43 + 43 + 43$. If you take 1 away from 44 and give it to 42, then you will have $43 + 43 + 43$.

B. $<$; The lefthand side is the same as 4×231 so it is less than 5×231.

C. $=$; If you take 1 away from 211 on the lefthand side and give it to 624, then you will have the same expression on both sides.

D. $>$; Since 3080 is larger than 3008, the lefthand side will produce a larger product.

AA Facts for 5s and 10s

A. $5 \times 6 =$ B. $10 \times 9 =$

C. $40 \div 5 =$ D. $40 \div 10 =$

E. $6 \times 10 =$ F. $10 \div 2 =$

G. $70 \div 7 =$ H. $4 \times 5 =$

TIMS Bit $\frac{5}{\times 7}$

A. 30   B. 90
C. 8   D. 4
E. 60   F. 5
G. 10   H. 20

BB Estimating Products

1. Estimate the answers to the following problems.

2. Then tell what convenient numbers you used to make your estimate.

3. Finally tell whether the actual product will be larger or smaller than your estimate.

A. 49×28 B. 598×9

C. 4074×3

TIMS Task Ⓝ 🗙

Answers will vary. Examples are given here.

1. A. 1500
2. A. 50×30
3. A. smaller
1. B. 6000
2. B. 600×10
3. B. smaller
1. C. 12,000
2. C. 4000×3
3. C. larger

Student Questions	Teacher Notes

CC Quiz: 5s and 10s

A. $7 \times 5 =$ B. $40 \div 4 =$

C. $10 \div 2 =$ D. $8 \times 10 =$

E. $9 \times 5 =$ F. $6 \times 10 =$

G. $30 \div 6 =$ H. $10 \times 2 =$

I. $15 \div 5 =$ J. $70 \div 10 =$

K. $40 \div 8 =$ L. $5 \times 10 =$

M. $10 \times 3 =$ N. $25 \div 5 =$

O. $90 \div 9 =$ P. $4 \times 5 =$

Q. $10 \times 10 =$

TIMS Bit

We recommend 5 minutes for this quiz. You might want to allow students to change pens after the time is up and complete the remaining problems in a different color. After students take the test, have them update their *Multiplication Facts I Know* and *Division Facts I Know* charts.

DD Scientific Notation

1. Explain how to multiply 29,000,000 × 600 without a calculator. What do you get for an answer?

2. Now use your calculator. What does the calculator window show? What do the symbols on the display mean?

TIMS Task

1. $29 \times 6 = 174$
   Append eight zeros after 174.
   17,400,000,000

2. Answers will vary.

Lesson ① Reading and Writing Big Numbers

Lesson Overview

Estimated Class Sessions **2-3**

There are three parts to this lesson. In part 1, students read a play that reviews place value. In part 2, students read, write, and order large numbers. Part 3 is a game that practices these skills.

Key Content

- Reading and writing large numbers.
- Representing large numbers using number lines.
- Using estimation to place numbers on a number line.
- Developing number sense for large numbers.
- Comparing and ordering large numbers.
- Rounding large numbers.

Key Vocabulary

- billion
- digit
- expanded form
- million
- period
- place
- place value chart
- rounding
- standard form
- value
- word form

Math Facts

Continue review of addition and subtraction facts as needed for individual students.

Homework

1. Assign the Homework section in the *Student Guide.*
2. Assign the *Writing Big Numbers* Activity Page in the *Discovery Assignment Book.*
3. Assign the *Spin and Read Number Game.*
4. Assign Part 2 of the Home Practice.

Assessment

Use the Reading and Writing Big Numbers section of the *Student Guide* to assess writing numbers.

Curriculum Sequence

Before This Unit

Large Numbers

In previous grades students read and wrote numbers through the millions and were introduced to place value terminology. They should be familiar with the organization of the base-ten number system. Students investigated large numbers in Unit 6 of fourth grade and used them in various contexts throughout the year.

Materials List

Supplies and Copies

Student	Teacher
Supplies for Each Student • calculator **Supplies for Each Student Group** • playing cards, optional • clear plastic spinner or pencil and paper clip	**Supplies**
Copies • 4 copies of *Digit Cards 0–9* per student group copied back to back (*Unit Resource Guides* Pages 43–44)	**Copies/Transparencies** • 1 transparency of *Population Lines,* optional (*Discovery Assignment Book* Page 15) • 1 transparency of *Place Value Chart* (*Discovery Assignment Book* Page 19)

All blackline masters including assessment, transparency, and DPP masters are also on the Teacher Resource CD.

Student Books

Reading and Writing Big Numbers (*Student Guide* Pages 26–34)
Writing Big Numbers (*Discovery Assignment Book* Page 13)
Population Lines (*Discovery Assignment Book* Page 15)
Spin and Read Number Game Spinners (*Discovery Assignment Book* Page 17)
Place Value Chart (*Discovery Assignment Book* Page 19)

Daily Practice and Problems and Home Practice

DPP items A–D (*Unit Resource Guide* Pages 19–20)
Home Practice Part 2 (*Discovery Assignment Book* Page 10)

Note: Classrooms whose pacing differs significantly from the suggested pacing of the units should use the Math Facts Calendar in Section 4 of the *Facts Resource Guide* to ensure students receive the complete math facts program.

Daily Practice and Problems

Suggestions for using the DPPs are on pages 40–41.

A. Bit: Addition and Subtraction Practice (URG p. 19)

Solve the following problems using paper and pencil. Estimate to check if your answer is reasonable.

A. $356 + 76 =$ B. $1037 - 763 =$

C. $484 + 158 =$ D. $4656 - 2937 =$

B. Challenge: Nickels and Dimes (URG p. 19)

There are some nickels and dimes on the kitchen table. The total is 65 cents.

1. How many nickels and how many dimes might there be? (Give several answers to this problem.)
2. What is the fewest number of dimes that might be on the counter? Then, how many nickels would there be?
3. What is the fewest number of nickels that might be on the counter? Then, how many dimes would there be?
4. There are 9 coins on the counter. How many nickels and how many dimes are on the counter?

C. Bit: Median Time (URG p. 20)

Michael's father takes the train to work. He arrives on the platform every morning at 6:20 A.M. On Monday, he waited 15 minutes for the train. On Tuesday he waited 8 minutes. On Wednesday he waited 7 minutes. On Thursday he waited 10 minutes and on Friday, 13 minutes. What is the median number of minutes Michael's father waited for the train?

D. Task: Adding Time (URG p. 20)

Felicia's skating practice lasted for 2 hours 45 minutes on Tuesday and 3 hours 35 minutes on Thursday. She found the total amount of time she practiced on these two days.

$$2 \text{ hours } 45 \text{ minutes}$$
$$+3 \text{ hours } 35 \text{ minutes}$$
$$5 \text{ hours } 80 \text{ minutes} = 5 \text{ hours} + 1 \text{ hour} + 20 \text{ minutes}$$

Felicia practiced 6 hours and 20 minutes.

Solve these problems.

A. 1 hour 35 minutes + 4 hours and 15 minutes

B. 4 hours 16 minutes + 3 hours and 37 minutes

C. 2 hours 28 minutes + 6 hours 54 minutes

D. 6 minutes 52 seconds + 3 minutes 43 seconds

Part 1 A Play: Reviewing Place Value

Have students read the introduction and the play on the *Reading and Writing Big Numbers* Activity Pages in the *Student Guide*. The play is a setting for students to refresh their ideas about place value and to review language used in reading and writing larger numbers.

When the play is finished, ask students to give examples of the vocabulary terms. Make sure students understand the organization of the place value chart and its use in reading large numbers.

Part 2 Reading, Writing, and Ordering Big Numbers

Check students' understanding of big numbers with transparencies of the *Place Value Chart* and the *Writing Big Numbers* Activity Pages from the *Discovery Assignment Book*. Write a number on the *Place Value Chart*. Have students read the number. Then have them write the number in words. Check students' understanding of the column values on the chart by asking them, for example, what value the number 4 has in the number 3,456,782. This kind of prompt assists students in writing the number in expanded form. Students can practice writing numbers in standard, expanded, and word form using the *Writing Big Numbers* Activity Page in the *Discovery Assignment Book*.

Trillions			Billions			Millions			Thousands			Ones		
								3	4	5	6	7	8	2

Figure 3: *Place Value Chart*

Reading and Writing Big Numbers

Students in a fifth-grade Social Studies class are learning about populations. Their teacher wrote some of the populations on the board for them to read and write.

2006 Populations

Our Classroom:	28	Our County:	286,742
Our School:	686	Our State:	3,677,985
Our City:	7122	Our Country:	290,809,777
		Our World:	6,511,000,000

Some students had difficulty reading and writing the big numbers. The teacher gave these students a play to read. The play was about students who worked together to solve a problem about big numbers.

The characters in the play are:
N.S. (Not Sure)
P.S. (Problem Solver)
L.L. (Loves Lists)
R.R. (Remembers Rules)
Teacher

Student Guide - page 26

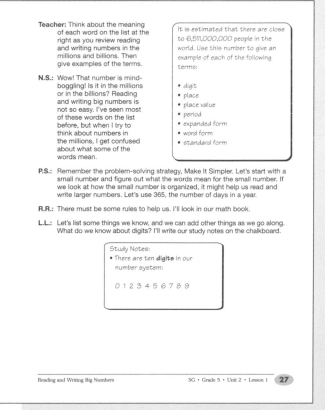

Teacher: Think about the meaning of each word on the list at the right as you review reading and writing numbers in the millions and billions. Then give examples of the terms.

It is estimated that there are close to 6,511,000,000 people in the world. Use this number to give an example of each of the following terms:

• digit
• place
• place value
• period
• expanded form
• word form
• standard form

N.S.: Wow! That number is mind-boggling! Is it in the millions or in the billions? Reading and writing big numbers is not so easy. I've seen most of these words on the list before, but when I try to think about numbers in the millions, I get confused about what some of the words mean.

P.S.: Remember the problem-solving strategy, Make It Simpler. Let's start with a small number and figure out what the words mean for the small number. If we look at how the small number is organized, it might help us read and write larger numbers. Let's use 365, the number of days in a year.

R.R.: There must be some rules to help us. I'll look in our math book.

L.L.: Let's list some things we know, and we can add other things as we go along. What do we know about digits? I'll write our study notes on the chalkboard.

Study Notes:
• There are ten **digits** in our number system:

  0 1 2 3 4 5 6 7 8 9

Student Guide - page 27

R.R.: I found this rule: The value of each **digit** in a number is determined by its position or **place**. This is called its **place value**. Add that to the study notes.

> **Study Notes:**
> • There are ten **digits** in our number system:
>
>   0 1 2 3 4 5 6 7 8 9
>
> • The value of each **digit** is determined by its position or **place**.

N.S.: Okay, back to 365. The 3 is three hundred because, because. . . . If I draw a place value chart on the chalkboard, it's easier to explain.

Ones		
Hundreds	Tens	Ones
3	6	5

When 3 is in this position or place, it really means 3 hundreds or 300. The 6 really means 6 tens or 60 and the 5 means 5 ones or 5.

R.R.: The value of each digit in 365 is $300 + 60 + 5$. This way of writing a number is called **expanded form.**

L.L.: Should I add that to our notes?

Student Guide - page 28

P.S.: I don't think so, but now I remember—**standard form** is just the regular way to write a number using digits, 365.

N.S.: Now I remember another term on that list! **Word form** just means that the digits are written in words, three hundred sixty-five.

P.S.: There's another problem-solving strategy that can help us. Find a Pattern. That way you don't have to remember so many rules. There is a pattern in reading and writing larger numbers, and it has something to do with knowing the **periods.**

R.R.: There's a rule about that: Read the number in each period and say the name of each period. A **period** is a group of three places in a large number. If you can read three-digit numbers, and you know the names of the periods, reading big numbers is easy. We need this rule on our study notes.

> **Study Notes:**
> • There are ten **digits** in our number system:
>
>   0 1 2 3 4 5 6 7 8 9
>
> • The value of each **digit** is determined by its position or **place**.
>
> • Read the number in each **period** and say the name of each **period**.

N.S.: I guess I need to get a better picture of the periods in my head.

P.S.: Okay. Let's go back to the place value chart.

Student Guide - page 29

L.L.: It was my tenth birthday a week ago. My family always figures out our age in days, so right now I can say my age in days, 3657. Three **thousand,** six hundred fifty-seven days. Hey, is that the **word form** or the **standard form?**

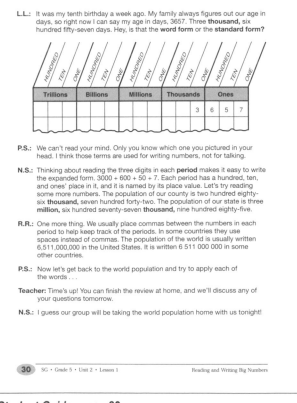

P.S.: We can't read your mind. Only you know which one you pictured in your head. I think those terms are used for writing numbers, not for talking.

N.S.: Thinking about reading the three digits in each **period** makes it easy to write the expanded form. $3000 + 600 + 50 + 7$. Each period has a hundred, ten, and ones' place in it, and it is named by its place value. Let's try reading some more numbers. The population of our county is two hundred eighty-six **thousand,** seven hundred forty-two. The population of our state is three **million,** six hundred seventy-seven **thousand,** nine hundred eighty-five.

R.R.: One more thing. We usually place commas between the numbers in each period to help keep track of the periods. In some countries they use spaces instead of commas. The population of the world is usually written 6,511,000,000 in the United States. It is written 6 511 000 000 in some other countries.

P.S.: Now let's get back to the world population and try to apply each of the words . . .

Teacher: Time's up! You can finish the review at home, and we'll discuss any of your questions tomorrow.

N.S.: I guess our group will be taking the world population home with us tonight!

Student Guide - page 30

Name _____   Date _____

Place Value Chart

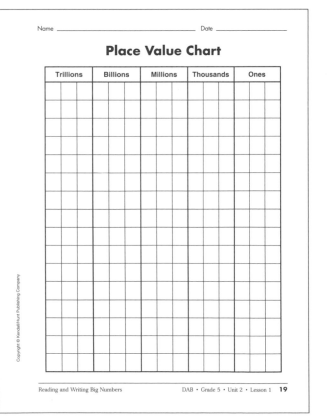

Trillions	Billions	Millions	Thousands	Ones

Discovery Assignment Book - page 19

The Discuss section on the *Reading and Writing Big Numbers* Activity Pages in the *Student Guide* will help you determine if students are able to apply the ideas reviewed in the play. Students should talk about their answers to **Questions 1–9.** The discussion may clarify some unclear notions. Note that for **Questions 4–5,** students refer to the numbers on the board in the illustration at the beginning of the play.

Question 10 challenges students to place numbers in a range on a number line. Have students take out the *Population Lines* Activity Page in the *Discovery Assignment Book.* You may want to make a transparency of this page. Guide students to number the first line according to the directions given. See Figure 4.

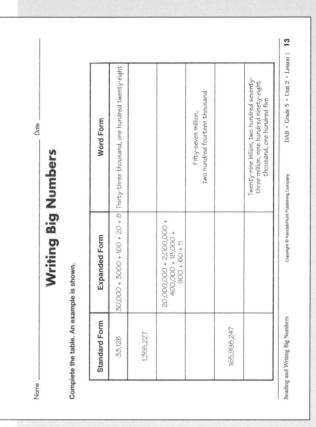

Name _____ Date _____

Writing Big Numbers

Complete the table. An example is shown.

Standard Form	Expanded Form	Word Form
33,128	30,000 + 3000 + 100 + 20 + 8	Thirty-three thousand, one hundred twenty-eight
1,355,227		
	20,000,000 + 2,000,000 + 400,000 + 18,000 + 900 + 60 + 5	
		Fifty-seven million, two hundred fourteen thousand
165,998,247		Twenty-nine billion, two hundred seventy-three million, nine hundred ninety-eight thousand, one hundred five

Reading and Writing Big Numbers   Copyright © Kendall/Hunt Publishing Company   DAB · Grade 5 · Unit 2 · Lesson 1   **13**

Discovery Assignment Book - page 13 (Answers on p. 48)

Discuss

Reading, Writing, and Ordering Big Numbers

2006 Populations Table 1

State	Nickname	Population
Alabama	Heart of Dixie	4,500,752
Alaska	Last Frontier	648,818
Arizona	Grand Canyon State	5,580,811
Arkansas	Natural State	2,725,714
California	Golden State	35,484,453
Colorado	Centennial State	4,550,688
Connecticut	Constitution State	3,483,372
Delaware	First State	817,491
Florida	Sunshine State	17,019,068

Using the 2006 Populations Table 1:

1. What is the reported population in Alabama?

2. What is the reported population in Florida?

3. **A.** Which state populations have an 8 in the ten thousands' place?
   B. The populations of which states have a 5 in the hundred thousands' place?

(*Hint:* There may be more than one answer for each question.)

4. **A.** In which state do the students in the play live?
   B. How many people live in that state?

Reading and Writing Big Numbers   SG · Grade 5 · Unit 2 · Lesson 1   **31**

Student Guide - page 31 (Answers on p. 45)

---

5. What is the estimated world population?

6. List the populations of Arizona, Colorado, and Connecticut in order from smallest to largest.

7. **A.** Write the reported population of Alabama in expanded form.
   B. Write the reported population of Florida in expanded form.

8. **A.** Write the reported population of Connecticut in word form.
   B. Write the reported population of Delaware in word form.

9. Which state has a reported population closest to 1 million?

10. Complete the number lines on the *Population Lines* Activity Page in the *Discovery Assignment Book.* Show the position of each state's population in the 2006 Populations Table 1 on the appropriate number line. Alaska has been written as an example on the correct number line.

11. Use the *Population Lines* Activity Page to help you:
   A. Round the population of Arizona to the nearest million.
   B. Round the population of Alabama to the nearest million.
   C. Round the population of Delaware to the nearest hundred thousand.

12. **A.** Round the population of Arkansas to the nearest million.
   B. Round the population of Arkansas to the nearest hundred thousand.

13. **A.** Round the population of Florida to the nearest ten million.
   B. Round the population of Florida to the nearest million.

Spin and Read Number Game

Players

This game is for groups of three students. Two students play and one student serves as a judge.

The purpose of the game is to practice reading large numbers.

Materials

• one deck of playing cards (use ace as "1" and the king as "0" and remove the queens, jacks, and tens) or four sets of *Digit Cards 0–9*
• *Spin and Read Number Game Spinners* Activity Page
• one clear plastic spinner or paper clip and pencil
• *Place Value Chart* Activity Page
• one calculator

32   SG · Grade 5 · Unit 2 · Lesson 1   Reading and Writing Big Numbers

Student Guide - page 32 (Answers on p. 46)

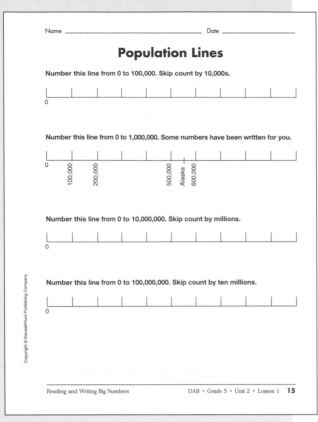

Name _____ Date _____

Population Lines

Number this line from 0 to 100,000. Skip count by 10,000s.

Number this line from 0 to 1,000,000. Some numbers have been written for you.

100,000 200,000 500,000 Alaska 600,000

Number this line from 0 to 10,000,000. Skip count by millions.

Number this line from 0 to 100,000,000. Skip count by ten millions.

Reading and Writing Big Numbers   DAB • Grade 5 • Unit 2 • Lesson 1   **15**

Discovery Assignment Book - page 15 (Answers on p. 48)

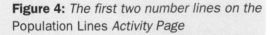

Number this line from 0 to 100,000. Skip count by 10,000s.

0 10,000 20,000 30,000 40,000 50,000 60,000 70,000 80,000 90,000 100,000

Number this line from 0 to 1,000,000. Some numbers have been written for you.

0 100,000 200,000 500,000 Alaska 600,000

Figure 4: *The first two number lines on the* Population Lines *Activity Page*

Then, ask, *"Where is 50,000? Where is 75,000? Where is 25,000?"* Ask a student to place 88,000. Ask:

- *Where would you place 88,000?* (Close to 90,000) 88,000 rounded to the nearest 10,000 is 90,000.

- *Where would you place 12,000?* (Close to 10,000) 12,000 rounded to the nearest 10,000 is 10,000.

- *What 10,000 is 37,000 closest to?* (40,000) 37,000 rounded to the nearest 10,000 is 40,000.

- *Where would you place 37,000?* (Close to 40,000)

Practice rounding to other benchmark numbers.

It is often useful to divide line segments by multiples of ten when we are estimating the placement of larger numbers. Proceed to the next number line. Fill in the numbers on the tick marks. Guide students to name interim points again. Ask a student to indicate where to place 217,000; 588,000; and 902,000. For each of these numbers, ask students to name the closest 100,000. This illustrates rounding to the nearest 100,000.

Ask, *"Can you place the population of Arizona (3,677,985) on the same number line as the population of Alaska?"* Since the population of Arizona is greater than one million, but less than ten million, students will need a number line numbered from 0 to 10,000,000. Assist students in writing the millions on the tick marks on the next number line. Follow the same sequence for each number line on the page. Give students numbers to place on the appropriate number lines.

Question 11 in the *Student Guide* asks students to round. Use the number lines to help them. For example, *Question 11A* asks them to round the population of Arizona to the nearest million. Ask,

- *The population of Arizona is between which two millions?* (Between 3 million and 4 million.)

- *Which million is it closest to?* (4 million)

- *So, 3,677,985 rounded to the nearest million is 4,000,000.*

In *Question 12* students round the population of Arkansas (2,362,239) to the nearest million and hundred thousand. The number line helps round to the nearest million. However, the number line doesn't help round to the nearest hundred thousand since it does not tell us which two hundred thousands the number lies between. Students can write the number on the *Place Value Chart* Activity Page in the *Discovery Assignment Book,* then answer the following questions:

- *Look at the thousands period for the number 2,362,239. Is the population of Alaska closer to 2,300,000 or 2,400,000? (2,400,000)*

- *Now, round the population of Arkansas to the nearest hundred thousand. (2,400,000. Remind students to give the rounded number as 2,400,000 and not simply 400,000.)*

Note: Since populations are constantly changing, the populations given in the population tables are estimates.

Part 3 **Spin and Read Number Game**

Introduce students to the *Spin and Read Number Game* in the *Student Guide.* A trio of students can play it whenever time permits. The game can also be used for homework for students to play with family members. Students will need a deck of playing cards or three copies per group of the *Digit Cards 0–9* Activity Page. Students will also need the *Spin and Read Number Game Spinners* Activity Page and the *Place Value Chart* Activity Page in the *Discovery Assignment Book.* They can use a pencil and a paper clip as a spinner as shown.

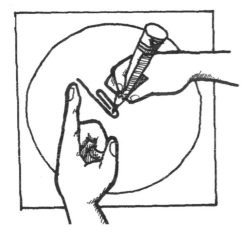

Figure 5: *A pencil and paper clip spinner*

Students can use Spinner 1, which has smaller numbers, to play the first few rounds of the game. This will give them practice reading numbers. Then students can use Spinner 2 to read larger numbers. As students correctly read the numbers, they can write them on the *Place Value Chart* Activity Page.

Rules

Shuffle the cards together to make one deck of 40 cards. Spin to determine the number of cards to pick up. (Use Spinner 1 on the Activity Page the first few times you play the game, then use Spinner 2 for a greater challenge.) The first player spins and lays down that many cards from the deck face-up on the table. That player then reads the number. If it is read correctly, the player records the number on the *Place Value Chart* and returns the cards to the deck. If it is not read correctly, the other player gets the opportunity. If neither reads it correctly, the cards go back into the deck and the deck is reshuffled. It is the judge's responsibility to determine whether the number was read correctly. If there is a dispute, it is resolved by a discussion of the number. Each game consists of four rounds, with each player beginning two rounds.

At the end of the game, players use their calculators to total the numbers they recorded. The calculator may go into scientific notation. The player with the larger total wins. Play rotates, and a new student serves as the judge.

Reading and Writing Big Numbers   SG • Grade 5 • Unit 2 • Lesson 1   **33**

Student Guide - page 33

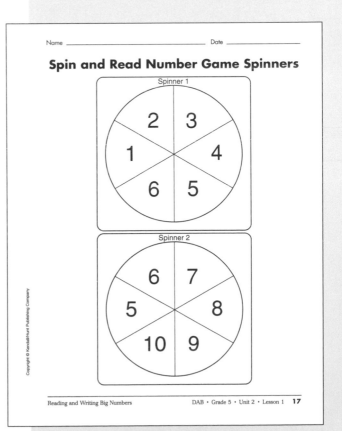

Name _____   Date _____

Spin and Read Number Game Spinners

Spinner 1

Spinner 2

Reading and Writing Big Numbers   DAB • Grade 5 • Unit 2 • Lesson 1   **17**

Discovery Assignment Book - page 17

Refer to the place value chart in your *Student Guide* and think about things you have learned to help you read and write large numbers. List at least three ideas. Share your ideas with your class. Add their helpful ideas to your list.

Math Facts

Use the Addition and Subtraction Math Facts Review in the *Grade 5 Facts Resource Guide* to review addition and subtraction facts as needed.

Homework and Practice

- The Homework section in the *Student Guide* gives additional practice in reading, writing, and ordering numbers.
- The *Writing Big Numbers* Activity Page in the *Discovery Assignment Book* can be used for homework.
- The *Spin and Read Number Game* can be used as homework.
- Assign Bits A and C for practice adding, subtracting, and finding medians.
- Assign Part 2 of the Home Practice to review placing numbers on number lines and estimation.
- DPP Task D is the first of a series of practice items involving time. Assign this item for practice with adding hours and minutes.

Answers for Part 2 of the Home Practice are in the Answer Key at the end of this lesson and at the end of this unit.

Homework

2006 Populations Table 2

State	Nickname	Population
Georgia	Peach State	8,684,715
Hawaii	Aloha State	1,257,608
Idaho	Gem State	1,366,332
Illinois	Prairie State	12,653,544
Indiana	Hoosier State	6,195,643
Iowa	Hawkeye State	2,944,062
Kansas	Sunflower State	2,723,507
Kentucky	Bluegrass State	4,117,827
Louisiana	Pelican State	4,496,334

1. Read each of the numbers aloud. List the numbers in order from the largest to the smallest.
2. Use expanded form to write the numbers that have a 5, 6, or 8 in the 10,000s' place.
3. Use word form to write the numbers for the four states that have reported populations closest to 2 million.
4. Round the population of Kansas to the nearest hundred thousand.
5. Round the population of Illinois to the nearest thousand.
6. The population of Georgia as reported in a 1995 atlas was 6,508,419 people. About how many more people were there in Georgia in 2006 than in 1995? If Georgia continues to grow at this rate, when might the population of Georgia go over twelve million? Estimate the year.

Note:
These populations were reported in the *2006 Rand McNally Road Atlas*. If you have access to a more current edition, you can determine how much each state has increased or decreased in population.

Student Guide - page 34 (Answers on p. 47)

Name _____ Date _____

PART 2   Numbers in the Hundreds and Thousands

1. Number the line below from 0 to 10,000. Skip count by 1000s.

Read each of the facts about the United States below. Then make a tick mark on the number line above to show where each number falls on the line. Label the tick mark with the appropriate letter.

A. The highest bridge over water in the world—1053 feet—is in Colorado. It is the suspension bridge over the Royal Gorge of the Arkansas River.
B. Mount Katahdin is the highest spot in Maine—5268 feet. This mountain is the first place in the entire United States to get hit with sunlight when the sun rises in the morning.
C. The world's tallest living redwood tree on record stands 367 feet tall. Redwood trees are native to California.

2. Without actually finding exact answers to these problems, give the number of digits in the answer. Explain how you know.
   A. 512 + 369

   B. 843 − 776

   C. 2190 + 8756

   D. 15 × 65

   E. 4589 − 637

Discovery Assignment Book - page 10 (Answers on p. 47)

After students complete the homework, ask them to turn to *Reading and Writing Big Numbers* in the *Student Guide.* Ask them to write the standard form, the word form, and the expanded form for each number listed in the 1995 Populations Table 1 chart.

Extension

Assign DPP item B for a challenge problem involving money.

Social Studies Connection

Ask students to find these facts:
    Population of your class
    Population of your school
    Population of your town
    Population of your state
    Population of your country

They can add these numbers to the *Population Lines* Activity Page.

At a Glance

Math Facts and Daily Practice and Problems

1. Complete items A–D.
2. Continue review of addition and subtraction facts as needed for individual students.

Part 1. A Play: Reviewing Place Value

Students read the play on the *Reading and Writing Big Numbers* Activity Pages in the *Student Guide*. They review language and ideas related to the importance of place value in reading and writing larger numbers.

Part 2. Reading, Writing, and Ordering Big Numbers

1. Students discuss and apply the ideas presented in the play by reading and writing big numbers in words, standard form, and expanded form using the *Place Value Chart* and the *Writing Big Numbers* Activity Page in the *Discovery Assignment Book*.
2. Students discuss *Questions 1–9* on the *Reading and Writing Big Numbers* Activity Pages in the *Student Guide*.
3. Make a transparency of the *Population Lines* Activity Page in the *Discovery Assignment Book*. Estimate the placement of numbers on the number lines. Review rounding.
4. Students answer *Question 10* by placing numbers on a number line using the *Population Lines* Activity Page in the *Discovery Assignment Book*.
5. Students use the number lines on the *Population Lines* Activity Page to help them round numbers in *Questions 11–13*.

Part 3. *Spin and Read Number Game*

Students play *Spin and Read Number Game*.

Homework

1. Assign the Homework section in the *Student Guide*.
2. Assign the *Writing Big Numbers* Activity Page in the *Discovery Assignment Book*.
3. Assign the *Spin and Read Number Game*.
4. Assign Part 2 of the Home Practice.

Assessment

Use the Reading and Writing Big Numbers section of the *Student Guide* to assess writing numbers.

Extension

Assign DPP item B as a challenge.

Connection

Have students look up population information about their school, class, town, state, and so on to add to their *Population Lines* Activity Page.

Answer Key is on pages 45–48.

Notes:

Digit Cards 0–9

4	9
3	8
2	7
1	6
0	5

Reverse Side of Digit Cards 0–9

Blackline Master

Student Guide (p. 31)

1. 4,062,608

2. 13,003,362

3. **A.** Alabama, Arkansas, and Delaware

   B. Arizona and Delaware

4. **A.** Arizona (On the board, in the opening vignette it says, "Our State: 3,677,985." Looking at the 1995 State Populations Table, this was Arizona's population in 1995.

   B. 3,677,985

Student Guide - page 31

5. What is the estimated world population?

6. List the populations of Arizona, Colorado, and Connecticut in order from smallest to largest.

7. A. Write the reported population of Alabama in expanded form.
   B. Write the reported population of Florida in expanded form.

8. A. Write the reported population of Connecticut in word form.
   B. Write the reported population of Delaware in word form.

9. Which state has a reported population closest to 1 million?

10. Complete the number lines on the *Population Lines* Activity Page in the *Discovery Assignment Book*. Show the position of each state's population in the 2006 Populations Table 1 on the appropriate number line. Alaska has been written as an example on the correct number line.

11. Use the *Population Lines* Activity Page to help you:
   A. Round the population of Arizona to the nearest million.
   B. Round the population of Alabama to the nearest million.
   C. Round the population of Delaware to the nearest hundred thousand.

12. A. Round the population of Arkansas to the nearest million.
   B. Round the population of Arkansas to the nearest hundred thousand.

13. A. Round the population of Florida to the nearest ten million.
   B. Round the population of Florida to the nearest million.

Spin and Read Number Game

Players

This game is for groups of three students. Two students play and one student serves as a judge.

The purpose of the game is to practice reading large numbers.

Materials

- one deck of playing cards (use ace as "1" and the king as "0" and remove the queens, jacks, and tens) or four sets of *Digit Cards 0–9*
- *Spin and Read Number Game Spinners* Activity Page
- one clear plastic spinner or paper clip and pencil
- *Place Value Chart* Activity Page
- one calculator

32 SG • Grade 5 • Unit 2 • Lesson 1   Reading and Writing Big Numbers

Student Guide - page 32

Student Guide (p. 32)

5. 5,642,000,000 (This is listed on the board in the opening vignette.)

6. Connecticut, 3,295,669; Colorado, 3,307,912; Arizona, 3,677,985

7. A. 4,000,000 + 60,000 + 2000 + 600 + 8
   B. 10,000,000 + 3,000,000 + 3000 + 300 + 60 + 2

8. A. three million, two hundred ninety-five thousand, six hundred sixty-nine
   B. six hundred sixty-eight thousand, six hundred ninety-six

9. Delaware

10.*

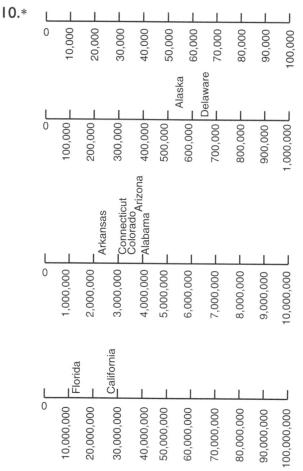

11. A. 4,000,000
   B. 4,000,000
   C. 700,000

12. A. 2,000,000
   B. 2,400,000

13. A. 10,000,000
   B. 13,000,000

Student Guide (p. 34)

Homework

1. 11,466,682; 6,508,419; 5,564,228; 4,238,216; 3,698,969; 2,787,424; 2,485,600; 1,115,274; 1,011,986

2. 11,466,682 = 10,000,000 + 1,000,000 + 400,000 + 60,000 + 6000 + 600 + 80 + 2

   5,564,228 = 5,000,000 + 500,000 + 60,000 + 4000 + 200 + 20 + 8

   2,787,424 = 2,000,000 + 700,000 + 80,000 + 7000 + 400 + 20 + 4

   2,485,600 = 2,000,000 + 400,000 + 80,000 + 5000 + 600

3. Kansas: two million, four hundred eighty-five thousand, six hundred

   Iowa: two million, seven hundred eighty-seven thousand, four hundred twenty-four

   Hawaii: one million, one hundred fifteen thousand, two hundred seventy-four

   Idaho: one million, eleven thousand, nine hundred eighty-six

4. 2,500,000   5. 11,467,000

6. 2,000,000. Estimates will vary. 2040–2045

Discovery Assignment Book (p. 10)

Home Practice*

Part 2. Numbers in the Hundreds and Thousands

1.

2. **A.** 3 digits. 512 + 369 is less than 1000; it is about 880.

   B. 2 digits. The difference is less than 100.

   C. 5 digits. Estimating, the sum will be over 10,000.

   D. 10 × 65 = 650, 20 × 65 = 1300. The answer is in the middle. Add 300 to 650 and get 950. Subtract 300 from 1300 and get 1000. The number in the middle of 950 and 1000 is 975—3 digits.

   E. 4 digits. The difference is about 4000.

2006 Populations Table 2

State	Nickname	Population
Georgia	Peach State	8,684,715
Hawaii	Aloha State	1,257,608
Idaho	Gem State	1,366,332
Illinois	Prairie State	12,653,544
Indiana	Hoosier State	6,195,643
Iowa	Hawkeye State	2,944,062
Kansas	Sunflower State	2,723,507
Kentucky	Bluegrass State	4,117,827
Louisiana	Pelican State	4,496,334

1. Read each of the numbers aloud. List the numbers in order from the largest to the smallest.

2. Use expanded form to write the numbers that have a 5, 6, or 8 in the 10,000s' place.

3. Use word form to write the numbers for the four states that have reported populations closest to 2 million.

4. Round the population of Kansas to the nearest hundred thousand.

5. Round the population of Illinois to the nearest thousand.

6. The population of Georgia as reported in a 1995 atlas was 6,508,419 people. About how many more people were there in Georgia in 2006 than in 1995? If Georgia continues to grow at this rate, when might the population of Georgia go over twelve million? Estimate the year.

Note:
These populations were reported in the *2006 Rand McNally Road Atlas*. If you have access to a more current edition, you can determine how much each state has increased or decreased in population.

34   SG • Grade 5 • Unit 2 • Lesson 1   Reading and Writing Big Numbers

Student Guide - page 34

Name _____ Date _____

PART 2 **Numbers in the Hundreds and Thousands**

1. Number the line below from 0 to 10,000. Skip count by 1000s.

Read each of the facts about the United States below. Then make a tick mark on the number line above to show where each number falls on the line. Label the tick mark with the appropriate letter.

   A. The highest bridge over water in the world—1053 feet—is in Colorado. It is the suspension bridge over the Royal Gorge of the Arkansas River.

   B. Mount Katahdin is the highest spot in Maine—5268 feet. This mountain is the first place in the entire United States to get hit with sunlight when the sun rises in the morning.

   C. The world's tallest living redwood tree on record stands 367 feet tall. Redwood trees are native to California.

2. Without actually finding exact answers to these problems, give the number of digits in the answer. Explain how you know.

   A. 512 + 369

   B. 843 − 776

   C. 2190 + 8756

   D. 15 × 65

   E. 4589 − 637

10   DAB • Grade 5 • Unit 2   BIG NUMBERS

Discovery Assignment Book - page 10

---

*Answers for all the Home Practice in the *Discovery Assignment Book* are at the end of the unit.

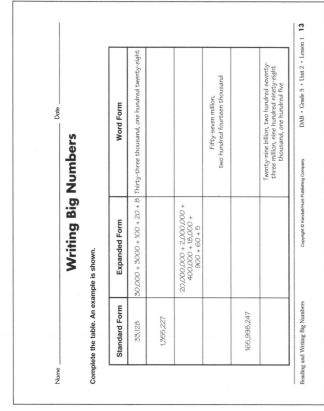

Discovery Assignment Book - page 13

Discovery Assignment Book (p. 13)

Writing Big Numbers

1,355,227; 1,000,000 + 300,000 + 50,000 + 5000 + 200 + 20 + 7; one million, three hundred fifty-five thousand, two hundred twenty-seven

22,418,965; twenty-two million, four hundred eighteen thousand, nine hundred sixty-five

57,214,000; 50,000,000 + 7,000,000 + 200,000 + 10,000 + 4000

100,000,000 + 60,000,000 + 5,000,000 + 900,000 + 90,000 + 8000 + 200 + 40 + 7; one hundred sixty-five million, nine hundred ninety-eight thousand, two hundred forty-seven

29,273,998,105; 20,000,000,000 + 9,000,000,000 + 200,000,000 + 70,000,000 + 3,000,000 + 900,000 + 90,000 + 8000 + 100 + 5

Population Lines

Number this line from 0 to 100,000. Skip count by 10,000s.

Number this line from 0 to 1,000,000. Some numbers have been written for you.

0   100,000   200,000   500,000   Alaska   600,000

Number this line from 0 to 10,000,000. Skip count by millions.

Number this line from 0 to 100,000,000. Skip count by ten millions.

Discovery Assignment Book - page 15

Discovery Assignment Book (p. 15)

Population Lines

Students use this page to record their answers to **Question 10** on the *Student Guide* pages in Lesson 1.

Lesson 2

Facts I Know

Lesson Overview

Estimated Class Sessions
1-2

This lesson introduces the yearlong review of the multiplication and division facts. Students use flash cards to review the multiplication and division facts for the first group of facts, the 5s and 10s. They record on charts both the multiplication and division facts they know and can answer quickly. They will continue to update these charts throughout the year. Specific DPP items in Unit 2 continue the practice of the 5s and 10s. In the DPP for Units 3–6 the other four groups of facts (2s and 3s, squares, 9s, and the last six facts—4×6, 4×7, 4×8, 6×7, 6×8, and 7×8) are practiced and assessed.

Key Content

- Self-assessing the multiplication and division facts.
- Maintaining fluency with the multiplication and division facts.

Key Vocabulary

- divisor
- fact families
- factors
- product
- quotient
- turn-around facts

Homework

Assign Part 1 of the Home Practice that asks students to practice the math facts.

Assessment

1. Students use flash cards and *Facts I Know* charts to assess themselves on the multiplication and division facts.
2. Record your observations on the *Observational Assessment Record*.

Curriculum Sequence

Before This Unit

Multiplication and Division Facts

Students using *Math Trailblazers* are expected to demonstrate fluency with the multiplication facts by the end of third grade. By the end of fourth grade, they are expected to demonstrate fluency with the division facts.

Students develop conceptual understanding and procedures for multiplication in third grade. The introduction of strategies to gain fluency with the multiplication facts begins in Unit 11 of third grade. A systematic approach to gaining fluency with the division facts is a component of the fourth-grade curriculum.

After This Unit

Multiplication and Division Facts

By the end of fourth grade, students in *Math Trailblazers* are expected to demonstrate fluency with all the facts. This lesson, which focuses on the 5s and 10s, begins a systematic review of the multiplication and division facts that will continue throughout the DPP in fifth grade. As students review each of five groups of multiplication facts, they study the related division facts. Using this approach, students maintain their fluency with the multiplication and division facts. The table below lists the five groups of facts and indicates when each is introduced in the DPP.

For a detailed explanation of our approach to learning and assessing the facts, see the *Grade 5 Facts Resource Guide*. Information is also in the TIMS Tutor: *Math Facts* in the *Teacher Implementation Guide* and *Information for Parents: Grade 5 Math Facts Philosophy*, which immediately follows the Unit 2 Background.

Unit	Math Fact Group
2	Group 1: 5s and 10s
3	Group 2: 2s and 3s
4	Group 3: squares
5	Group 4: 9s
6	Group 5: The last six facts: 4×6, 4×7, 4×8, 6×7, 6×8, 7×8
7	Review all five groups.
8	Assess all five groups.

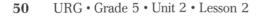

Materials List

Supplies and Copies

Student	Teacher
Supplies for Each Student • ruler • scissors	**Supplies** • scissors
Copies • 1 copy of *Multiplication* and *Division Facts I Know* charts per student (*Unit Resource Guide* Pages 61–62) • 1 copy of *Information for Parents: Grade 5 Math Facts Philosophy* per student (*Unit Resource Guide* Pages 13–14) • 1 copy of *Centimeter Dot Paper* per student (*Unit Resource Guide* Page 63)	**Copies/Transparencies** • 1 transparency of *Triangle Flash Cards: 5s* (*Discovery Assignment Book* Page 21) • 1 transparency of *Triangle Flash Cards: 10s* (*Discovery Assignment Book* Page 23) • 1 transparency of *Centimeter Dot Paper* (*Unit Resource Guide* Page 63) • 1 copy of *Observational Assessment Record* to be used throughout this unit (*Unit Resource Guide* Pages 15–16)

All blackline masters including assessment, transparency, and DPP masters are also on the Teacher Resource CD.

Student Books
Facts I Know (*Student Guide* Pages 35–38)
Triangle Flash Cards: 5s (*Discovery Assignment Book* Page 21)
Triangle Flash Cards: 10s (*Discovery Assignment Book* Page 23)

Daily Practice and Problems and Home Practice
DPP items E–F (*Unit Resource Guide* Page 21)
Home Practice Part 1 (*Discovery Assignment Book* Page 9)

Note: Classrooms whose pacing differs significantly from the suggested pacing of the units should use the Math Facts Calendar in Section 4 of the *Facts Resource Guide* to ensure students receive the complete math facts program.

Assessment Tools
Observational Assessment Record (*Unit Resource Guide* Pages 15–16)

Daily Practice and Problems

Suggestions for using the DPPs are on page 58.

E. Bit: Making Change (URG p. 21)

David buys a CD that costs $14.49 with tax. He gives the sales clerk a $20 bill. How much change will he receive? Name the least number of coins and bills he can receive.

F. Task: Measuring Pencils (URG p. 21)

Measure the length of four classmates' pencils to the nearest centimeter. Record the information in a data table. Then find the median length of the pencils.

TIMS Tip

Although students work in pairs, each student needs a set of flash cards so he or she can sort the cards in class and at home. Students need the flash cards repeatedly throughout the Daily Practice and Problems and the Home Practice. Have students write their initials on the back of each card and save them in envelopes or folders for future use. Some teachers have students make two sets—one for home and one for school. Others laminate the cards for durability. Blackline masters of the cards are provided in the *Facts Resource Guide*. Use these masters throughout the year to make additional copies as the need arises.

Before the Activity

Each student needs *Triangle Flash Cards: 5s* and *10s* from the *Discovery Assignment Book* and one copy each of the *Multiplication Facts I Know* and *Division Facts I Know* charts. Send home a copy of the *Information for Parents: Grade 5 Math Facts Philosophy* with each student.

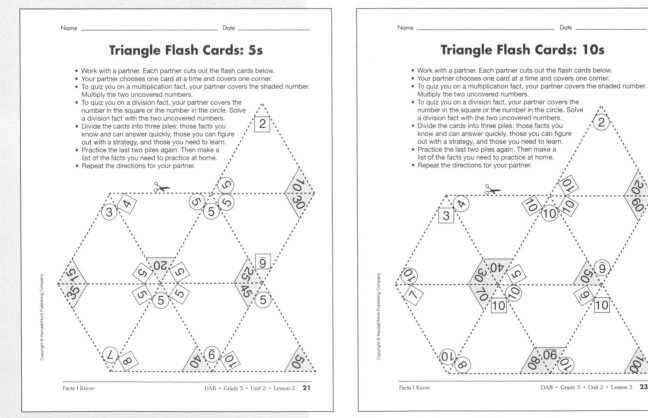

Discovery Assignment Book - page 21

Discovery Assignment Book - page 23

Part 1 Multiplication Facts and Triangle Flash Cards

The Multiplication Facts and Triangle Flash Cards section of the *Facts I Know* Activity Pages in the *Student Guide* introduces students to the use of Triangle Flash Cards. In this lesson students use *Triangle Flash Cards: 5s* and *10s* which are in the *Discovery Assignment Book.* Students who had *Math Trailblazers* in fourth grade will probably recognize the flash cards and remember how to use them. Read the directions in **Questions 1A and 1B** on the *Facts I Know* Activity Pages along with your students. To use the flash cards, one partner covers the corner containing the highest number with his or her thumb (this number is lightly shaded). This number is the answer—or **product**—to a multiplication problem. The second person multiplies the two uncovered numbers. These are the two **factors.** Partners should take turns quizzing each other on the multiplication facts for the 5s and 10s. As students are quizzed, they place each flash card into one of three piles: those facts they know and can answer quickly, those they can figure out with a strategy, and those they need to learn.

Once students sort all their cards, they record their results on their copies of the *Multiplication Facts I Know* chart, which is in the *Unit Resource Guide* **(Question 1C).** Figure 6 illustrates how to do this with one set of facts. Throughout the year, students will be reminded to update these charts.

> ## TIMS Tip
>
> To help students organize the three stacks of flash cards, they can cut an index card into three pieces. Then they write "Know Quickly" on one piece, "Know with Strategy" on another, and "Don't Know" on a third.

> ## Content Note
>
> **Multiplication Facts.** Since third grade, students in *Math Trailblazers* have used the term **turn-around facts** to describe multiplication facts that contain the same factors but in a different order. For example, $4 \times 5 = 20$ and $5 \times 4 = 20$ are turn-around facts.
>
> When students begin their *Multiplication Facts I Know* charts, you might want to discuss the facts for 0s and 1s. Many students know these facts and will want to circle them right away. Have students explain multiplication by 0 and 1. Any number times 0 is 0. Any number times 1 is itself.

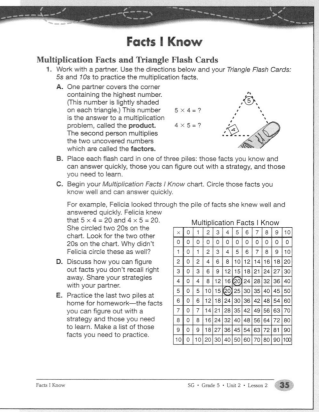

Student Guide - page 35 (Answers on p. 64)

Multiplication Facts I Know											
×	0	1	2	3	4	5	6	7	8	9	10
0	0	0	0	0	0	0	0	0	0	0	0
1	0	1	2	3	4	5	6	7	8	9	10
2	0	2	4	6	8	10	12	14	16	18	20
3	0	3	6	9	12	15	18	21	24	27	30
4	0	4	8	12	16	⑳	24	28	32	36	40
5	0	5	10	15	⑳	25	30	35	40	45	50
6	0	6	12	18	24	30	36	42	48	54	60
7	0	7	14	21	28	35	42	49	56	63	70
8	0	8	16	24	32	40	48	56	64	72	80
9	0	9	18	27	36	45	54	63	72	81	90
10	0	10	20	30	40	50	60	70	80	90	100

Recording $4 \times 5 = 20$ and $5 \times 4 = 20$ as "Facts I Know."

Figure 6: *Circling a fact I know on the* Multiplication Facts I Know *chart*

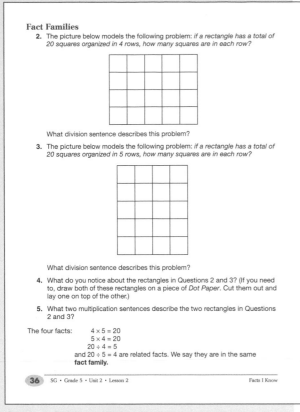

Fact Families

2. The picture below models the following problem: *if a rectangle has a total of 20 squares organized in 4 rows, how many squares are in each row?*

What division sentence describes this problem?

3. The picture below models the following problem: *if a rectangle has a total of 20 squares organized in 5 rows, how many squares are in each row?*

What division sentence describes this problem?

4. What do you notice about the rectangles in Questions 2 and 3? (If you need to, draw both of these rectangles on a piece of *Dot Paper*. Cut them out and lay one on top of the other.)

5. What two multiplication sentences describe the two rectangles in Questions 2 and 3?

The four facts:
$4 \times 5 = 20$
$5 \times 4 = 20$
$20 \div 4 = 5$
and $20 \div 5 = 4$ are related facts. We say they are in the same **fact family.**

Student Guide - page 36 *(Answers on p. 64)*

TIMS Tip

Remind students that rows go across and columns go up and down.

Question 1D asks students to discuss strategies for figuring out answers to the multiplication facts they need to practice. Some examples of strategies follow. For more information about math fact strategies, see the TIMS Tutor: *Math Facts* in the *Teacher Implementation Guide.*

- Skip counting: This strategy is only efficient for a small number of facts. $2 \times 3 = \ldots$ 2, 4, 6.

- Doubling: 7×4 may be solved by doubling the answer to 7×2; $7 \times 2 = 14$; $14 + 14 = 28$.

- Using known facts: Knowing 5×5 is 25 may help in solving 5×6; $5 \times 5 = 25$; $25 + 5 = 30$.

- Patterns in the 9s: The sum of the digits of the products is 9. For example, $9 \times 5 = \mathbf{45.}$ $\mathbf{4 + 5} = 9$.

Students should not spend time practicing the facts they already know. Therefore, after the flash cards are sorted and the *Multiplication Facts I Know* charts have been updated, *Question 1E* asks students to list the facts in the other two piles—those they can figure out using a strategy and those they need to learn. Students should take this list home along with their flash cards to study the facts. Part 1 of the Home Practice reminds students to take home this list and their flash cards.

Part 2 Fact Families

Distribute a copy of *Centimeter Dot Paper* to each student. Pose the following problem: *If a rectangle on the dot paper is made up of 30 squares and there are 5 rows of squares, how many squares are in each row?* Have students solve the problem by creating such a rectangle on *Centimeter Dot Paper.* The rectangle should be made up of 5 rows of 6 squares. See Figure 7.

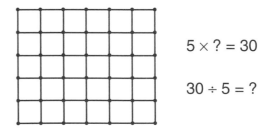

$5 \times ? = 30$

$30 \div 5 = ?$

Figure 7: *5 rows of 6 squares*

Ask students, *"What operation can you use to answer this question? Write a number sentence for the problem."* This question can be viewed as a multiplication problem with a missing number: $5 \times ? = 30$. It can also be viewed as a division problem: $30 \div 5 = ?$ Have students label their rectangles with both number sentences: $5 \times 6 = 30$ and $30 \div 5 = 6$.

Pose a similar problem: *If a rectangle is made up of 30 squares and there are 6 rows of squares, how many squares are in each row?* Ask students to solve this problem using the *Centimeter Dot Paper.* Your students should recognize that this problem results in a rectangle similar to the one they created earlier. This time there are 6 rows of 5 squares. Ask, *"What operation can you use to answer this question? Write a number sentence for the problem."* Both $6 \times ? = 30$ and $30 \div 6 = ?$ are appropriate number sentences. Ask students to label their second rectangle with both number sentences: $6 \times 5 = 30$ and $30 \div 6 = 5$. See Figure 8. Emphasize the fact that the two rectangles are the same, by having students cut out both rectangles and laying one directly on top of the other. You can demonstrate this using overhead transparencies of the *Centimeter Dot Paper.*

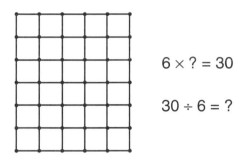

$6 \times ? = 30$

$30 \div 6 = ?$

Figure 8: *6 rows of 5 squares*

Since the four number sentences—$6 \times 5 = 30$, $5 \times 6 = 30$, $30 \div 5 = 6$, and $30 \div 6 = 5$—all represent the same rectangle, we can see that these four facts are related. Introduce students to the term fact family. These four related facts are in the same **fact family.**

If necessary, have students create more rectangles on *Centimeter Dot Paper* to illustrate fact families. *Questions 2–5* in the Fact Families section on the *Facts I Know* Activity Pages in the *Student Guide* provide another example using the facts 4×5, 5×4, $20 \div 4$, and $20 \div 5$. You may complete these questions as a class or have student pairs complete them. *Questions 6–11* provide multiplication and division fact practice for the 5s and 10s. Fact families are emphasized throughout. Students' knowledge of the multiplication facts and turn-around facts helps them review the division facts.

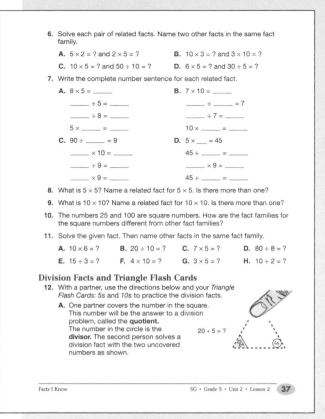

6. Solve each pair of related facts. Name two other facts in the same fact family.

   A. $5 \times 2 = ?$ and $2 \times 5 = ?$ **B.** $10 \times 3 = ?$ and $3 \times 10 = ?$

   C. $10 \times 5 = ?$ and $50 \div 10 = ?$ **D.** $6 \times 5 = ?$ and $30 \div 5 = ?$

7. Write the complete number sentence for each related fact.

   A. $8 \times 5 = \underline{\hspace{0.5cm}}$

   $\underline{\hspace{0.5cm}} \div 5 = \underline{\hspace{0.5cm}}$

   $\underline{\hspace{0.5cm}} \div 8 = \underline{\hspace{0.5cm}}$

   $5 \times \underline{\hspace{0.5cm}} = \underline{\hspace{0.5cm}}$

   B. $7 \times 10 = \underline{\hspace{0.5cm}}$

   $\underline{\hspace{0.5cm}} \div \underline{\hspace{0.5cm}} = 7$

   $\underline{\hspace{0.5cm}} \div 7 = \underline{\hspace{0.5cm}}$

   $10 \times \underline{\hspace{0.5cm}} = \underline{\hspace{0.5cm}}$

   C. $90 \div \underline{\hspace{0.5cm}} = 9$

   $\underline{\hspace{0.5cm}} \times 10 = \underline{\hspace{0.5cm}}$

   $\underline{\hspace{0.5cm}} \div 9 = \underline{\hspace{0.5cm}}$

   $\underline{\hspace{0.5cm}} \times 9 = \underline{\hspace{0.5cm}}$

   D. $5 \times \underline{\hspace{0.5cm}} = 45$

   $45 \div \underline{\hspace{0.5cm}} = \underline{\hspace{0.5cm}}$

   $\underline{\hspace{0.5cm}} \times 9 = \underline{\hspace{0.5cm}}$

   $45 \div \underline{\hspace{0.5cm}} = \underline{\hspace{0.5cm}}$

8. What is 5×5? Name a related fact for 5×5. Is there more than one?

9. What is 10×10? Name a related fact for 10×10. Is there more than one?

10. The numbers 25 and 100 are square numbers. How are the fact families for the square numbers different from other fact families?

11. Solve the given fact. Then name other facts in the same fact family.

   A. $10 \times 6 = ?$ **B.** $20 \div 10 = ?$ **C.** $7 \times 5 = ?$ **D.** $80 \div 8 = ?$

   E. $15 \div 3 = ?$ **F.** $4 \times 10 = ?$ **G.** $3 \times 5 = ?$ **H.** $10 \div 2 = ?$

Division Facts and Triangle Flash Cards

12. With a partner, use the directions below and your *Triangle Flash Cards: 5s and 10s* to practice the division facts.

   A. One partner covers the number in the square. This number will be the answer to a division problem, called the **quotient.** The number in the circle is the **divisor.** The second person solves a division fact with the two uncovered numbers as shown.

   $20 \div 5 = ?$

Student Guide - page 37 (Answers on p. 65)

B. Place each flash card in one of three piles: those facts you know well and can answer quickly, those you can figure out with a strategy, and those you need to learn.

C. Begin your *Division Facts I Know* chart. Circle the facts you know well and can answer quickly.

For example, Edward knew 20 ÷ 5 = 4. So Edward circled the 20 in the row for a divisor of 5.

Division Facts I Know

×	0	1	2	3	4	5	6	7	8	9	10
0	0	0	0	0	0	0	0	0	0	0	0
1	0	1	2	3	4	5	6	7	8	9	10
2	0	2	4	6	8	10	12	14	16	18	20
3	0	3	6	9	12	15	18	21	24	27	30
4	0	4	8	12	16	20	24	28	32	36	40
5	0	5	10	15	(20)	25	30	35	40	45	50
6	0	6	12	18	24	30	36	42	48	54	60
7	0	7	14	21	28	35	42	49	56	63	70
8	0	8	16	24	32	40	48	56	64	72	80
9	0	9	18	27	36	45	54	63	72	81	90
10	0	10	20	30	40	50	60	70	80	90	100

Divisor

D. Sort the cards again. This time your partner covers the number in the circle. The number in the square is now the divisor. Solve a division fact with the two uncovered numbers.

20 ÷ 4 = ?

E. Update your *Division Facts I Know* chart. Circle the facts you know well and can answer quickly.

F. Discuss how you can figure out facts you don't recall right away. Share your strategies with your partner.

G. Practice the last two piles at home for homework—the facts you can figure out with a strategy and those you need to learn. Make a list of these facts.

13. Compare your *Multiplication Facts I Know* chart to your *Division Facts I Know* chart. Look for facts in the same fact family. Do you know any complete fact families? Which family or families? Explain.

You will continue to use *Triangle Flash Cards* to study other groups of facts. You will be reminded to update your *Multiplication* and *Division Facts I Know* charts. If you know one or two of the facts in a fact family, use those facts to help you learn the others.

38 SG • Grade 5 • Unit 2 • Lesson 2 Facts I Know

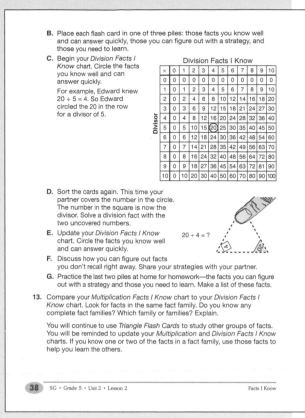

Student Guide* - page 38 *(Answers on p. 65)

Division Facts I Know

×	0	1	2	3	4	5	6	7	8	9	10
0	0	0	0	0	0	0	0	0	0	0	0
1	0	1	2	3	4	5	6	7	8	9	10
2	0	2	4	6	8	10	12	14	16	18	20
3	0	3	6	9	12	15	18	21	24	27	30
4	0	4	8	12	16	20	24	28	32	36	40
5	0	5	10	15	(20)	25	30	35	40	45	50
6	0	6	12	18	24	30	36	42	48	54	60
7	0	7	14	21	28	35	42	49	56	63	70
8	0	8	16	24	32	40	48	56	64	72	80
9	0	9	18	27	36	45	54	63	72	81	90
10	0	10	20	30	40	50	60	70	80	90	100

Divisor

Recording 20 ÷ 5 = 4 as a "Fact I Know."

Figure 10: *Using the* Division Facts I Know *chart*

Questions 8–10 focus on the square facts 5 × 5 = 25 and 10 × 10 = 100. Since the two factors in each of these number sentences are the same, the fact families for these are different from other families. 5 × 5 = 25 and 25 ÷ 5 = 5 are the only two facts in this fact family. Likewise, 10 × 10 = 100 and 100 ÷ 10 = 10 are the only two facts in this fact family.

Part 3 Division Facts and Triangle Flash Cards

After students practice the multiplication facts for the 5s and 10s by completing ***Questions 6–11*** in the *Student Guide,* have student pairs use their flash cards to assess the division facts. ***Question 12*** outlines how students can use the flash cards for division. The procedure here is similar to the way the cards were used earlier for multiplication. However, there is one difference. When using the cards for division, students need to sort the *Triangle Flash Cards: 5s* and *10s* twice. The first time through the cards, partners cover the numbers in squares ***(Question 12A–12B).*** Then, after sorting the cards, students update the *Division Facts I Know* chart ***(Question 12C).*** The second time through, partners cover the numbers in circles ***(Question 12D).*** After sorting the entire set of cards for the second time, students update their division chart ***(Question 12E).*** See Figure 9. Demonstrate this sequence using a transparency of the flash cards and the *Division Facts I Know* chart.

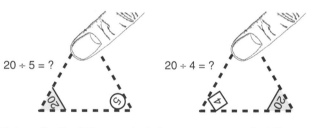

Figure 9: *Sort the cards twice—once covering the numbers in squares and a second time covering the numbers in circles.*

Question 12C provides an example of how to use the *Division Facts I Know* chart. Turn students' attention to the chart in ***Question 12C.*** Since Edward divided by 5 (20 ÷ 5 = 4), 5 is the **divisor.** He followed the 5 across its row to find the 20 he should circle. See Figure 10. Remind students that they circle only those facts that were in the pile of facts they know and can answer quickly. They should list the facts in the other two piles. Students should take this list home along with their flash cards to study the facts. Part 1 of the Home Practice reminds students to take home this list and their flash cards.

Question 13 asks students to compare their *Multiplication Facts I Know* chart with their *Division Facts I Know* chart. If students are using their knowledge of the multiplication facts and fact families to help them learn the division facts, they will see some patterns in their charts. For example, if a student knows 4 × 5 and 5 × 4, it is very likely he or she will know 20 ÷ 4 and 20 ÷ 5. Thus, two 20s should be circled on the division chart as well. Discuss students' results. Note that both *Facts I Know* charts have a multiplication symbol in the first square since both charts are simply multiplication tables used for recording known facts.

DPP items I, M, O, Q, U, W, X, Y, and AA, provide further practice with the multiplication and division facts for the 5s and 10s. A quiz on the 5s and 10s is provided in Item CC. Inform students when you will give the quiz so they can practice at home.

Part 4 Fact Practice in the DPP

Students practice the multiplication and division facts as they use them to solve problems in labs, activities, and games. However, the systematic practice and assessment of the math facts takes place primarily in the DPP. The study of math facts in the DPP for Units 3–6 parallels what takes place in Unit 2:

1. A DPP item instructs students to quiz each other on a group of facts using the *Triangle Flash Cards*. Students sort the cards into three piles as previously described. They update their *Multiplication* and *Division Facts I Know* charts.

2. Additional DPP items provide practice with the multiplication and division fact families for a particular group.

3. A final DPP item includes a quiz that assesses students on a mixture of multiplication and division facts for a particular group. Students take the quiz and update their *Multiplication Facts I Know* and *Division Facts I Know* charts.

The DPP for Units 7 and 8 review all five groups of facts. As students complete these items, students update their *Multiplication* and *Division Facts I Know* charts. A final DPP item in Unit 8 includes an inventory test on multiplication and division facts from all five groups. The tests help you and students assess the facts they know and those they still need to learn. During the second semester, students can use their *Triangle Flash Cards* to practice the multiplication and division facts they have not circled. The second semester's DPP includes additional math fact review, especially of the division facts. This provides further opportunities for students to strengthen their fluency with the math facts.

Content Note

The math facts program is closely linked to the recommended schedule for teaching lessons. Thus, classrooms that deviate significantly from the suggested pacing will need to make special accommodations to ensure students receive a consistent program of math facts practice and assessment throughout the year. The *Grade 5 Facts Resource Guide* outlines a schedule for math facts practice and assessment in classrooms that are moving much more slowly through lessons than recommended in the Lesson Guides. The *Grade 5 Facts Resource Guide* contains all components of the math facts program, including DPP items, flash cards, *Facts I Know* charts, and assessments.

Math Facts

Begin reviewing the multiplication and division facts for the 5s and 10s.

Homework and Practice

- Part 1 of the Home Practice reminds students to take home their flash cards for the 5s and 10s. Students should practice the multiplication and division facts they need to learn at home with a family member.
- Assign DPP Bit E which provides practice with money and DPP Task F which reviews measurement and finding a median.

Answers for the Home Practice are in the Answer Key at the end of this lesson and at the end of this unit.

Assessment

- Students use flash cards and *Facts I Know* charts to complete self assessments with the multiplication and division facts for the 5s and 10s.
- Record your observations on the *Observational Assessment Record*.

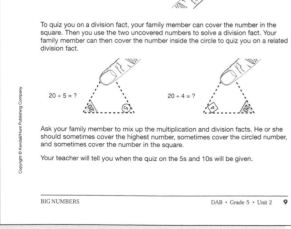

Name _____ Date _____

Unit 2 Home Practice

PART 1 *Triangle Flash Cards: 5s and 10s*

Study for the quiz on the multiplication and division facts for the 5s and 10s. Take home your *Triangle Flash Cards: 5s and 10s* and your list of facts you need to study.

Ask a family member to choose one flash card at a time. To quiz you on a multiplication fact, he or she should cover the corner containing the highest number. (The highest number on each card is lightly shaded.) This number will be the answer to two multiplication facts. Multiply the two uncovered numbers.

$5 \times 4 = ?$

$4 \times 5 = ?$

To quiz you on a division fact, your family member can cover the number in the square. Then you use the two uncovered numbers to solve a division fact. Your family member can then cover the number inside the circle to quiz you on a related division fact.

$20 \div 5 = ?$ $20 \div 4 = ?$

Ask your family member to mix up the multiplication and division facts. He or she should sometimes cover the highest number, sometimes cover the circled number, and sometimes cover the number in the square.

Your teacher will tell you when the quiz on the 5s and 10s will be given.

BIG NUMBERS   DAB • Grade 5 • Unit 2   **9**

Discovery Assignment Book - page 9

At a Glance

Math Facts and Daily Practice and Problems

Complete items E–F in the Daily Practice and Problems.

Part 1. Multiplication Facts and Triangle Flash Cards

1. Students prepare the *Triangle Flash Cards: 5s* and *10s* found in the *Discovery Assignment Book.* Each student cuts out a complete set.
2. Students use the flash cards to quiz each other on the multiplication facts. Directions on how to use the cards are on the *Facts I Know* Activity Pages in the *Student Guide. (Question 1)*
3. As students are quizzed, they sort their cards into three piles: facts I know and can answer quickly, facts I know using a strategy, and facts I need to learn.
4. Students begin their *Multiplication Facts I Know* chart by circling the facts they know well and can answer quickly.
5. Students discuss efficient strategies to use when trying to find the answer to a multiplication fact.
6. Students list the multiplication facts they still need to practice. They take home the list of facts and the flash cards.

Part 2. Fact Families

1. Distribute a copy of *Centimeter Dot Paper* to each student. Pose the following problem: *"If a rectangle on the dot paper is made up of 30 squares and there are 5 rows of squares, how many squares are in each row?"*
2. Students create the rectangle by connecting dots on the dot paper with a ruler. Discuss how they can solve this problem using a multiplication and a division sentence—$5 \times ? = 30$ and $30 \div 5 = ?$ Students label their rectangles with both number sentences: $5 \times 6 = 30$ and $30 \div 5 = 6$.
3. Pose a similar problem: *"If a rectangle is made up of 30 squares and there are 6 rows of squares, how many squares are in each row?"*
4. Ask students to solve this problem using the dot paper. Discuss how they can solve this problem using a multiplication and a division sentence—$6 \times ? = 30$ and $30 \div 6 = ?$ Students label their rectangles with both number sentences: $6 \times 5 = 30$ and $30 \div 6 = 5$.
5. Have students cut out both rectangles and lay one directly on top of the other. Both rectangles are the same.
6. Introduce the term fact family. All four number sentences—$6 \times 5 = 30$, $5 \times 6 = 30$, $30 \div 5 = 6$, and $30 \div 6 = 5$—represent the same rectangle. These four related facts are in the same fact family.
7. If necessary, have your students create more rectangles on *Centimeter Dot Paper* to illustrate fact families.
8. Students complete *Questions 2–11* in the Fact Families section on the *Facts I Know* Activity Pages in the *Student Guide.*

Part 3. Division Facts and Triangle Flash Cards

1. Students quiz each other on the division facts using the flash cards. Directions on how to use the cards are on the *Facts I Know* Activity Pages in the *Student Guide. (Question 12)* Student pairs first cover the numbers in squares.

2. As students are quizzed, they sort their cards into three piles: facts I know and can answer quickly, facts I know using a strategy, and facts I need to learn.

3. Students begin their *Division Facts I Know* chart by circling the facts they know well and can answer quickly.

4. Students sort the cards again. This time partners cover the numbers in circles.

5. Students update their *Division Facts I Know* chart a second time.

6. Students list the facts they need to practice.

7. Students compare their *Multiplication Facts I Know* chart to their *Division Facts I Know* chart.

8. They take home their list of facts and their flash cards to practice with a family member.

Part 4. Fact Practice in the DPP

Throughout the year, the practice and assessment of the facts continue in the DPP.

Homework

Assign Part 1 of the Home Practice that asks students to practice the math facts.

Assessment

1. Students use flash cards and *Facts I Know* charts to assess themselves on the multiplication and division facts.

2. Record your observations on the *Observational Assessment Record.*

Answer Key is on pages 64–65.

Notes:

Multiplication Facts I Know

- **Circle the facts you know well.**
- **Keep this table and use it to help you multiply.**
- **As you learn more facts, circle them too.**

×	0	1	2	3	4	5	6	7	8	9	10
0	0	0	0	0	0	0	0	0	0	0	0
1	0	1	2	3	4	5	6	7	8	9	10
2	0	2	4	6	8	10	12	14	16	18	20
3	0	3	6	9	12	15	18	21	24	27	30
4	0	4	8	12	16	20	24	28	32	36	40
5	0	5	10	15	20	25	30	35	40	45	50
6	0	6	12	18	24	30	36	42	48	54	60
7	0	7	14	21	28	35	42	49	56	63	70
8	0	8	16	24	32	40	48	56	64	72	80
9	0	9	18	27	36	45	54	63	72	81	90
10	0	10	20	30	40	50	60	70	80	90	100

Division Facts I Know

- **Circle the facts you know well.**
- **Keep this table and use it to help you divide.**
- **As you learn more facts, circle them too.**

Divisor

×	0	1	2	3	4	5	6	7	8	9	10
0	0	0	0	0	0	0	0	0	0	0	0
1	0	1	2	3	4	5	6	7	8	9	10
2	0	2	4	6	8	10	12	14	16	18	20
3	0	3	6	9	12	15	18	21	24	27	30
4	0	4	8	12	16	20	24	28	32	36	40
5	0	5	10	15	20	25	30	35	40	45	50
6	0	6	12	18	24	30	36	42	48	54	60
7	0	7	14	21	28	35	42	49	56	63	70
8	0	8	16	24	32	40	48	56	64	72	80
9	0	9	18	27	36	45	54	63	72	81	90
10	0	10	20	30	40	50	60	70	80	90	100

Name _____   Date _____

Centimeter Dot Paper

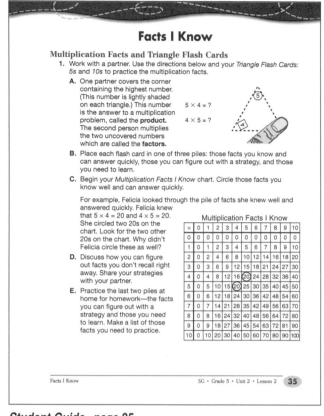

Student Guide - page 35

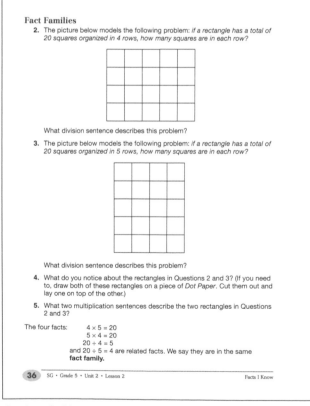

Student Guide - page 36

Student Guide (pp. 35–36)

Facts I Know

1.*

2. $20 \div 4 = 5$

3. $20 \div 5 = 4$

4. The rectangles are the same. If you cut one out and turn it around, you can lay it directly on top of the other.

5. $4 \times 5 = 20$ and $5 \times 4 = 20$

---

*Answers and/or discussion are included in the Lesson Guide.

Student Guide (pp. 37–38)

6. A. 10; 10; $10 \div 2 = 5$; $10 \div 5 = 2$

    B. 30; 30; $30 \div 3 = 10$; $30 \div 10 = 3$

    C. 50; 5; $5 \times 10 = 50$; $50 \div 5 = 10$

    D. 30; 6; $5 \times 6 = 30$; $30 \div 6 = 5$

7. A. 40; $40 \div 5 = 8$; $40 \div 8 = 5$; $5 \times 8 = 40$

    B. 70; $70 \div 10 = 7$; $70 \div 7 = 10$;
       $10 \times 7 = 70$

    C. $90 \div 10 = 9$; $9 \times 10 = 90$; $90 \div 9 = 10$;
       $10 \times 9 = 90$

    D. $5 \times 9 = 45$; $45 \div 5 = 9$; $5 \times 9 = 45$;
       $45 \div 9 = 5$

8. 25; $25 \div 5 = 5$; No.*

9. 100; $100 \div 10 = 10$; No.*

10. There are only two facts in the fact families for square numbers.*

11. A. 60; $6 \times 10 = 60$; $60 \div 6 = 10$;
       $60 \div 10 = 6$

    B. 2; $20 \div 2 = 10$; $2 \times 10 = 20$; $10 \times 2 = 20$

    C. 35; $5 \times 7 = 35$; $35 \div 7 = 5$; $35 \div 5 = 7$

    D. 10; $80 \div 10 = 8$; $8 \times 10 = 80$;
       $10 \times 8 = 80$

    E. 5; $15 \div 5 = 3$; $3 \times 5 = 15$; $5 \times 3 = 15$

    F. 40; $10 \times 4 = 40$; $40 \div 4 = 10$;
       $40 \div 10 = 4$

    G. 15; $5 \times 3 = 15$; $15 \div 3 = 5$; $15 \div 5 = 3$

    H. 5; $10 \div 5 = 2$; $2 \times 5 = 10$; $5 \times 2 = 10$

12. *

13. Answers will vary.*

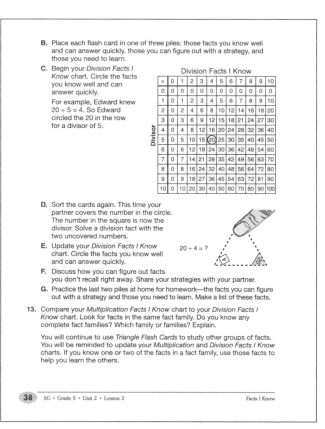

Student Guide - page 37

Student Guide - page 38

*Answers and/or discussion are included in the Lesson Guide.

The Base-Ten Number System

Lesson Overview

The activities in this optional review lesson are adapted from material in the fourth grade *Math Trailblazers* program. Use this lesson if your students did not have *Math Trailblazers* in fourth grade.

The lesson is divided into three parts. Use any or all parts of the lesson to review with your students as needed. Alternatively, parts of the lesson can be assigned to individual students. Part 1 uses base-ten pieces to review our number system. Part 2 uses the base-ten pieces to model addition. Part 3 models subtraction.

Key Content

- Understanding place value.
- Representing large numbers with base-ten pieces.
- Translating between different representations of large numbers (concrete, pictorial, symbolic).
- Modeling addition and subtraction with base-ten pieces.
- Estimating with base-ten pieces.
- Developing number sense for large numbers.

Key Vocabulary

- base-ten pieces
- bits
- Fewest Pieces Rule
- flats
- packs
- place value
- skinnies

Math Facts

Assign DPP item I.

Homework

Assign the Homework sections in *The Base-Ten Number System, Addition with Base-Ten Pieces,* and *Subtraction with Base-Ten Pieces* Activity Pages.

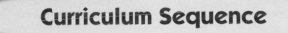

Curriculum Sequence

Before This Unit

Base-ten pieces were used in grades 2 through 4 to discuss place value and to introduce addition, subtraction, and multiplication algorithms. This lesson is an adaptation of fourth-grade work. It is intended for fifth graders who have some understanding of place value and the algorithms but have little experience with the base-ten pieces. It is a good review for students who can perform computations by rote, but need to improve their understanding of place value.

After This Unit

Multiplication in Lesson 5 and division in Unit 4 will be discussed using the base-ten pieces.

Materials List

Supplies and Copies

Student	Teacher
Supplies for Each Student Pair • 1 set of base-ten pieces (2 packs, 14 flats, 30 skinnies, 50 bits) or 2 copies of bits and skinnies *Base-Ten Pieces Master* and 3 copies of flats and packs *Base-Ten Pieces Master* (*Unit Resource Guide* Pages 87–88) **Supplies for Each Student Group** • 40 connecting cubes, optional • scissors, optional • tape	**Supplies** • overhead base-ten pieces, optional
Copies • 1 copy of *The Base-Ten Number System* per student (*Unit Resource Guide* Pages 79–83) • 1 copy of *Addition with Base-Ten Pieces* per student (*Unit Resource Guide* Pages 89–91) • 1 copy of *Subtraction with Base-Ten Pieces* per student (*Unit Resource Guide* Pages 92–95) • 1 copy of *Recording Sheet* per student (*Unit Resource Guide* Page 86) • 1 copy of *Base-Ten Board Part 1* per student group (*Unit Resource Guide* Page 84) • 1 copy of *Base-Ten Board Part 2* per student group (*Unit Resource Guide* Page 85)	**Copies/Transparencies** • 1 transparency of *Recording Sheet*, optional (*Unit Resource Guide* Page 86) • 1 transparency of *Base-Ten Board Part 1*, optional (*Unit Resource Guide* Page 84)

All blackline masters including assessment, transparency, and DPP masters are also on the Teacher Resource CD.

Daily Practice and Problems and Home Practice

DPP items G–J (*Unit Resource Guide* Pages 21–22)

Note: Classrooms whose pacing differs significantly from the suggested pacing of the units should use the Math Facts Calendar in Section 4 of the *Facts Resource Guide* to ensure students receive the complete math facts program.

G. Bit: Write the Number (URG p. 21) $\boxed{N}$

Write a number that has:

A. 6 tens and 3 ones
B. 91 hundreds and 6 tens
C. 73 tens
D. 8 hundreds and 14 ones
E. 50 tens and 8 ones

I. Bit: Multiplication and Division Sentences (URG p. 22) $\boxed{\begin{array}{r}5\\ \times\,7\end{array}}$

Lin has 15 flowers to place in 3 vases. How many flowers go in each vase if she divides them evenly?

A. Draw a picture to illustrate this problem.
B. Write a multiplication sentence and a division sentence that describe this problem.

H. Task: Smallest and Largest (URG p. 22) $\boxed{N}$

1. Rearrange the digits in 1997 to make the smallest possible number.
2. Rearrange the digits in 1997 to make the largest possible number.

For Questions 3 and 4, you may use a digit more than once; however, the number should begin with a nonzero digit.

3. Write the smallest four-digit number possible using the digits 0 through 9.
4. Write the largest four-digit number possible using the digits 0 through 9.

J. Challenge: Leaves on a Tree (URG p. 22) $\boxed{N}$

Find a tree. Estimate the number of leaves on your tree. Explain how you made your estimate.

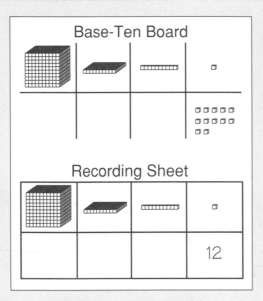

Figure 11: *Recording 12 bits*

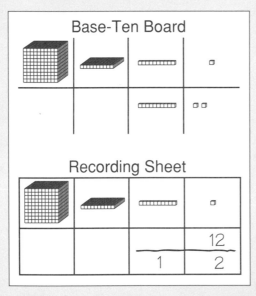

Figure 12: *Exchanging 12 bits for 1 skinny and 2 bits*

Teaching the Activity

Part 1 The TIMS Candy Company: Reviewing Place Value

Note: Refer to the Unit 2 Background for an overview of the vocabulary terms used with the base-ten pieces.

Hand out base-ten pieces, *Recording Sheets,* and *Base-Ten Boards Parts 1* and *2.* Explain to students that base-ten pieces are used to model numbers and operations. Introduce (or review) the TIMS Candy Company. The company makes chocolates called Chocos. They use the base-ten pieces to keep track of how many Chocos they make. A bit represents an individual Choco. If the company makes 12 Chocos, they place 12 bits in the bits' column of the *Base-Ten Board.* Record 12 bits (12 ones) on the *Recording Sheet* as shown in Figure 11. Note that the illustrations show the Base-Ten Board as one piece; students can tape together their two pieces of paper.

The TIMS Candy Company packages as many Chocos as they can. The company always packages in groups of 10. When there are 10 **bits,** they are packaged into a **skinny** (a ten). Show the class how to take 10 bits and exchange them for 1 skinny. Take a skinny out of its container and place the 10 bits back into the container. The skinny must be placed in the skinnies' column. Thus, you now have 1 skinny and 2 bits. Make sure all the students see that 12 bits represent the same amount of candy as 1 skinny and 2 bits. Record this modeling on the *Recording Sheet* as shown in Figure 12.

Have each group take a handful of unit cubes (bits) and pretend this represents the number of Chocos they made at the TIMS Candy Company. Ask students to place the cubes on the *Base-Ten Board.* Ask them to find different ways of grouping these bits by exchanging 10 bits for a skinny.

As an example, see Figure 13 which shows how 43 bits can be recorded on the *Recording Sheet.* The *Recording Sheet* records the action of the trades.

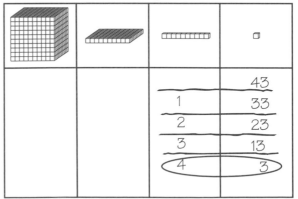

Figure 13: *Recording Sheet for 43 bits*

Explain that using 4 skinnies and 3 bits is the most efficient since it uses the least number of pieces. We call this the **Fewest Pieces Rule.** The representation using the Fewest Pieces Rule is circled in Figure 13. This representation corresponds to the base-ten system. Only one digit is allowed in each column. Children should express their amount of candy using the Fewest Pieces Rule. They should place any pieces that are not part of the number they are working on in a container. This emphasizes the trading action. Remind them that the bits always live in the bits' column and the skinnies live in the skinnies' column.

Explain to the class that for the TIMS Candy Company to operate as efficiently as possible, it decided that ten skinnies should form a flat. Illustrate this by placing ten skinnies side-by-side to show they are exactly the same size as a **flat.** Ask, *"How many bits are in a flat?"* If students are not sure, have them skip count by 10s to 100. When they have 10 skinnies, they can exchange them for a flat and vice versa. The *Base-Ten Board Part 2* has a column for the flats. Show them 3 flats and ask how many skinnies there would be if they broke up the flats. They should see that 3 flats is the same as 30 skinnies or 300 bits. Do several more examples as needed.

Show 2 flats, 6 skinnies, and 4 bits. Ask, *"How many bits would there be if you broke up the flats and skinnies and they were all in the bits' column?"* Make sure everyone sees that there are 264 bits. Ask, *"How else could you show or represent 264?"* There are many answers to this question. Two possible answers are:

1 flat, 16 skinnies, 4 bits

and

1 flat, 15 skinnies, 14 bits

Now, introduce the **packs** as 10 flats. Make a pack together with the class as you stack flats atop one another. Have students count with you by 100s to 1000 to determine how many bits there are in a pack. Students should see the layers of flats that make a pack, otherwise they may think there are 600 bits in a pack (100 for each side of the cube rather than 100 for each layer). Repeat the stacking process and count how many skinnies there are in a pack. Note to the class that they can exchange 10 flats for a pack and vice versa. To work with these larger amounts, use all four columns of the *Base-Ten Board Parts 1* and *2*.

TIMS Tip

It is not practical because of size limitations to have an overhead transparency of the *Base-Ten Board* with all four columns. If you are using an overhead and are working with flats and packs, explain the difficulty to the class. Then either lay the pieces on the overhead, however they fit, or switch to a magnetic board or a table for illustrating. Sketch the *Recording Sheet* on the board.

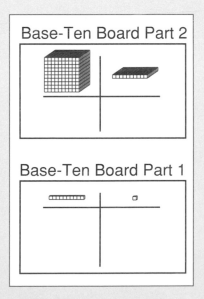

Figure 14: *Base-Ten Board*

Content Note

You may wish to refer to the bits as ones, skinnies as tens, flats as hundreds, and packs as thousands. Likewise, you can refer to the bits' column as the ones' column, and so on. However, when studying decimals, we will assign other values to the pieces. For example, to help students understand decimals, the flat can be the unit, then the skinny is .1 (one-tenth) and the bit is .01 (one-hundredth).

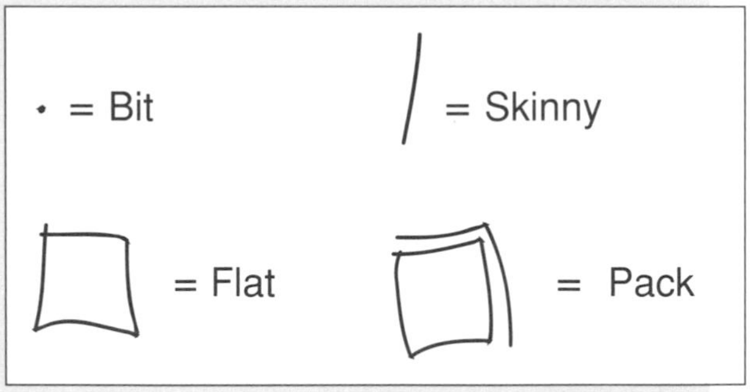

Figure 15: *Base-ten shorthand*

Practice trading with the class by asking them to express amounts using the Fewest Pieces Rule. For example, on their *Base-Ten Boards* students can place the amounts given below. They should then trade pieces until they have expressed the amount using the fewest number of pieces. They should record their work on the *Recording Sheet* as well.

1. 4 bits, 15 skinnies, 11 flats, 1 pack
2. 12 bits, 11 skinnies, 11 flats
3. 21 bits, 11 skinnies, 3 flats

The *Recording Sheets* have vertical lines that separate columns. If no one has questioned the necessity for them, ask, *"Do you think the column marks are needed? Are they sometimes needed?"* If there is only one digit in each column, then the column markings are not necessary. The right-most column records bits, the next column records skinnies, and so on. Problems arise only if we are not using the Fewest Pieces Rule. For example, if we have 4 flats, 12 skinnies, and 35 bits, we cannot write 41235 without column marks. Thus, the way we record numbers is a convention where we assume there is one digit in each column and each column is a place with a certain value attached (the **place value** of a column). Discuss with the class that this is the basis of our number system.

Write a number, such as 376, on the board or overhead. Ask, *"How many candies is this? How many candies does the 7 represent? How many candies does the 3 represent?"*

The 7 means 70 candies while the 3 is 300 candies. Thus, 376 is 300 + 70 + 6 candies. Do more of these problems as needed.

When the class is ready, introduce base-ten shorthand. Students who used the *Math Trailblazers* curriculum previously used the shorthand in Grades 3 and 4. **Base-ten shorthand** is a pictorial representation of the blocks that helps students move from the concrete to the symbolic. It also provides a written record of students' work with the manipulatives. The shorthand is shown in Figure 15.

Explain to the class that the shorthand is helpful in recording their work with the base-ten pieces. It is especially helpful for completing homework and illustrating base-ten pieces on the board or overhead projector. The manipulatives, however, should not be abandoned.

To practice base-ten shorthand, ask children to draw several numbers. Two examples are shown in Figure 16.

3421 ▱▱▱ ▱▱▱▱ //·

and

5768 ▱▱▱▱▱ ▱▱▱▱▱ //// ∷∴
             ▱▱   \

Figure 16: *Examples of base-ten shorthand*

Have the class complete The TIMS Candy Company: Reviewing Place Value and the Base-Ten Shorthand sections of *The Base-Ten Number System* Activity Pages. You can assign Homework ***Questions 1–9.***

Part 2 *Addition with Base-Ten Pieces*

Hand out base-ten pieces and copies of the *Base-Ten Board Parts 1* and *2* and *Recording Sheet* Activity Pages. Begin by describing the following situation. Rhonda and Joe work for the TIMS Candy Company. In one hour, Rhonda made 36 pieces of candy. She packed these as 3 skinnies and 6 bits. Joe made 47 pieces of candy and he packed his as 4 skinnies and 7 bits. *How much candy was packed?* Illustrate the problem with base-ten pieces using a *Base-Ten Board* transparency, a magnetic board, or model the use of base-ten shorthand on the board as shown in Figure 17.

Rhonda and Joe have 7 skinnies and 13 bits. Ask, *"Could Rhonda and Joe record the candy they made together using fewer base-ten pieces?"* They have 13 bits altogether. They can make one skinny and have 3 bits left over. They now have 8 skinnies and 3 bits. We can use the *Recording Sheet* to record the computation as shown in Figure 18.

Since most students know the standard addition algorithm, tie it in with the base-ten pieces immediately. Point out that when they add the 6 bits with the 7 bits, they can regroup and think, "That's 1 skinny and 3 bits." This can be directly translated to what we do when we write the 3 in the ones' column and write a 1 on top by the tens' column. The little "1" is the extra skinny we formed. In the last step, we add our skinnies to get 8 (see Figure 19). Explain that since we are skipping steps (or doing the problem in our heads) we refer to this as the quick paper-and-pencil method for addition.

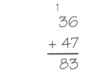

Figure 19: *Adding 36 and 47*

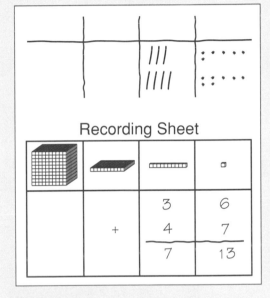

Figure 17: *Rhonda and Joe's first record*

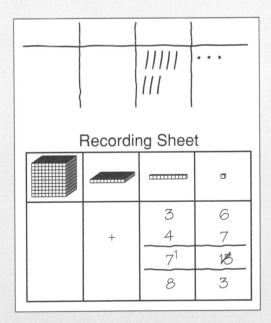

Figure 18: *Rhonda and Joe's second record*

Recording Sheet			
+	1 4	8 5	5 7
	5 5^1 6	13^1 1̸4̸ 4	1̸2̸ 2 2

Figure 20: *Joe's 185 pieces plus Rhonda's 457 pieces*

Repeat the above activity with several more examples. Model the situation on the *Base-Ten Board* and work the problem using the standard algorithm. Students who are proficient at carrying can benefit from reinforcment with the base-ten pieces.

Move to larger numbers. For example, Joe made 185 pieces of candy which he represented by 1 pack, 8 skinnies, and 5 bits. Rhonda packed 457 pieces of candy, which she wrote as 4 packs, 5 skinnies, and 7 bits. Ask, *"How much candy did they pack altogether?"*

This problem involves a double carry, since the total number of pieces includes 5 flats, 13 skinnies, and 12 bits. There is nothing wrong with beginning in the tens' column: trading 10 skinnies for a flat, leaving 6 flats, 3 skinnies, and 12 bits. The problem is completed by trading 10 bits for a skinny, leaving 6 flats, 4 skinnies, and 2 bits. It works just as well to start with the bits' column and work to the left. This is shown in Figure 20. Sometimes with harder problems, however, it may become confusing to begin working with the column to the left.

Estimating Sums. Picturing base-ten pieces is a good way for children to estimate. For example, there are 527 students at one school and 619 students at another school. Ask students to imagine base-ten pieces representing the number of students at the schools. Since 527 is 5 flats (and some skinnies and bits) and 619 is 6 flats (and some skinnies and bits), the number of students is about 11 flats (1 pack and 1 flat) or 1100 students. This type of reasoning is called front-end estimation. Thinking about the base-ten pieces when doing front-end estimation comes easily because we think about the largest size base-ten piece involved. We could use front-end estimation if the number of students were 527 and 689, but the estimate would not be as good as if we used other numbers such as 500 and 700.

Ask students to picture the base-ten pieces to estimate the following sums.

$$843 + 426 \qquad 134 + 234 \qquad 550 + 435$$

They can complete *Addition with Base-Ten Pieces* Activity Pages individually or in groups. Assign Homework *Questions 1–15.*

Part 3 *Subtraction with Base-Ten Pieces*

To review the concept of subtraction, do the following problems using the base-ten pieces or base-ten shorthand on the *Base-Ten Board*. Ask students to estimate before doing the problems.

Pose the following problem. Rhonda and Joe need to keep track of how much candy is in the store. One day, the store had 576 pieces of candy. That is, they had 5 flats, 7 skinnies, and 6 bits. A customer came in and bought 2 flats, 4 skinnies, and no bits (240 pieces of candy). Ask, *"How much candy was left after the purchase?"*

Students should show 576 on the *Base-Ten Board* and then record 576. Since they sold 240 pieces of candy, we are subtracting 240 from 576. Students should physically remove 2 flats, 4 skinnies, and 0 bits from their boards leaving 3 flats, 3 skinnies, and 6 bits in the store. This is shown in Figure 21. Convention dictates that we begin at the right. However, it is intuitive to begin on the left. No harm is done if students do so though it may involve some extra trading. Work the problem using the standard algorithm (the quick paper-and-pencil method for subtraction) alongside the manipulatives. In the examples here, the columns are eliminated. Use the columns on the recording sheet if it would aid students' understanding.

Now pose the following example. On another day, the store had 674 pieces of candy, represented by 6 flats, 7 skinnies, and 4 bits. Another customer came in and bought 183 pieces of candy (1 flat, 8 skinnies, and 3 bits). Ask, *"How much candy will be left?"* This problem is pictured in Figure 22 using base-ten shorthand.

As shown in Figure 22, many will first remove 1 flat and then try to remove 8 skinnies. However, there are only 7 skinnies available. The only solution is to break apart a flat. Make sure every child sees the problem here and physically takes a flat from the flats' column and exchanges it for 10 skinnies. Since skinnies only live in the skinnies' column, we now have 4 flats, 17 skinnies, and 4 bits. We can now take 8 skinnies away, leaving 9 skinnies. We finish the problem by taking 3 bits away, leaving 4 flats, 9 skinnies, and 1 bit in the store. See Figure 23.

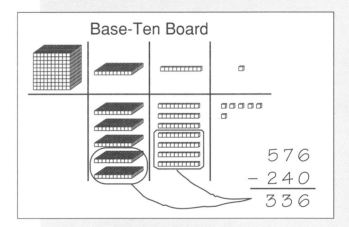

Base-Ten Board

$$576 - 240 \over 336$$

Figure 21: *576 – 240*

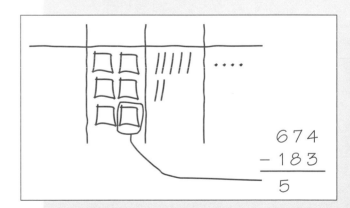

$$674 - 183 \over 5$$

Figure 22: *674 – 183, first try*

Figure 23: *674 − 183, second try*

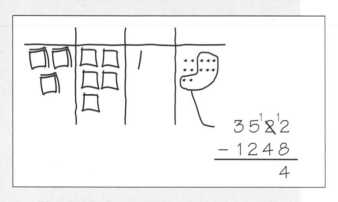

Figure 24: *Break apart 1 skinny into 10 bits. Then, take away 8 bits.*

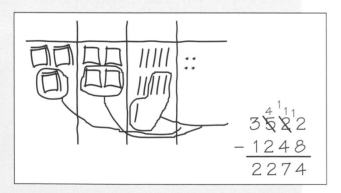

Figure 25: *Break apart 1 flat into 10 skinnies. Then, take away 4 skinnies, 2 flats, and 1 pack.*

Note that while working from the left works, we need to revisit the flats' column. Rework the problem starting on the right and note how it models the traditional subtraction algorithm. The subtraction algorithm is a procedure that many students can perform, but often do not understand. This leads to many errors, especially when regrouping more than once. Do many examples of regrouping so students develop a mental image of working with the blocks even when they are not available.

Some more problems involving one regrouping are:

$$576 − 238 \qquad 2178 − 1422$$
$$607 − 532 \qquad 5364 − 219$$

Now introduce the following problem with two regroupings. The TIMS Candy Company had 3 packs, 5 flats, 2 skinnies, and 2 bits of candy. It sells 1 pack, 2 flats, 4 skinnies, and 8 bits. Ask, *"How many candies are left?"* Students should place the base-ten pieces representing 3522 on their boards and record the problem with numbers on a separate sheet of paper. One solution is shown in Figures 24 and 25.

Below are more problems for the class to work on individually or in groups. Students should have the base-ten pieces available if they need them. Others may rely on base-ten shorthand as shown in Figures 24 and 25.

$$501 − 199 \qquad 5628 − 1834$$
$$7124 − 985 \qquad 3003 − 1658$$

Subtracting Across Zeros. Problems that contain several zeros in the minuend (the number from which we are subtracting) are often very difficult for students. Practice with the base-ten pieces alleviates these difficulties. Students should use the base-ten pieces whenever they experience confusion with the algorithm. Later, reminding them to think about the base-ten pieces helps them realize the correct manner in which to proceed.

Discuss different ways to solve the problems. Remind students that often there are easier methods for some subtraction problems than paper-and-pencil solutions. For example, the first problem, 501 − 199, can be solved by mental addition. A student may count up: 199-299-399-499 (that's 300) and 2 more makes 302. Another method is to start at 199 and move 1 forward to 200. Then from 200 to 500 we move 300. One more move forward takes us to 501 for a total number of 302 moves. Give students a chance to discover and discuss different methods of solving these and similar problems.

Estimating Differences. Ask students to estimate the answers to the following subtraction problems. They may use front-end estimation by thinking about the base-ten pieces or other convenient numbers.

$$659 - 78 \qquad 609 - 426 \qquad 759 - 132$$
$$4001 - 86 \qquad 2468 - 561$$

For example, for $659 - 78$, students can think about 6 flats with 7 skinnies taken away. This leaves about 5 flats and 3 skinnies or about 530. After discussing students' estimates, ask students to compute the answers to the problems. Then compare their answers to the estimates.

Encourage students to estimate answers whenever they compute. This will help them recognize when their answer is not reasonable.

Have students read and discuss the *Subtraction with Base-Ten Pieces* Activity Pages. Assign Homework *Questions 1–8.*

Math Facts

DPP item I presents problems with multiplication and division by 5.

Homework and Practice

- As students work through each part of the activity, assign the corresponding homework problems at the end of each set of activity pages.
- Assign DPP items G and H to review place value concepts.

Extension

Assign DPP Challenge J.

At a Glance

Math Facts and Daily Practice and Problems

Assign DPP items G–J.

Part 1. The TIMS Candy Company: Reviewing Place Value

1. Introduce the base-ten pieces—bits and skinnies—as a system for keeping track of the candy made by the TIMS Candy Company.
2. Students take a handful of bits. They make exchanges on the *Base-Ten Board Part 1,* trading 10 bits for a skinny, and record each trade on the *Recording Sheet.*
3. Discuss the Fewest Pieces Rule.
4. Introduce the flat. Discuss how they can exchange 10 skinnies for 1 flat and vice versa.
5. Represent a number using flats, skinnies, and bits. Students offer other ways of representing the same number. Repeat with other numbers.
6. Introduce the packs. Discuss how they can exchange 10 flats for 1 pack and vice versa.
7. Discuss the need for columns.
8. Introduce base-ten shorthand.
9. Students read and discuss The TIMS Candy Company: Reviewing Place Value section in *The Base-Ten Number System* Activity Pages. They complete *Questions 1–6.*

Part 2. *Addition with Base-Ten Pieces*

1. As a class, solve addition problems using base-ten pieces, *Base-Ten Board Part 1 and 2,* and the *Recording Sheets.* Use the context of the TIMS Candy Company.
2. Along with working with the pieces, use the quick paper-and-pencil method for addition or another paper-and-pencil method to solve the problems. Use the *Recording Sheet* to show work and solve problems.
3. Discuss estimating by visualizing the base-ten pieces.
4. Students read and discuss the *Addition with Base-Ten Pieces* Activity Pages. *(Questions 1–6)*

Part 3. *Subtraction with Base-Ten Pieces*

1. As a class, solve subtraction problems using base-ten pieces and *Base-Ten Boards.* Using the context of the TIMS Candy Company, solve problems that involve no regrouping, one regrouping, and two regroupings.
2. Along with your work with the pieces, use the quick paper-and-pencil method for subtraction. Use the *Recording Sheet* for some problems.
3. Discuss different ways of mentally computing subtraction problems. Discuss estimating the answers to subtraction problems.
4. Students read and discuss the *Subtraction with Base-Ten Pieces* Activity Pages. *(Questions 1–8)*

Homework

Assign the Homework sections in the *Base-Ten Number System, Addition with Base-Ten Pieces,* and *Subtraction with Base-Ten Pieces* Activity Pages.

Extension

Assign DPP Challenge J.

Answer Key is on pages 96–105.

Notes:

The Base-Ten Number System

The TIMS Candy Company: Reviewing Place Value

Mr. and Mrs. Haddad own a chocolate factory that makes Chocos. The name of their company is the TIMS Candy Company. They use base-ten pieces to keep track of how much candy they make.

They use a **bit** for each Choco.

Whenever there are 10 bits, they can be packed together to make a **skinny.**

When there are 10 skinnies, they can be packaged together to make a **flat.**

A group of 10 flats makes a **pack.**

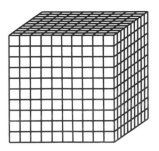

Mr. and Mrs. Haddad use a **Base-Ten Board** to show the bits, skinnies, flats, and packs. They also write the amounts in numbers on the **Recording Sheet.**

One day the company made 236 Chocos. This is one way to record the candy:

Base-Ten Board				Recording Sheet			

Recording Sheet

	2	3	6

1. Here is another way to show 236 Chocos. How is this way different from the way shown before?

Base-Ten Board

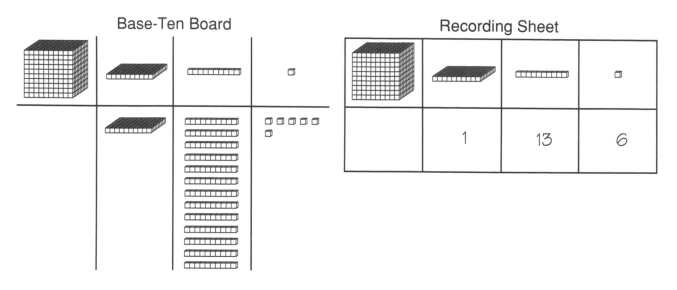

Recording Sheet

	1	13	6

Rhonda and Joe work for the TIMS Candy Company. Whenever possible, Rhonda and Joe exchange pieces so they use the fewest pieces possible. They call this the **Fewest Pieces Rule.**

2. Rhonda had 3 flats, 3 skinnies, and 15 bits. Rhonda can exchange 10 of the bits for a skinny. She then has 5 bits, 4 skinnies, and 3 flats. How many pieces of candy is that?

Base-Ten Board

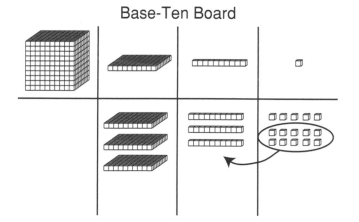

Blackline Master

Rhonda recorded her work on the Recording Sheet writing the amount as 5 bits, 4 skinnies, and 3 flats using the Fewest Pieces Rule.

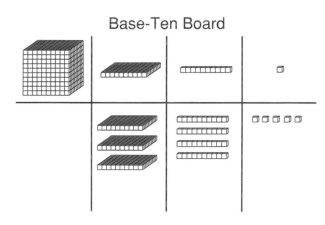

Base-Ten Board				Recording Sheet			

3. Another day Rhonda showed 12 flats, 7 skinnies, and 17 bits on her Base-Ten Board.

   A. Show this amount on your Base-Ten Board.

   B. How many pieces of candy is this?

Recording Sheet

	12	7	17

   C. Rhonda can exchange 10 flats for a pack. She then has 1 pack, 2 flats, 7 skinnies, and 17 bits. Make this trade on your Base-Ten Board.

Recording Sheet

1	2	7	17

   D. Can Rhonda exchange any more pieces? If so, make the trade on your Base-Ten Board. Show this amount on your Recording Sheet.

   E. Compare the amount on your Recording Sheet in Part D to your answer in Part B. Are they the same?

4. Joe had 15 flats, 12 skinnies, and 28 bits.

   A. What exchanges can Joe make? Record these on your Recording Sheet.

   B. Which way of recording the amount uses the Fewest Pieces Rule?

   C. How much candy did Joe make?

Sometimes Rhonda and Joe do not use the Base-Ten Boards. They put the blocks on a table.

5. Rhonda had 14 flats, 4 skinnies, and 15 bits. She said this was 1445 pieces of candy. Is she correct?

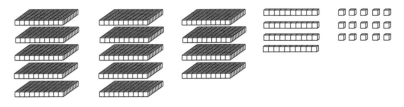

   A. Use base-ten pieces to model the amount of candy Rhonda made.

   B. Record the amount of candy Rhonda made on your Recording Sheet.

   C. Make all the exchanges you can so that the amount of candy is shown using the Fewest Pieces Rule. Record this on your Recording Sheet.

   D. How much candy did Rhonda make?

Base-Ten Shorthand

Sometimes, base-ten pieces are not available but drawing a picture of the base-ten pieces is helpful. Mr. Haddad decided to use a shorthand for the base-ten pieces.

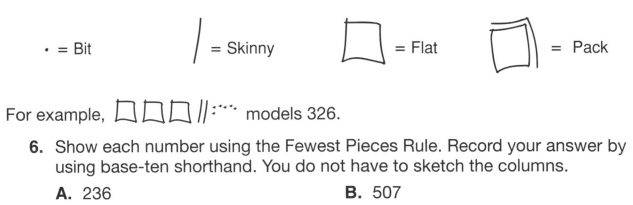

For example, ☐☐☐ //∶···· models 326.

6. Show each number using the Fewest Pieces Rule. Record your answer by using base-ten shorthand. You do not have to sketch the columns.

   A. 236

   B. 507

   C. 5235

   D. 6008

Copyright © Kendall/Hunt Publishing Company

Blackline Master

Dear Family Member:

Your child is reviewing place value—that the value of a digit in a number depends on where it is placed. For example, the 2 in 329 stands for 2 tens but the 2 in 7293 is 2 hundreds. In class your child uses base-ten pieces to represent numbers. When the pieces are not available, students are encouraged to draw pictures of the base-ten pieces. We call these drawings of the base-ten pieces, base-ten shorthand.

The workers at the TIMS Candy Company recorded the amount of candy they made in numbers. Sketch each amount using base-ten shorthand.

1. 356

2. 4206

3. 240

4. 3005

The sketches below show the number of Chocos made by workers at the TIMS Candy Company. Check if the Fewest Pieces Rule is followed. If not, use base-ten shorthand to sketch the amount of candy using the fewest pieces. Write the amount of candy using numbers.

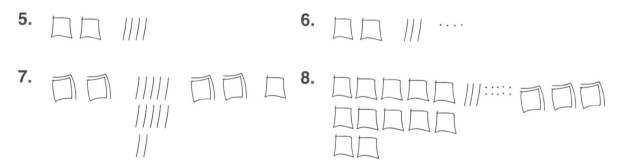

9. One way to show 352 using base-ten shorthand is:

Sketch 352 two other ways using base-ten shorthand. Tell which one shows the Fewest Pieces Rule.

Base-Ten Board Part 1

Skinnies

Bits

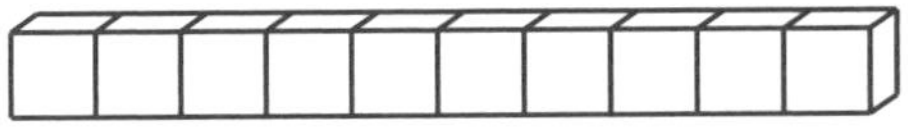

Name _____

Copyright © Kendall/Hunt Publishing Company

Date _____

Base-Ten Board Part 2

Flats

Packs

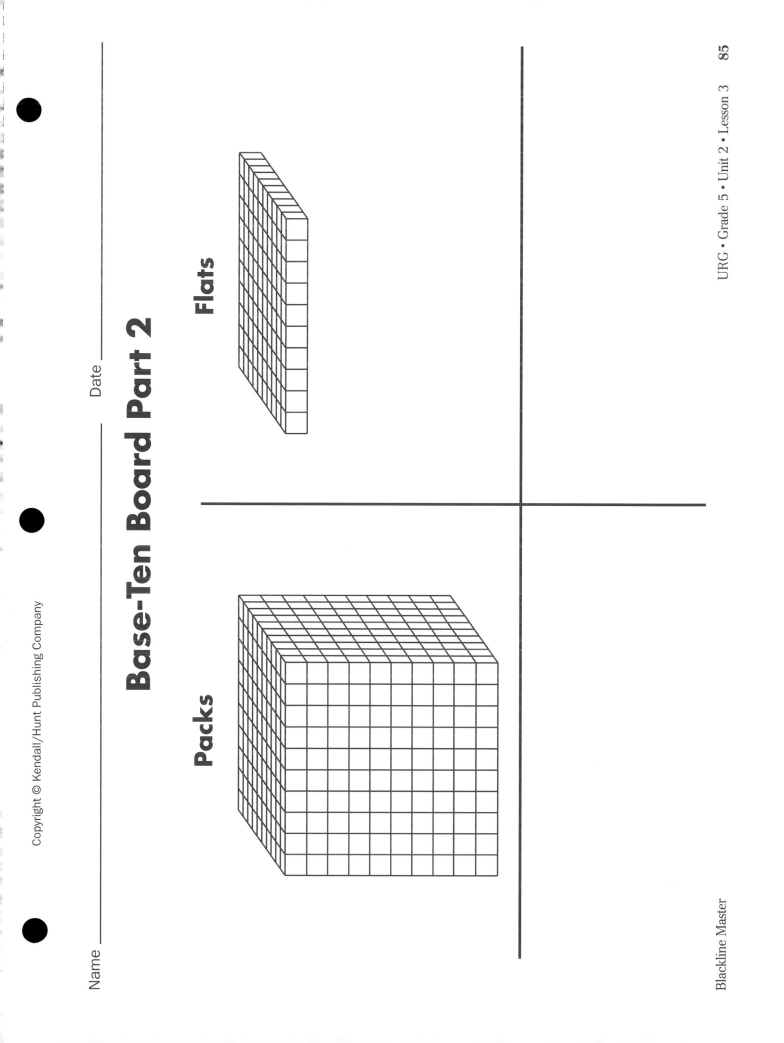

Recording Sheet

Blackline Master

Base-Ten Pieces Masters

Base-Ten Pieces Masters

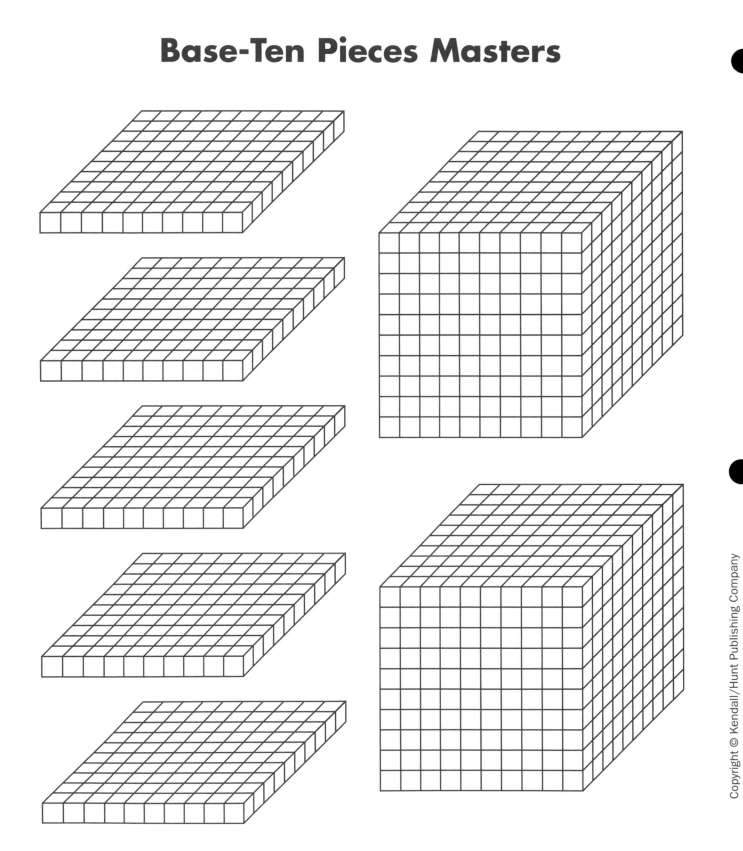

Addition with Base-Ten Pieces

One day, Rhonda made 326 pieces of candy. She used the base-ten pieces to show her work. She recorded 3 flats, 2 skinnies, and 6 bits. Joe made 258 candies, which he recorded as 2 flats, 5 skinnies, and 8 bits. Mrs. Haddad wanted to know how much candy they made altogether. She recorded her addition like this:

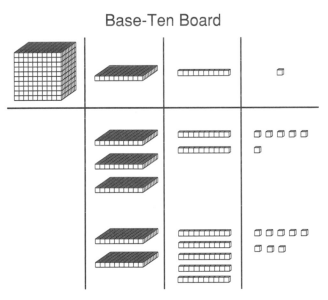

Base-Ten Board

Recording Sheet

	3	2	6
+	2	5	8
	5	7	14

Mrs. Haddad saw that she was not using the fewest base-ten pieces possible. Since there are 14 bits, she can make 1 more skinny with 4 bits left over by exchanging 10 bits for a skinny. Mrs. Haddad recorded her work like this:

Recording Sheet

	3	2	6
+	2	5	8
	5	7¹	1̶4̶
	5	8	4

1. On another day, Rhonda made 1326 candies and Joe made 575. Use your base-ten pieces to find the number of candies they made altogether.

Joe remembered the Fewest Pieces Rule and wrote:

1	3	2	6
+	5	7	5
1	8	9¹	~~11~~
1	8¹	~~10~~	1
1	9	0	1

Mrs. Haddad noticed that drawing columns on the Recording Sheet was not necessary if they always used the Fewest Pieces Rule. Mrs. Haddad called this the **quick paper-and-pencil method for addition.** She wrote the problem like this:

$$
\begin{array}{r}
{\scriptstyle 1\ 1} \\
1326 \\
+\ \ 575 \\
\hline
1901
\end{array}
$$

2. **A.** Dominique has 325 baseball cards. Her sister Rosie has 416. About how many baseball cards do the two girls have altogether?

   One way to estimate is to think about base-ten pieces. The number of baseball cards Dominique has can be shown with 3 flats and some more. The number of baseball cards Rosie has can be shown with 4 flats and some more. Together they have 7 flats and some more—or more than 700 baseball cards.

   B. Find how many baseball cards the two girls have altogether.

Use the base-ten pieces or base-ten shorthand to model Questions 3–6. Estimate the sum. Record the problem using a paper-and-pencil method. Does your answer match your estimate?

3. 236
   + 417

4. 397
   + 169

5. 1203
   + 1779

6. 971
   + 829

Blackline Master

In Questions 1–3, draw a picture of the problem using base-ten shorthand. Use a separate piece of paper or the back of this paper. Then, solve the problem using the picture to help you.

1. 672	2. 1024	3. 2828
+ 283	+ 592	+ 1347

In Questions 4–15 estimate the sum by thinking about the base-ten pieces. Then solve the problem. Is your answer reasonable?

4. 246	5. 678	6. 1339	7. 1747
+ 372	+ 1546	+ 643	+ 2096

8. 212	9. 100	10. 1427	11. 265
+ 619	+ 237	+ 428	+ 1344

12. 1679	13. 9999	14. 241	15. 8719
+ 1438	+ 1001	+ 2733	+ 367

Subtraction with Base-Ten Pieces

Next to the factory, Mr. and Mrs. Haddad have a store where they sell their Chocos. They use the base-ten pieces to keep track of how much candy they sell. Sometimes they have to break apart skinnies, flats, or packs to keep track of how much candy they have in the store.

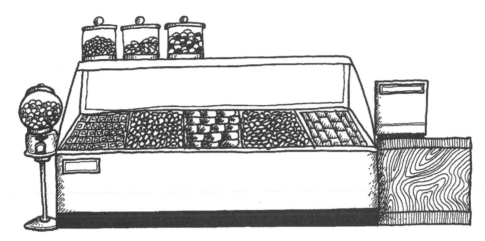

One morning, there were 3 flats, 6 skinnies, and 4 bits worth of candy in the store. A customer came in and bought 147 pieces of candy. To find how much candy was left, Mrs. Haddad did the following:

Base-Ten Board

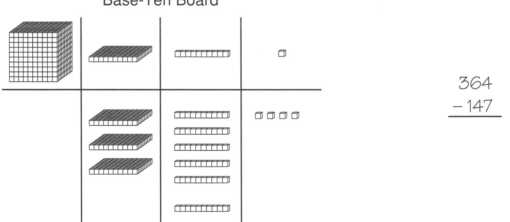

$$\begin{array}{r} 364 \\ -147 \\ \hline \end{array}$$

Since 7 bits cannot be taken away from 4 bits, a skinny must be broken apart. She exchanged 1 skinny for 10 bits. Now there are 3 flats, 5 skinnies, and 14 bits and she can take away 1 flat, 4 skinnies, and 7 bits.

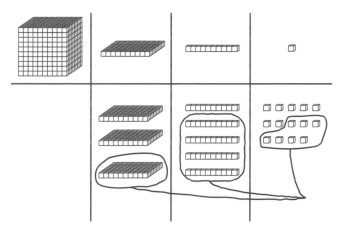

This leaves 2 flats, 1 skinny, and 7 bits. Mrs. Haddad said she knew a different method to figure out how much candy is left. This is what Mrs. Haddad did:

$$\begin{array}{r} {\scriptstyle 5\,1} \\ 364 \\ -1\,\cancel{4}\,7 \\ \hline 217 \end{array}$$

1. Explain Mrs. Haddad's method in your own words.

Another day there were 1237 pieces of candy in the store. They sold 459 pieces of candy that day. To find how much was left, Rhonda used Mrs. Haddad's method. Rhonda called this the **quick paper-and-pencil method for subtraction.** Rhonda first made a sketch of the base-ten pieces.

$$\begin{array}{r} 1237 \\ -459 \\ \hline \end{array}$$

Rhonda saw that she had to trade 1 skinny for 10 bits to subtract 9 bits.

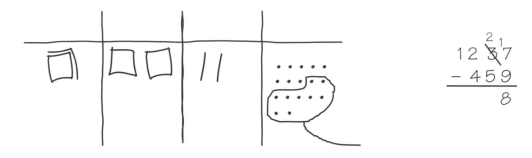

$$12\,\overset{2}{\cancel{3}}\overset{1}{7}$$
$$-\ 4\ 5\ 9$$
$$\overline{8}$$

She ran into the same problem in the next column since she could not take
5 skinnies from 2 skinnies.

Rhonda then broke up one flat so that she had 12 skinnies and was able to subtract.

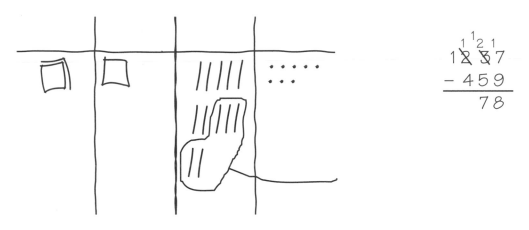

$$1\overset{1}{\cancel{2}}\,\overset{1}{\cancel{3}}\overset{1}{7}$$
$$-\ 4\ 5\ 9$$
$$\overline{7\ 8}$$

At the next step, Rhonda broke up her only pack so she had 11 flats. Rhonda found
there were 778 pieces of candy left in the store.

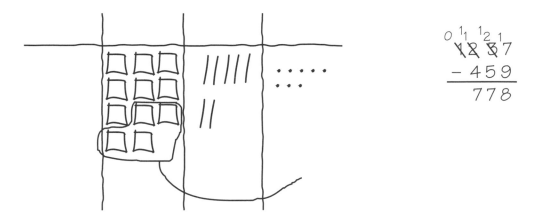

$$\overset{0}{\cancel{1}}\overset{1}{\cancel{2}}\,\overset{1}{\cancel{3}}\overset{1}{7}$$
$$-\ 4\ 5\ 9$$
$$\overline{7\ 7\ 8}$$

For Questions 2–5, use base-ten pieces or base-ten shorthand to solve the problem. Then do the problem using the quick paper-and-pencil method.

2. There were 578 pieces of candy in the store (5 flats, 7 skinnies, and 8 bits). They sold 349 pieces of candy. How many pieces of candy are left?

3. Another day there were 4443 pieces of candy and 1718 of them were sold. How many pieces of candy are left?

4. There are 2075 Chocos. They sell 1539. How many are left?

5. There are 5204 Chocos. A customer comes in and buys 565. Another customer comes in and wants to buy 4859 pieces of candy. Is there enough candy in the store so the second customer can buy 4859 pieces?

For Questions 6–8, estimate by thinking about the base-ten pieces or another estimation method. Then solve the problem. Use your estimate to check that your answer is reasonable.

6.	329	7.	402	8.	1013
	− 108		− 249		− 737

In Questions 1–3 sketch the problem using base-ten shorthand. Estimate and then find the solution. Is your answer reasonable?

1.	372	2.	409	3.	2009
	− 243		− 236		− 1572

In Questions 4–7 estimate the difference first. Find the solution using any method you wish. Use your estimate to check if your answer is reasonable.

4.	2357	5.	2001	6.	674	7.	1239
	− 528		− 432		− 279		− 643

8. Kris had 4006 stamps in his stamp collection. He sold 1650 of them. How many stamps does he have left? How can you solve this problem mentally?

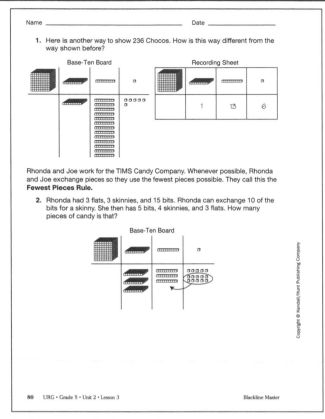

Unit Resource Guide - page 80

Unit Resource Guide (p. 80)

1. The amount of candy in both pictures is the same. The first way uses the fewest pieces. The second picture shows 1 flat and 13 skinnies whereas the first picture shows 2 flats and 3 skinnies. One flat in the first picture was exchanged for 10 skinnies.*

2. 345

*Answers and/or discussion are included in the Lesson Guide.

Unit Resource Guide (p. 81)

3. A.

Base-Ten Board

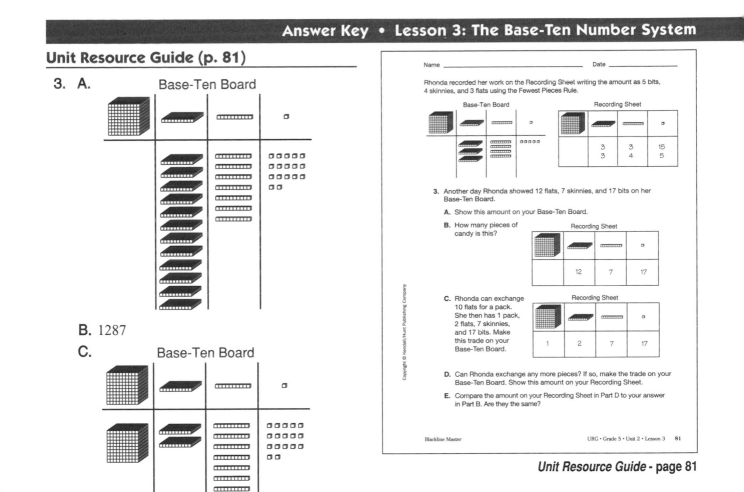

B. 1287

C.

Base-Ten Board

D. Yes

Base-Ten Board

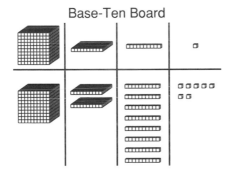

Recording Sheet

1	2	8	7

E. The amount on the *Recording Sheet* and the answer to ***Question 3B*** should both be 1287.

Name _____ Date _____

Rhonda recorded her work on the Recording Sheet writing the amount as 5 bits, 4 skinnies, and 3 flats using the Fewest Pieces Rule.

Base-Ten Board   Recording Sheet

	3	3	15
	3	4	5

3. Another day Rhonda showed 12 flats, 7 skinnies, and 17 bits on her Base-Ten Board.

A. Show this amount on your Base-Ten Board.

B. How many pieces of candy is this?

Recording Sheet

	12	7	17

C. Rhonda can exchange 10 flats for a pack. She then has 1 pack, 2 flats, 7 skinnies, and 17 bits. Make this trade on your Base-Ten Board.

Recording Sheet

1	2	7	17

D. Can Rhonda exchange any more pieces? If so, make the trade on your Base-Ten Board. Show this amount on your Recording Sheet.

E. Compare the amount on your Recording Sheet in Part D to your answer in Part B. Are they the same?

Blackline Master   URG • Grade 5 • Unit 2 • Lesson 3   81

Unit Resource Guide - page 81

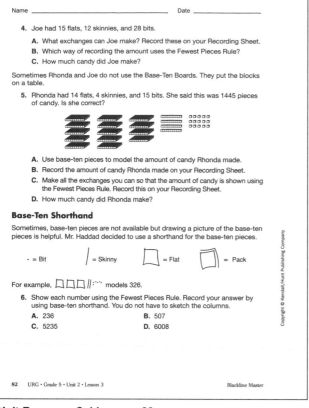

Name _____ Date _____

4. Joe had 15 flats, 12 skinnies, and 28 bits.

 A. What exchanges can Joe make? Record these on your Recording Sheet.

 B. Which way of recording the amount uses the Fewest Pieces Rule?

 C. How much candy did Joe make?

Sometimes Rhonda and Joe do not use the Base-Ten Boards. They put the blocks on a table.

5. Rhonda had 14 flats, 4 skinnies, and 15 bits. She said this was 1445 pieces of candy. Is she correct?

 A. Use base-ten pieces to model the amount of candy Rhonda made.

 B. Record the amount of candy Rhonda made on your Recording Sheet.

 C. Make all the exchanges you can so that the amount of candy is shown using the Fewest Pieces Rule. Record this on your Recording Sheet.

 D. How much candy did Rhonda make?

Base-Ten Shorthand

Sometimes, base-ten pieces are not available but drawing a picture of the base-ten pieces is helpful. Mr. Haddad decided to use a shorthand for the base-ten pieces.

· = Bit   / = Skinny   ▱ = Flat   ▱ = Pack

For example, ▱▱▱//∴ models 326.

6. Show each number using the Fewest Pieces Rule. Record your answer by using base-ten shorthand. You do not have to sketch the columns.

 A. 236   B. 507
 C. 5235   D. 6008

Unit Resource Guide - **page 82**

Unit Resource Guide (p. 82)

4. A.

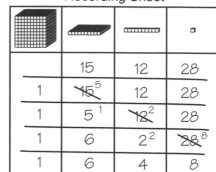

Recording Sheet

	15	12	28
1	15⁵	12	28
1	5¹	12²	28
1	6	2²	28⁸
1	6	4	8

B. 1 pack, 6 flats, 4 skinnies, and 8 bits

C. 1648 pieces of candy

5. A.

B.–C.   Recording Sheet

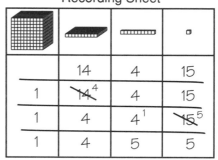

	14	4	15
1	14⁴	4	15
1	4	4¹	15⁵
1	4	5	5

D. 1455, so Rhonda was not correct by saying 1445.

6. A. ▱▱/// ∶∙∙∙∙

 B. ▱▱▱▱▱ ∶∷∙∙∙

 C. ▱▱▱▱▱ ▱▱ /// ∙∙∙∙∙

 D. ▱▱▱▱▱ ∷∷∙
     ▱

Unit Resource Guide (p. 83)

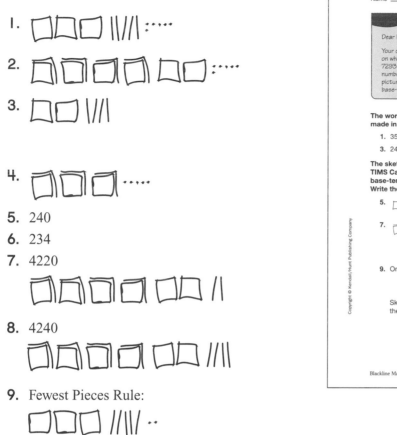

1. (base-ten shorthand drawing)

2. (base-ten shorthand drawing)

3. (base-ten shorthand drawing)

4. (base-ten shorthand drawing)

5. 240

6. 234

7. 4220

(base-ten shorthand drawing)

8. 4240

(base-ten shorthand drawing)

9. Fewest Pieces Rule:

(base-ten shorthand drawing)

One other way:

(base-ten shorthand drawing)

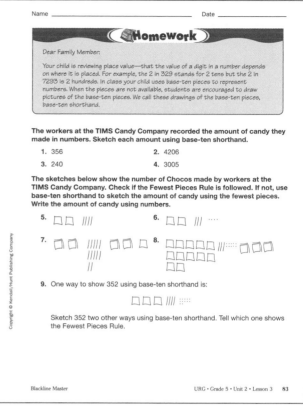

Unit Resource Guide - page 83

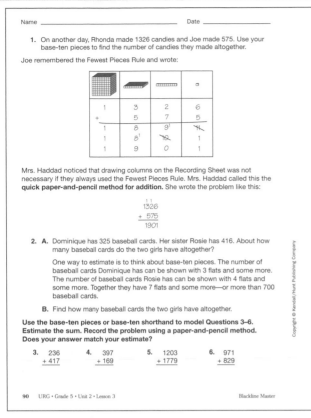

Unit Resource Guide - page 90

Unit Resource Guide (p. 90)

I. 1901

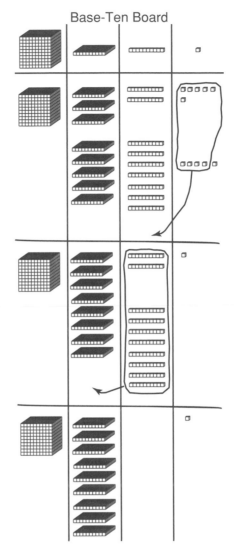

Base-Ten Board

2. A. Estimates will vary. One reasonable estimate is 700 baseball cards.

B. 741 baseball cards

3. 653

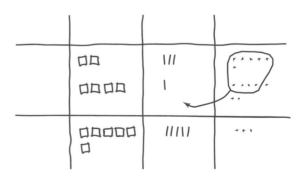

4. 566

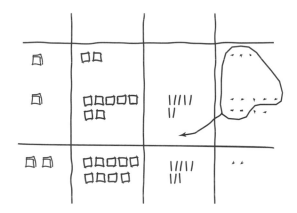

5. 2982

6. 1800

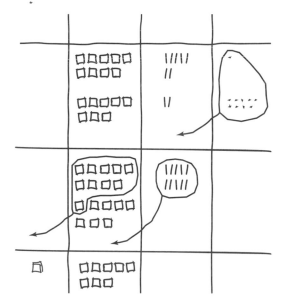

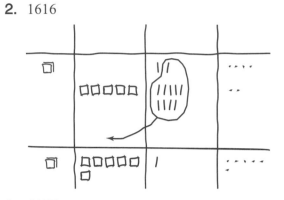

Name _____ **Date** _____

Homework

In Questions 1–3, draw a picture of the problem using base-ten shorthand. Use a separate piece of paper or the back of this paper. Then, solve the problem using the picture to help you.

1.	672	2.	1024	3.	2828
	+ 283		+ 592		+ 1347

In Questions 4–15 estimate the sum by thinking about the base-ten pieces. Then solve the problem. Is your answer reasonable?

4.	246	5.	678	6.	1339	7.	1747
	+ 372		+ 1546		+ 643		+ 2096

8.	212	9.	100	10.	1427	11.	265
	+ 619		+ 237		+ 428		+ 1344

12.	1679	13.	9999	14.	241	15.	8719
	+ 1438		+ 1001		+ 2733		+ 367

Copyright © Kendall/Hunt Publishing Company

Blackline Master   URG • Grade 5 • Unit 2 • Lesson 3   **91**

Unit Resource Guide - page 91

Unit Resource Guide (p. 91)

Homework

1. 955

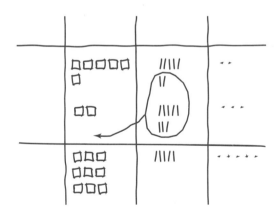

2. 1616

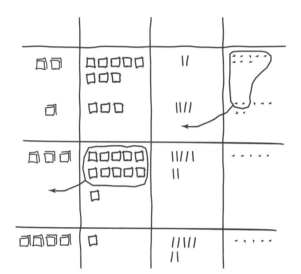

3. 4175

For *Questions 4–15,* estimates will vary.
One example is provided.

4. 600; 618		**5.** 2100; 2224	
6. 2000; 1982		**7.** 3700; 3843	
8. 800; 831		**9.** 300; 337	
10. 1800; 1855		**11.** 1600; 1609	
12. 3000; 3117		**13.** 11,000; 11,000	
14. 2900; 2974		**15.** 9000; 9086	

Unit Resource Guide (p. 93)

1. Since Mrs. Haddad couldn't subtract 7 from 4, she traded in 1 ten or 1 skinny for 10 ones or 10 bits. To show this, she crossed out the 6 tens and changed it to 5 tens. She recorded a 1 above the 4 in the ones' column to show that there are now 14 ones or 14 bits. She could then subtract to get 217.

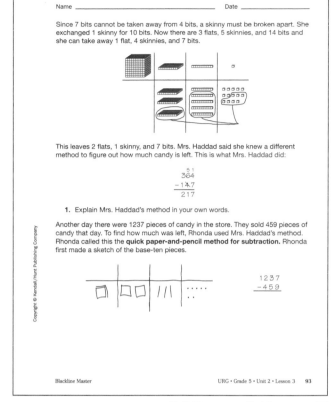

Name _____ Date _____

Since 7 bits cannot be taken away from 4 bits, a skinny must be broken apart. She exchanged 1 skinny for 10 bits. Now there are 3 flats, 5 skinnies, and 14 bits and she can take away 1 flat, 4 skinnies, and 7 bits.

This leaves 2 flats, 1 skinny, and 7 bits. Mrs. Haddad said she knew a different method to figure out how much candy is left. This is what Mrs. Haddad did:

$$\begin{array}{r} {\scriptstyle 5\,1} \\ 3\,6\,\cancel{4} \\ -\,1\,\cancel{4}\,7 \\ \hline 2\,1\,7 \end{array}$$

1. Explain Mrs. Haddad's method in your own words.

Another day there were 1237 pieces of candy in the store. They sold 459 pieces of candy that day. To find how much was left, Rhonda used Mrs. Haddad's method. Rhonda called this the **quick paper-and-pencil method for subtraction.** Rhonda first made a sketch of the base-ten pieces.

$$\begin{array}{r} 1\,2\,3\,7 \\ -\,4\,5\,9 \end{array}$$

Blackline Master   URG • Grade 5 • Unit 2 • Lesson 3   93

Unit Resource Guide **- page 93**

Name _____ Date _____

For Questions 2–5, use base-ten pieces or base-ten shorthand to solve the problem. Then do the problem using the quick paper-and-pencil method.

2. There were 578 pieces of candy in the store (5 flats, 7 skinnies, and 8 bits). They sold 349 pieces of candy. How many pieces of candy are left?

3. Another day there were 4443 pieces of candy and 1718 of them were sold. How many pieces of candy are left?

4. There are 2075 Chocos. They sell 1539. How many are left?

5. There are 5204 Chocos. A customer comes in and buys 565. Another customer comes in and wants to buy 4859 pieces of candy. Is there enough candy in the store so the second customer can buy 4859 pieces?

For Questions 6–8, estimate by thinking about the base-ten pieces or another estimation method. Then solve the problem. Use your estimate to check that your answer is reasonable.

6.	329	7.	402	8.	1013
	− 108		− 249		− 737

In Questions 1–3 sketch the problem using base-ten shorthand. Estimate and then find the solution. Is your answer reasonable?

1.	372	2.	409	3.	2009
	− 243		− 236		− 1572

In Questions 4–7 estimate the difference first. Find the solution using any method you wish. Use your estimate to check if your answer is reasonable.

4.	2357	5.	2001	6.	674	7.	1239
	− 528		− 432		− 279		− 643

8. Kris had 4006 stamps in his stamp collection. He sold 1650 of them. How many stamps does he have left? How can you solve this problem mentally?

Blackline Master   URG • Grade 5 • Unit 2 • Lesson 3   95

Unit Resource Guide - page 95

Unit Resource Guide (p. 95)

2. 229

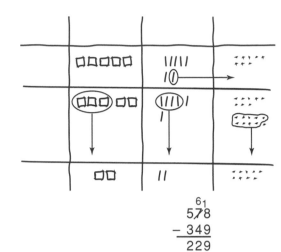

$$
\begin{array}{r}
{}^{6}5\overset{1}{7}8 \\
-\ 349 \\
\hline
229
\end{array}
$$

3. 2725

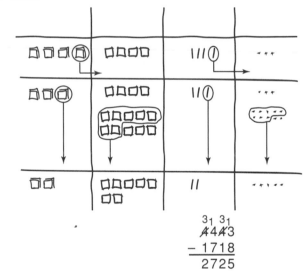

$$
\begin{array}{r}
{}^{3}\!\!\!{}_{1}\,{}^{3}\!\!\!{}_{1} \\
\cancel{4}4\cancel{4}3 \\
-\ 1718 \\
\hline
2725
\end{array}
$$

4. 536

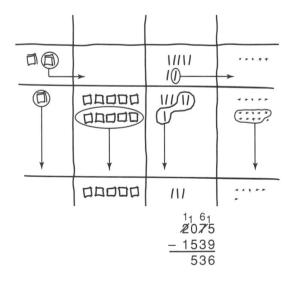

$$
\begin{array}{r}
{}^{1}\!\!\!{}_{1}\,{}^{6}\!\!\!{}_{1} \\
\cancel{2}0\cancel{7}5 \\
-\ 1539 \\
\hline
536
\end{array}
$$

5. No. After 565 were sold, there were only 4639 pieces of candy left.

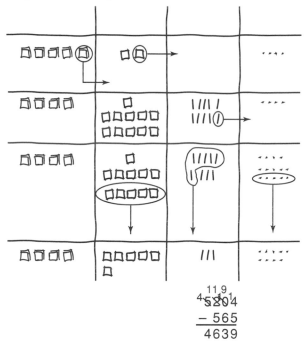

$$\begin{array}{r} 11\,9 \\ 4\,\overset{11\ 9}{\cancel{5}\cancel{2}\cancel{0}}4 \\ -\ 565 \\ \hline 4639 \end{array}$$

6. Estimates will vary. One reasonable estimate is 229. The actual answer is 221.

7. Estimates will vary. One reasonable estimate is 150. The actual answer is 153.

8. Estimates will vary. One reasonable estimate is 300. The actual answer is 276.

Homework

1. 100; 129

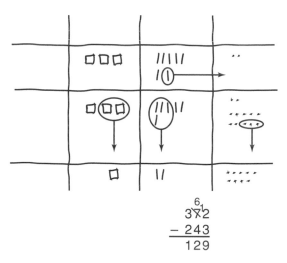

$$\begin{array}{r} 6 \\ 3\,\overset{6}{\cancel{7}}2 \\ -\ 243 \\ \hline 129 \end{array}$$

2. 150; 173

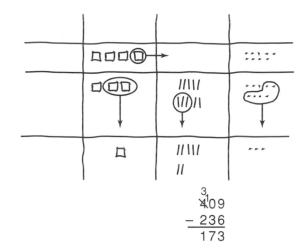

$$\begin{array}{r} 3 \\ \overset{3}{\cancel{4}}09 \\ -\ 236 \\ \hline 173 \end{array}$$

3. 500; 437

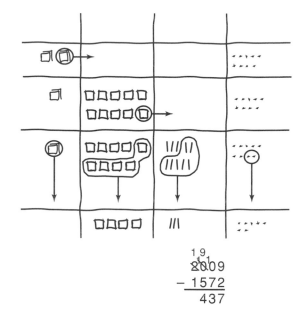

$$\begin{array}{r} 1\,9 \\ 2\,\overset{1\ 9}{\cancel{0}\cancel{0}}9 \\ -\ 1572 \\ \hline 437 \end{array}$$

4. 1800; 1829

5. 1600; 1569

6. 400; 395

7. 600; 596

8. 2356; you can count up. 1650 + 350 = 2000. 2000 + 2000 = 4000. 4000 + 6 = 4006. 2000 + 350 + 6 = 2356.

Optional Lesson 4

The Chinese Abacus

Lesson Overview

This lesson reviews place value for those classes that did not complete Lesson 3. Those that worked through Lesson 3 should not complete this lesson.

The lesson contains three parts. In Part 1 students build a Chinese abacus. In Part 2 they represent numbers and explore place-value concepts. They compare our base-ten system to the Chinese abacus. In Part 3, students add and subtract numbers on the abacus. Use the parts as needed by your students. Part 2 reinforces and extends students' place-value concepts using a new concrete model. Part 3 challenges students to think about the operations of addition and subtraction in new ways.

Key Content

- Understanding place value.
- Representing large numbers with an abacus.
- Translating between different representations of large numbers (concrete, pictorial, and symbolic).
- Developing number sense for large numbers.

Math Facts

Assign DPP item I.

Homework

1. Assign *Question 1* in the Homework section of the *Student Guide*. Students need two copies of the *Abacus Pictures* Activity Page to complete the assignment.
2. Assign *Questions 2–13* in the Homework section of the *Student Guide*. Students may use their abacuses to solve the problems.

Assessment

Use the *Number Changes* Assessment Pages to assess students' understanding of place value as modeled on the abacus.

Materials List

Supplies and Copies

Student	Teacher
Supplies for Each Student • 14 cm by 24 cm piece of cardboard • 11 pieces of string 16 cm long • 77 pony beads or ditali macaroni pieces • 24 cm strip of half-inch masking tape • scissors • cm ruler	**Supplies** • overhead abacus
Copies • 1 copy of *Number Changes* per student (*Unit Resource Guide* Pages 120–121) • 1 copy of *Column Place Value Guides* per student (*Unit Resource Guide* Page 122) • several copies of *Abacus Pictures* per student (*Unit Resource Guide* Page 123)	**Copies/Transparencies** • 1 transparency of *Column Place Value Guides* (*Unit Resource Guide* Page 122) • 1 transparency of *Abacus Pictures* (*Unit Resource Guide* Page 123)

All blackline masters including assessment, transparency, and DPP masters are also on the Teacher Resource CD.

Student Books

The Chinese Abacus (*Student Guide* Pages 39–45)

Daily Practice and Problems and Home Practice

DPP items G–J (*Unit Resource Guide* Pages 21–22)

Note: Classrooms whose pacing differs significantly from the suggested pacing of the units should use the Math Facts Calendar in Section 4 of the *Facts Resource Guide* to ensure students receive the complete math facts program.

Daily Practice and Problems

Suggestions for using the DPPs are on page 117.

G. Bit: Write the Number (URG p. 21) [N]

Write a number that has:

A. 6 tens and 3 ones

B. 91 hundreds and 6 tens

C. 73 tens

D. 8 hundreds and 14 ones

E. 50 tens and 8 ones

I. Bit: Multiplication and Division Sentences (URG p. 22) $\boxed{^5_{x\,7}}$

Lin has 15 flowers to place in 3 vases. How many flowers go in each vase if she divides them evenly?

A. Draw a picture to illustrate this problem.

B. Write a multiplication sentence and a division sentence that describe this problem.

H. Task: Smallest and Largest
   (URG p. 22) [N]

1. Rearrange the digits in 1997 to make the smallest possible number.

2. Rearrange the digits in 1997 to make the largest possible number.

For Questions 3 and 4, you may use a digit more than once; however, the number should begin with a nonzero digit.

3. Write the smallest four-digit number possible using the digits 0 through 9.

4. Write the largest four-digit number possible using the digits 0 through 9.

J. Challenge: Leaves on a Tree
   (URG p. 22) [N]

Find a tree. Estimate the number of leaves on your tree. Explain how you made your estimate.

Build an overhead abacus using a blank transparency or plastic page sleeve and the general instructions in *The Chinese Abacus* Activity Pages in the *Student Guide*. Use tape to secure the top and bottom of the string in each column, rather than cutting slits along the edges of the transparency.

TIMS Tip

Have one or two handmade abacuses in the classroom for students to model as they create their own.

TIMS Tip

Alternative suggestions for materials:

- Ditali macaroni is an inexpensive alternative to pony beads.
- 6-inch chenille sticks or wire can be used instead of string.
- Cardboard from food or shoe boxes can be used for the base of the abacus. (If you use an entire shoe box lid, you can anchor the strings to the rims giving more room for the beads.)

Teaching the Activity

Part 1 Building the Abacus

Read the first page of *The Chinese Abacus* Activity Pages in the *Student Guide*. This page tells students what an abacus is and lists the materials they need to construct one. After distributing the necessary materials, read the directions for constructing an abacus. While students follow the instructions, use the overhead abacus to demonstrate the steps, if needed. Students can also refer to the pictures in the *Student Guide*. See Figure 26.

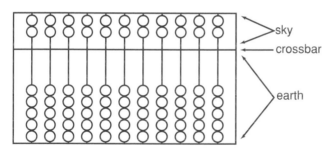

Figure 26: *A Chinese abacus*

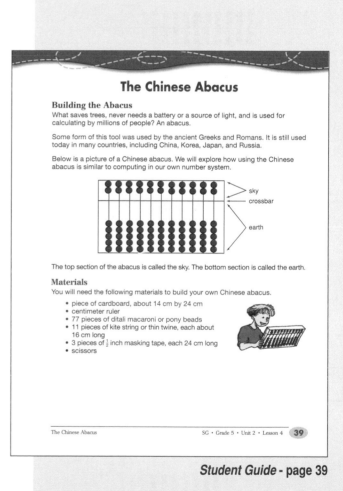

The Chinese Abacus

Building the Abacus
What saves trees, never needs a battery or a source of light, and is used for calculating by millions of people? An abacus.

Some form of this tool was used by the ancient Greeks and Romans. It is still used today in many countries, including China, Korea, Japan, and Russia.

Below is a picture of a Chinese abacus. We will explore how using the Chinese abacus is similar to computing in our own number system.

The top section of the abacus is called the sky. The bottom section is called the earth.

Materials
You will need the following materials to build your own Chinese abacus.

- piece of cardboard, about 14 cm by 24 cm
- centimeter ruler
- 77 pieces of ditali macaroni or pony beads
- 11 pieces of kite string or thin twine, each about 16 cm long
- 3 pieces of ½ inch masking tape, each 24 cm long
- scissors

The Chinese Abacus   SG • Grade 5 • Unit 2 • Lesson 4   **39**

Student Guide - page 39

Using beads (a nonproportional manipulative) to represent numbers on the abacus is more abstract than using base-ten pieces (a proportional model). Building numbers on the abacus helps students internalize the base-ten structure of our number system. Because a change in column position indicates a different value, numbers shown on the abacus parallel the system we use for writing numbers. The relationship between the value of two adjacent beads on the abacus is the same as the relationship between adjacent columns in our number system, i.e., the one on the left has a value ten times greater than the one on the right. Engaging students in problem solving with the abacus increases their understanding of place value.

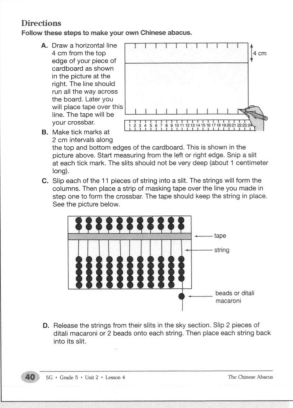

Directions
Follow these steps to make your own Chinese abacus.

A. Draw a horizontal line 4 cm from the top edge of your piece of cardboard as shown in the picture at the right. The line should run all the way across the board. Later you will place tape over this line. The tape will be your crossbar.

B. Make tick marks at 2 cm intervals along the top and bottom edges of the cardboard. This is shown in the picture above. Start measuring from the left or right edge. Snip a slit at each tick mark. The slits should not be very deep (about 1 centimeter long).

C. Slip each of the 11 pieces of string into a slit. The strings will form the columns. Then place a strip of masking tape over the line you made in step one to form the crossbar. The tape should keep the string in place. See the picture below.

tape
string
beads or ditali macaroni

D. Release the strings from their slits in the sky section. Slip 2 pieces of ditali macaroni or 2 beads onto each string. Then place each string back into its slit.

Student Guide - page 40

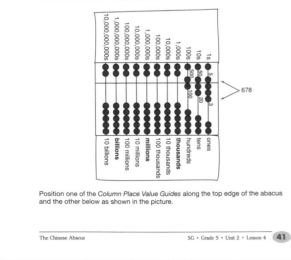

E. Release the strings from their slits in the earth section. Slip 5 pieces of macaroni or 5 beads onto each string. Then place each string back into its slit.

F. Tape the string ends to the back of the abacus, and you are ready to show some numbers.

Numbers on the Abacus
Like our number system, the Chinese abacus has place value columns. The column on the right is the 1s column, the next column is the 10s column, then the 100s column, and so on. This is similar to our own system. The beads in the earth section in the ones column stand for 1 when they are pushed to the crossbar. Each of the sky beads in the ones column, however, stands for 5 times 1, or 5. Likewise, each of the earth beads in the tens column stands for 10. Each of the sky beads in the tens column stands for 5 times 10, or 50. The number 678 is shown on the abacus in the picture below.

Position one of the *Column Place Value Guides* along the top edge of the abacus and the other below as shown in the picture.

Student Guide - page 41

Once students construct their abacuses, distribute one copy of the *Column Place Value Guides* Activity Page to each student. Ask them to cut the page along the dashed line. Students use both guides, placing one along the top edge of the abacus and the other along the bottom edge. This is shown in the *Student Guide*.

Compare the Chinese abacus to our number system. Both use place-value columns and have base-ten headings, i.e., ones, tens, hundreds, thousands, and so on. However, each column on the Chinese abacus is divided into two regions, the sky and the earth (see Figure 26). A crossbar separates the sky and earth sections of the abacus. A number is represented by pushing beads towards the crossbar. Explain the value of the beads on the abacus. Each earth bead, a bead below the crossbar, has a value 1 times the column place value. Each sky bead has a value 5 times the column place value. For example, a bead in the earth section of the ones' column stands for 1. Each bead in the sky section, however, stands for 5×1, or 5. Likewise, each bead in the earth section of the tens' column stands for 10, whereas each bead in the sky section stands for 5×10 or 50. (See Figure 27 for some examples of numbers represented on the abacus. Note: The figures in this lesson guide will show only the beads pushed to the crossbar.)

Read the Numbers on the Abacus section of the *Student Guide* Pages. This section introduces students to the place value system of the Chinese abacus. It also shows students how to move beads toward the crossbar with their forefinger and thumb to represent numbers or perform operations. The abacus is cleared when all beads are pushed away from the crossbar.

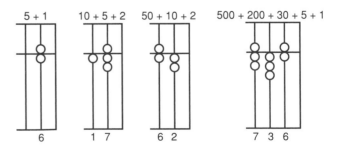

Figure 27: *Numbers represented on the abacus*

The Representing Numbers Using Three Beads section on *The Chinese Abacus* Activity Pages explores different numbers using a fixed number of beads in different place-value columns. This exercise focuses on the patterns in large and small numbers in a place-value system. Have students record their work for **Questions 1A–1C** on the *Abacus Pictures* Activity Page or by sketching pictures of the abacus. (To cut down on the drawing time, have students record only those beads they push towards the crossbar.) The powers of ten are dramatically displayed when students record their work with the abacus on paper and compare the various numbers represented. See Figure 28 for answers to **Questions 1A–1C.**

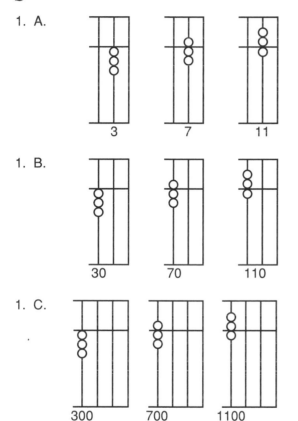

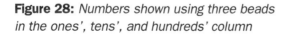

Figure 28: *Numbers shown using three beads in the ones', tens', and hundreds' column*

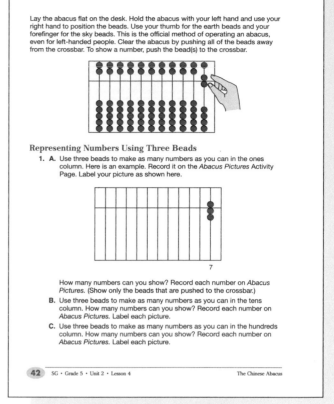

Lay the abacus flat on the desk. Hold the abacus with your left hand and use your right hand to position the beads. Use your thumb for the earth beads and your forefinger for the sky beads. This is the official method of operating an abacus, even for left-handed people. Clear the abacus by pushing all of the beads away from the crossbar. To show a number, push the bead(s) to the crossbar.

Representing Numbers Using Three Beads

1. **A.** Use three beads to make as many numbers as you can in the ones column. Here is an example. Record it on the *Abacus Pictures* Activity Page. Label your picture as shown here.

How many numbers can you show? Record each number on *Abacus Pictures*. (Show only the beads that are pushed to the crossbar.)

B. Use three beads to make as many numbers as you can in the tens column. How many numbers can you show? Record each number on *Abacus Pictures*. Label each picture.

C. Use three beads to make as many numbers as you can in the hundreds column. How many numbers can you show? Record each number on *Abacus Pictures*. Label each picture.

42   SG • Grade 5 • Unit 2 • Lesson 4   The Chinese Abacus

Student Guide **- page 42 (Answers on p. 124)**

D. Describe any patterns you see for the numbers you made for each of the columns. Will this pattern continue to the millions and billions?

2. A. Use four beads to make as many numbers as you can in the ones column. Record and label your work on the *Abacus Pictures* Activity Page.
   B. How many numbers can you make with four beads in the tens column? Record and label your work.
   C. How many numbers can you make with four beads in the hundreds column? Record and label your work.
   D. Describe any patterns you see for the numbers you made for each of the columns. Compare these patterns with those you found in Question 1D.

Representing Numbers in More than One Way

Felicia showed the number 75 two different ways using the abacus.

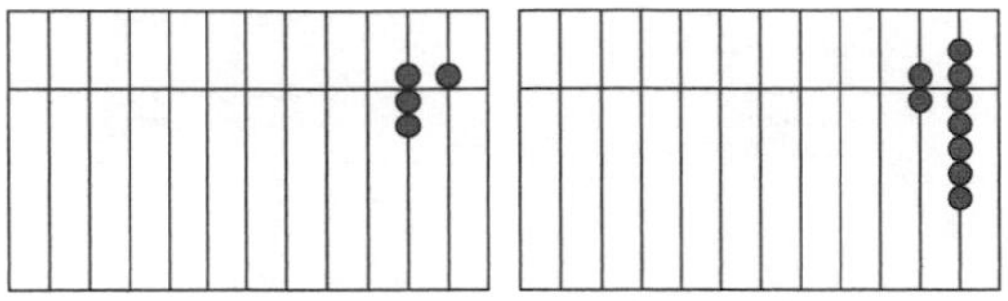

50 + 20 + 5 = 75   50 + 10 + 5 + 5 + 5 = 75

3. Find three ways to make each of the following numbers. Record each way on *Abacus Pictures.* Compare your pictures with those of your classmates to see if they found different ways. Be sure to label each picture.
   A. 15   B. 150   C. 1500
4. Find two ways to make the following numbers. Record and label both ways on *Abacus Pictures.* Compare your pictures with those of your classmates.
   A. 84   B. 4121
5. For each number in Questions 3 and 4, circle the picture that shows the fewest number of beads.

The Chinese Abacus   SG • Grade 5 • Unit 2 • Lesson 4   43

***Student Guide* - page 43** *(Answers on pp. 124–125)*

When the three beads are used in the ones' column, 3, 7, and 11 can be represented. When three beads are used in the tens' column, 30, 70, and 110 can be made. In the hundreds' column, 300, 700, and 1100 will result. Students are asked in ***Question 1D*** to describe the pattern they see and to tell whether this pattern will generalize to larger numbers. Students may say that the first digits in each of the three numbers are the same: 3, 7, 11. As you make a number in a new column to the left, the numbers are 10 times as great. The pattern will continue to larger and larger numbers. To see if this pattern continues, ***Question 2*** asks students to represent numbers in the ones', tens', and hundreds' column, using four beads. The numbers that result are: 4, 8, and 12 in the ones' column; 40, 80, and 120 in the tens' column; and 400, 800, and 1200 in the hundreds' column. You may complete ***Question 1*** (using three beads) as a class and then have students work in pairs to complete ***Question 2*** (using four beads).

In the Representing Numbers in More Than One Way section in the *Student Guide,* students explore ways to represent the same number on the abacus. (See Figure 29 for an example for ***Question 3A***.) This section also focuses on the values of the beads within a column. Students record their findings on the *Abacus Pictures* Activity Page.

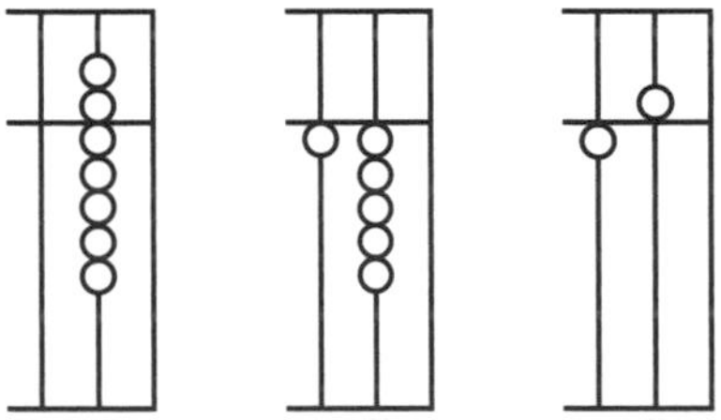

Figure 29: *Showing the number 15 three ways on the abacus (Question 3A)*

Question 5 asks students to circle the pictures in ***Questions 3–4*** that use the fewest number of beads. When a number is shown using the fewest number of beads, there is a quicker readout of the number. If appropriate, discuss how this relates to the Fewest Pieces Rule that students used with base-ten pieces in fourth grade. When the fewest base-ten pieces are used, it is easy to write the number in standard form.

Questions 6–7 emphasize place value on the abacus as students represent larger numbers—city and state populations.

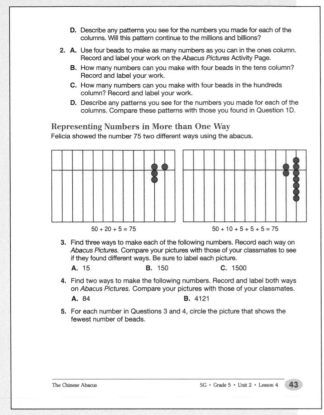

TIMS Tip

To assess whether students are able to use and interpret the abacus appropriately, tell students a number to represent on their abacuses. Then represent a number on your abacus and have students read the number. Students also can do this activity in pairs or groups of three.

Part 3 Adding and Subtracting Numbers on the Abacus

Adding on the Abacus. Show students how to add small numbers on the abacus by using your overhead abacus. Encourage them to explore the use of the abacus for computing with larger numbers.

Start with a simple fact. 8 + 4
Clear the abacus.
Input 8.

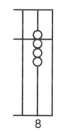

8

Add 4. If you push two earth beads (2) to the crossbar, you can exchange the five earth beads for one sky bead. Then, push two more earth beads (2) to the crossbar.

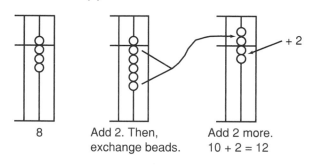

| 8 | Add 2. Then, exchange beads. | Add 2 more. 10 + 2 = 12 + 2 |

If you're speedy, you can push a sky bead to the crossbar—adding 5 instead of 4—and then push away one earth bead—subtracting 1.

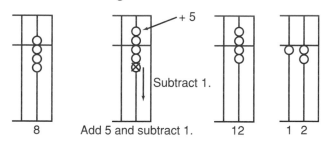

| 8 | Add 5 and subtract 1. | 12 | 1 2 |

The abacus will show 5 + 5 + 2 = 12. For an easier readout, use the fewest number of beads, 10 + 2.

Here are some other problems to do using the abacus. Have student volunteers demonstrate how to do these problems. Use your overhead abacus so the entire class can see.

| 6 + 5 | 13 + 7 | 8 + 9 |
| 53 + 27 | 24 + 17 | 72 + 49 |

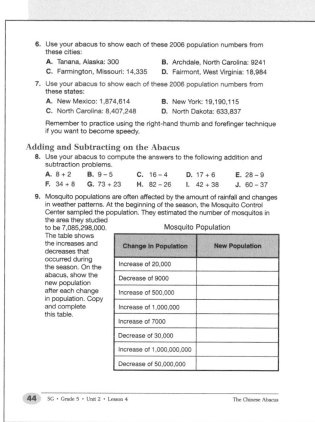

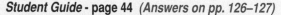

6. Use your abacus to show each of these 2006 population numbers from these cities:
   A. Tanana, Alaska: 300
   B. Archdale, North Carolina: 9241
   C. Farmington, Missouri: 14,335
   D. Fairmont, West Virginia: 18,984

7. Use your abacus to show each of these 2006 population numbers from these states:
   A. New Mexico: 1,874,614
   B. New York: 19,190,115
   C. North Carolina: 8,407,248
   D. North Dakota: 633,837

   Remember to practice using the right-hand thumb and forefinger technique if you want to become speedy.

Adding and Subtracting on the Abacus

8. Use your abacus to compute the answers to the following addition and subtraction problems.
   A. 8 + 2   B. 9 – 5   C. 16 – 4   D. 17 + 6   E. 28 – 9
   F. 34 + 8   G. 73 + 23   H. 82 – 26   I. 42 + 38   J. 60 – 37

9. Mosquito populations are often affected by the amount of rainfall and changes in weather patterns. At the beginning of the season, the Mosquito Control Center sampled the population. They estimated the number of mosquitos in the area they studied to be 7,085,298,000. The table shows the increases and decreases that occurred during the season. On the abacus, show the new population after each change in population. Copy and complete this table.

Mosquito Population

Change in Population	New Population
Increase of 20,000	
Decrease of 9000	
Increase of 500,000	
Increase of 1,000,000	
Increase of 7000	
Decrease of 30,000	
Increase of 1,000,000,000	
Decrease of 50,000,000	

Student Guide - page 44 (Answers on pp. 126–127)

Discuss students' strategies. For example:

- To add 8 + 9, begin with 8. Add 9 by adding 10 with one earth bead in the tens' column and subtracting one earth bead in the ones' column. This is shown below.

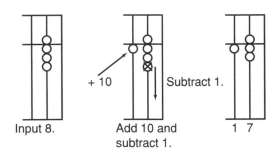

Input 8.   Add 10 and   1 7
           subtract 1.

- To add 27 in the problem 53 + 27, you can add 30 by pushing three earth beads in the tens' column to the crossbar and subtracting 3 by pushing away three earth beads in the ones' column.
- To add 49 to 72 in the last problem, you can push a sky bead in the tens' column (adding 50) to the crossbar and then push away one of the earth beads in the ones' column (subtracting 1).

Mental math is used as numerous exchanges are made with the abacus. Focus class discussion on the ways each problem can be solved.

Progressively lead into larger problems such as 428 + 306. Adding from left to right often results in fewer exchanges. However, students may start from the right since it more closely matches their work with traditional algorithms. In this example, we start at the left.

Add 300. Either:
Push the one remaining earth bead in the hundreds' column to the crossbar (this is adding only 100), then exchange the five earth beads for one sky bead in the hundreds' column, and finally add 200 more by pushing 2 earth beads in the hundreds' column to the crossbar.

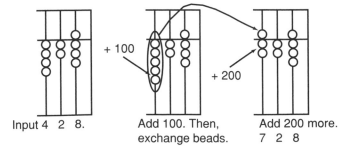

Input 4 2 8.   Add 100. Then,   Add 200 more.
                    exchange beads.   7 2 8

Or, instead of adding 300, add 500 by pushing one sky bead in the hundreds' column to the crossbar and then subtract 200 by pushing away 2 earth beads in the hundreds' column.

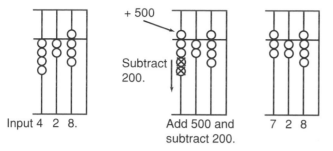

Input 4 2 8.   Add 500 and   7 2 8
                        subtract 200.

Add 6 to 728.

Push the second sky bead and 1 earth bead to the crossbar in the ones' column. Exchange two sky beads in the ones' column for one earth bead in the tens' column. The abacus should read 734.

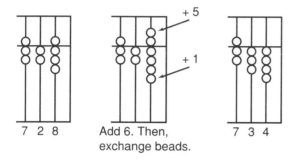

7 2 8   Add 6. Then,   7 3 4
                 exchange beads.

The Adding and Subtracting on the Abacus section in the *Student Guide* provides several addition problems students can solve using their abacuses.

Subtracting on the Abacus. Show students how to subtract using the abacus. Start with a simple fact that involves no regrouping or exchanging of beads: 9 – 3. Clear the abacus. Then, input 9. To subtract 3, push 3 earth beads (3) in the ones' column away from the crossbar.

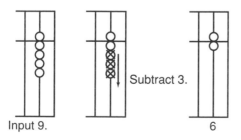

Input 9.   Subtract 3.   6

Your abacus should show 1 sky bead and 1 earth bead in the ones' column. The answer is 6.

Then use the abacus to solve a fact that involves regrouping: 8 − 4. One strategy for subtracting 4 is to subtract 5 and add 1. Subtract 5 by pushing away 1 sky bead in the ones' column. Then, add 1 by pushing an earth bead to the crossbar.

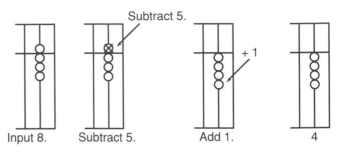

Your abacus should show 4 earth beads in the ones' column. The answer is 4. Other strategies involve more exchanges. Ask students to find an alternative method and demonstrate it to the class.

Here are other problems to explore with students.

$$11 - 3 \qquad 15 - 6 \qquad 32 - 12 \qquad 33 - 18$$
$$58 - 23 \qquad 53 - 27 \qquad 83 - 35$$

Have student volunteers demonstrate their strategies. For example, to subtract 18 from 33, you can subtract 20 first by pushing away 2 earth beads in the tens' column. Then since you subtracted 2 too many, add 2 by pushing 2 earth beads in the ones' column to the crossbar. This is shown below.

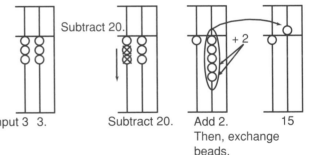

The Adding and Subtracting on the Abacus section in the *Student Guide* provides subtraction problems students can solve using their abacuses.

Progressively lead into harder problems or encourage students to explore computations with larger problems on their own.

Journal Prompt

Compare place value on the abacus and on a place value chart. Describe how they are alike and how they are different.

Math Facts

DPP item I presents problems with multiplication and division by 5.

Homework and Practice

- Assign the Homework section of *The Chinese Abacus* Activity Pages in the *Student Guide*. In the Showing Numbers on the Abacus section, students represent numbers using the abacus and then record their work on the *Abacus Pictures* Activity Page. Students will need two copies of this page, which is in the *Unit Resource Guide*. Students can use their abacuses to solve some of the problems in the Moon Problems section of the homework. They can use paper-and-pencil calculations and estimations (mental math) to solve others. They should choose the appropriate tool and method for solving each problem.

- Assign DPP items G and H to review place value concepts.

Assessment

Have students complete the *Number Changes* Assessment Pages in the *Unit Resource Guide*. Students represent a large number on the abacus. Then they use the abacus to add and subtract various amounts from the original number. They record their work using pictures. Remind students to use the original number in *Question 1* to solve each problem.

Extension

Assign DPP Challenge J.

Homework

Showing Numbers on the Abacus

You will need two copies of the *Abacus Pictures* Activity Page to complete this assignment.

1. Show the following numbers on your abacus using the fewest beads. Then record and label your work on copies of the *Abacus Pictures* Activity Page.

A. 6	B. 600	C. 6000	D. 60,000
E. 17	F. 170	G. 1700	H. 17,000
I. 54	J. 540	K. 5400	L. 54,000
M. 589	N. 735	O. 2550	P. 38,964

Moon Problems

The earth's closest neighbor in space is our moon. It is the earth's only natural satellite.

Solve the following problems about the earth and the moon. You can use any of these tools to solve Questions 2–5: paper and pencil, calculator, or your abacus.

2. The earth has a diameter of about 7926 miles. The moon's diameter is about 2160 miles. What is the difference between the diameter of the moon and the diameter of the earth?

3. Although from space the earth may look like a perfect ball, it really is not. The circumference of the earth at the equator is nearly 24,901 miles. The distance around the earth at the meridian (an imaginary line circling the earth through both poles) is nearly 24,860 miles. Find the difference between these numbers.

4. The average distance from the earth to the moon is about 238,800 miles. Estimate the number of miles in a round trip. Explain your thinking.

5. The average distance from the earth to the moon is about 238,800 miles. However, it can be as far away as 252,710 miles and as close as 221,463 miles. Estimate the difference between the farthest distance and the nearest distance. How did you make your estimate?

Use your abacus or paper and pencil to solve Questions 6–13.

6. 367 + 213	7. 309 − 176	8. 1348 + 471	9. 2078 − 563
10. 2472 − 1895	11. 6882 + 6754	12. 62,395 − 48,778	13. 23,334 + 95,767

The Chinese Abacus   SG • Grade 5 • Unit 2 • Lesson 4   **45**

Student Guide - page 45 (Answers on p. 128)

At a Glance

Math Facts and Daily Practice and Problems

Assign DPP items G–J.

Part 1. Building the Abacus

1. Introduce students to the activity by having them read the first page of *The Chinese Abacus* Activity Pages in the *Student Guide*.
2. Students construct abacuses using the supplied materials and following the directions in the *Student Guide*. Use a transparent abacus on the overhead for demonstration purposes.

Part 2. Numbers on the Abacus

1. Distribute one copy of the *Column Place Value Guides* Activity Page to each student. Students cut along the dashed line on the page. They place the guides along the top and bottom edges of the abacus.
2. Explain the value of the beads in the earth and sky sections of the abacus. Compare the abacus to our base-ten number system.
3. Read together the Numbers on the Abacus section in the *Student Guide*.
4. Students explore different numbers that can be shown using a fixed number of beads in different place-value columns. They complete *Questions 1–2* and record their work with the abacus on copies of the *Abacus Pictures* Activity Page found in the *Unit Resource Guide*.
5. Students complete *Questions 3–5* in the Representing Numbers in More Than One Way section in the *Student Guide*. They compare different representations of the same number and recognize those that use the fewest beads. They record their work on the *Abacus Pictures* Activity Page.
6. In *Questions 6–7* students represent larger numbers on the abacus.

Part 3. Adding and Subtracting Numbers on the Abacus

1. Using an overhead abacus, demonstrate how to add small numbers on the abacus. Start with a simple fact such as $8 + 4$.
2. Have student volunteers demonstrate how to solve other problems on the abacus. Focus your discussion on the variety of ways each problem can be solved.
3. Progressively lead into larger problems such as $428 + 306$.
4. Using an overhead abacus, demonstrate how to subtract small numbers on the abacus. Start with simple facts such as $9 - 3$ and $8 - 4$.
5. Progressively lead into harder problems such as $345 - 152$.
6. *Questions 8 and 9* in the *Student Guide* ask students to add and subtract using their abacuses.

At a Glance

Homework

1. Assign *Question 1* in the Homework section of the *Student Guide*. Students need two copies of the *Abacus Pictures* Activity Page to complete the assignment.
2. Assign *Questions 2–13* in the Homework section of the *Student Guide*. Students may use their abacuses to solve the problems.

Assessment

Use the *Number Changes* Assessment Pages to assess students' understanding of place value as modeled on the abacus.

Extension

Assign DPP Challenge J.

Answer Key is on pages 124–130.

Notes:

Number Changes

You need your abacus to complete this page.

1. Show the number 4,287,398,729 on your abacus. Then, record the number on the abacus picture below. Show only the beads that are pushed to the crossbar.

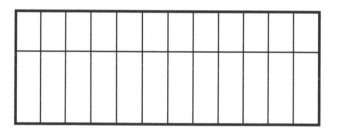

Now, make the changes described below. After each change, go back to the original number in Question 1 before you make the next change.

2. **A.** Show 500 less than 4,287,398,729.

B. Write the new number. _____

3. **A.** Show 1 million more than 4,287,398,729.

B. Write the new number. _____

4. A. Show 3 million more than 4,287,398,729.

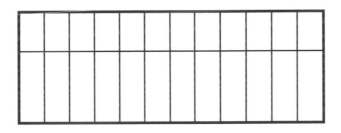

B. Write the new number. _____

5. A. Show 100 million less than 4,287,398,729.

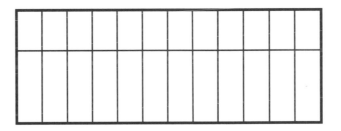

B. Write the new number. _____

6. A. Show 13 million more than 4,287,398,729.

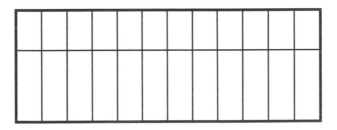

B. Write the new number. _____

7. A. Show 19 thousand less than 4,287,398,729.

B. Write the new number. _____

Column Place Value Guides

ones	1s
tens	10s
hundreds	100s
thousands	**1000s**
10 thousands	10,000s
100 thousands	100,000s
millions	**1,000,000s**
10 millions	10,000,000s
100 millions	100,000,000s
billions	**1,000,000,000s**
10 billions	10,000,000,000s

Abacus Pictures

3 6 5

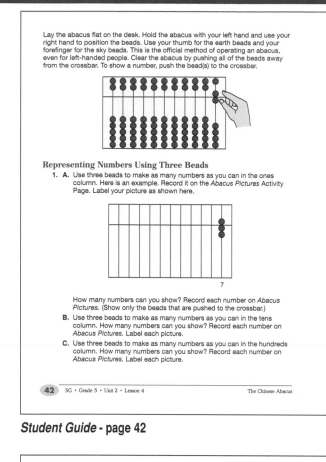

Lay the abacus flat on the desk. Hold the abacus with your left hand and use your right hand to position the beads. Use your thumb for the earth beads and your forefinger for the sky beads. This is the official method of operating an abacus, even for left-handed people. Clear the abacus by pushing all of the beads away from the crossbar. To show a number, push the bead(s) to the crossbar.

Representing Numbers Using Three Beads

1. **A.** Use three beads to make as many numbers as you can in the ones column. Here is an example. Record it on the *Abacus Pictures* Activity Page. Label your picture as shown here.

How many numbers can you show? Record each number on *Abacus Pictures*. (Show only the beads that are pushed to the crossbar.)

  B. Use three beads to make as many numbers as you can in the tens column. How many numbers can you show? Record each number on *Abacus Pictures*. Label each picture.

  C. Use three beads to make as many numbers as you can in the hundreds column. How many numbers can you show? Record each number on *Abacus Pictures*. Label each picture.

Student Guide - page 42

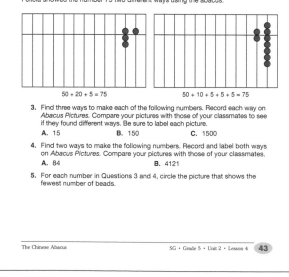

  D. Describe any patterns you see for the numbers you made for each of the columns. Will this pattern continue to the millions and billions?

2. **A.** Use four beads to make as many numbers as you can in the ones column. Record and label your work on the *Abacus Pictures* Activity Page.

  B. How many numbers can you make with four beads in the tens column? Record and label your work.

  C. How many numbers can you make with four beads in the hundreds column? Record and label your work.

  D. Describe any patterns you see for the numbers you made for each of the columns. Compare these patterns with those you found in Question 1D.

Representing Numbers in More than One Way
Felicia showed the number 75 two different ways using the abacus.

50 + 20 + 5 = 75   50 + 10 + 5 + 5 + 5 = 75

3. Find three ways to make each of the following numbers. Record each way on *Abacus Pictures*. Compare your pictures with those of your classmates to see if they found different ways. Be sure to label each picture.
   A. 15   **B.** 150   **C.** 1500

4. Find two ways to make the following numbers. Record and label both ways on *Abacus Pictures*. Compare your pictures with those of your classmates.
   A. 84   **B.** 4121

5. For each number in Questions 3 and 4, circle the picture that shows the fewest number of beads.

Student Guide - page 43

Student Guide (pp. 42–43)

1.* See Figure 28 in Lesson Guide 4.

  A. 3, 7, and 11

  B. 30, 70, and 110

  C. 300, 700, and 1100

  D. The leftmost digits are always 3, 7, and 11. The numbers built in the hundreds' column are ten times greater than those in the tens' column. Those in the tens' column are ten times greater than those in the ones' column.

2. **A.** 4, 8, and 12*

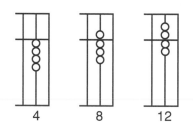

  B. 40, 80, and 120*

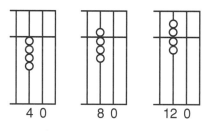

  C. 400, 800, and 1200*

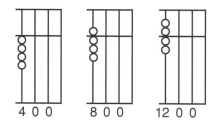

  D. The leftmost digits are always 4, 8, and 12. The numbers built in the hundreds' column are ten times greater than those in the tens' column. Those in the tens' column are ten times greater than those in the ones' column.

*Answers and/or discussion are included in the Lesson Guide.

3. A.

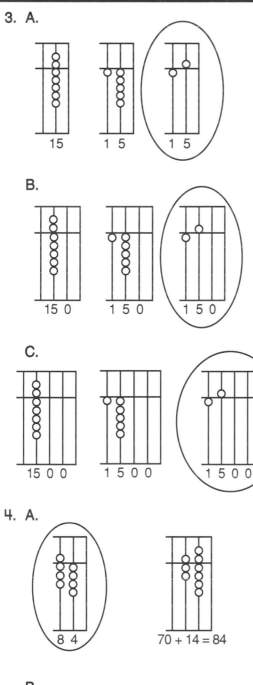

B.

C.

4. A.

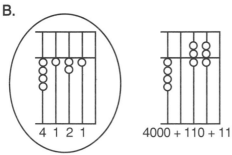

B.

5. See the answers to *Questions 3* and *4.*

6. Use your abacus to show each of these 2006 population numbers from these cities:

   A. Tanana, Alaska: 300   **B.** Archdale, North Carolina: 9241

   C. Farmington, Missouri: 14,335   **D.** Fairmont, West Virginia: 18,984

7. Use your abacus to show each of these 2006 population numbers from these states:

   A. New Mexico: 1,874,614   **B.** New York: 19,190,115

   C. North Carolina: 8,407,248   **D.** North Dakota: 633,837

Remember to practice using the right-hand thumb and forefinger technique if you want to become speedy.

Adding and Subtracting on the Abacus

8. Use your abacus to compute the answers to the following addition and subtraction problems.

   A. 8 + 2   **B.** 9 − 5   **C.** 16 − 4   **D.** 17 + 6   **E.** 28 − 9

   F. 34 + 8 **G.** 73 + 23 **H.** 82 − 26   **I.** 42 + 38 **J.** 60 − 37

9. Mosquito populations are often affected by the amount of rainfall and changes in weather patterns. At the beginning of the season, the Mosquito Control Center sampled the population. They estimated the number of mosquitos in the area they studied to be 7,085,298,000. The table shows the increases and decreases that occurred during the season. On the abacus, show the new population after each change in population. Copy and complete this table.

Mosquito Population

Change in Population	New Population
Increase of 20,000	
Decrease of 9000	
Increase of 500,000	
Increase of 1,000,000	
Increase of 7000	
Decrease of 30,000	
Increase of 1,000,000,000	
Decrease of 50,000,000	

44   SG • Grade 5 • Unit 2 • Lesson 4   The Chinese Abacus

Student Guide - page 44

Student Guide (p. 44)

6. There is more than one way to represent each number. We show the representation that uses the fewest beads.

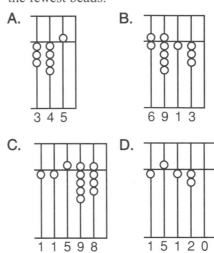

7. There is more than one way to represent each number. We show the representation that uses the fewest beads.

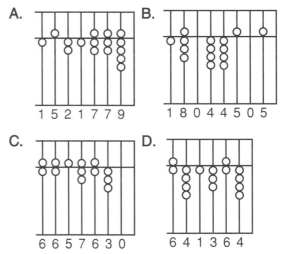

8. There is more than one way to solve each problem using the abacus. One strategy is shown for each.

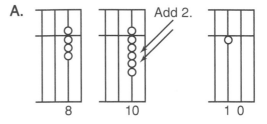

B.

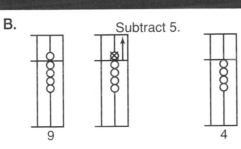

Subtract 5.

9   4

C.

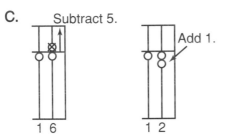

Subtract 5.

Add 1.

1 6   1 2

D.

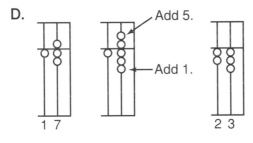

Add 5.

Add 1.

1 7   2 3

E.

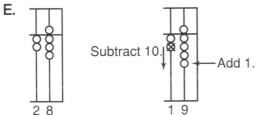

Subtract 10.   Add 1.

2 8   1 9

F.

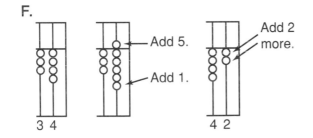

Add 5.   Add 2 more.

Add 1.

3 4   4 2

G.

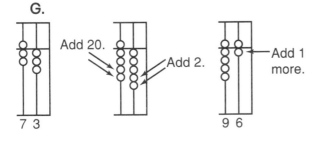

Add 20.   Add 2.

Add 1 more.

7 3   9 6

H.

Subtract 5.

Subtract 20.   Subtract 1.

8 2   5 6

I.

Add 5.

Add 10.   Add 3.

Add 20 more.

4 2   8 0

J.

Subtract 10.   Subtract 20.   Subtract 5.

Subtract 2.

6 0   2 3

9.

Change in Population	New Population
Increase of 20,000	7,085,318,000
Decrease of 9000	7,085,309,000
Increase of 500,000	7,085,809,000
Increase of 1,000,000	7,086,809,000
Increase of 7000	7,086,816,000
Decrease of 30,000	7,086,786,000
Increase of 1,000,000,000	8,086,786,000
Decrease of 50,000,000	8,036,786,000

Student Guide (p. 45)

Homework

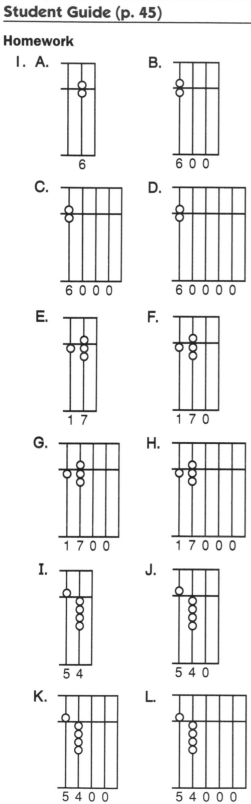

I. A. 6
B. 600
C. 6000
D. 60000
E. 17
F. 170
G. 1700
H. 17000
I. 54
J. 540
K. 5400
L. 54000

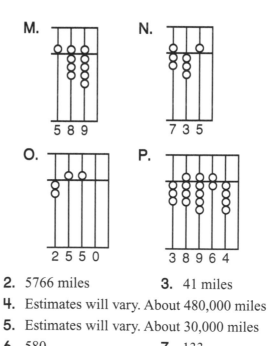

Student Guide - page 45

M. 589
N. 735
O. 2550
P. 38964

2. 5766 miles
3. 41 miles
4. Estimates will vary. About 480,000 miles
5. Estimates will vary. About 30,000 miles
6. 580
7. 133
8. 1819
9. 1515
10. 577
11. 13,636
12. 13,617
13. 119,101

Unit Resource Guide (p. 120)

Number Changes

I. 4,287,398,729

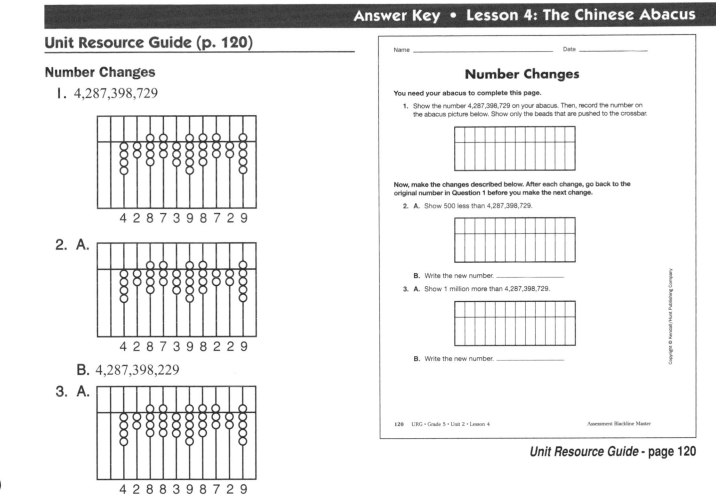

2. A.

B. 4,287,398,229

3. A.

B. 4,288,398,729

Name _____ Date _____

Number Changes

You need your abacus to complete this page.

1. Show the number 4,287,398,729 on your abacus. Then, record the number on the abacus picture below. Show only the beads that are pushed to the crossbar.

Now, make the changes described below. After each change, go back to the original number in Question 1 before you make the next change.

2. **A.** Show 500 less than 4,287,398,729.

B. Write the new number. _____

3. **A.** Show 1 million more than 4,287,398,729.

B. Write the new number. _____

Unit Resource Guide - page 120

---

*Answers and/or discussion are included in the Lesson Guide.

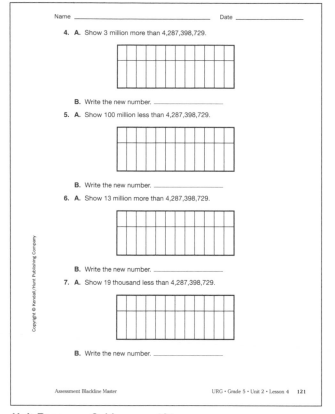

Unit Resource Guide - page 121

Unit Resource Guide (p. 121)

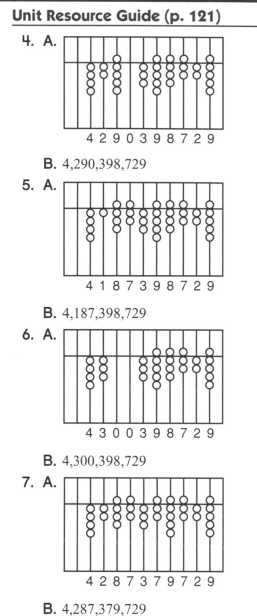

4. A.

4 2 9 0 3 9 8 7 2 9

B. 4,290,398,729

5. A.

4 1 8 7 3 9 8 7 2 9

B. 4,187,398,729

6. A.

4 3 0 0 3 9 8 7 2 9

B. 4,300,398,729

7. A.

4 2 8 7 3 7 9 7 2 9

B. 4,287,379,729

Multiplication

Lesson Overview

Estimated Class Sessions

5

In the first part of the lesson, Reach for the Stars, we review multiplying numbers that end in zeros. In the second part, word problems about the solar system are the context for reviewing the concept of multiplication using base-ten pieces. Children practice different multiplication methods and do various types of multiplication problems. Multiplication practice focuses on 1-digit times multidigit numbers and 2-digit times 2-digit problems.

Key Content

- Multiplying numbers with ending zeros.
- Modeling multiplication with base-ten pieces.
- Understanding paper-and-pencil methods for multiplication.
- Multiplying using paper-and-pencil methods.

Key Vocabulary

- all-partials multiplication method
- commutative property
- compact multiplication method
- partial product

Math Facts

Assign items M, O, and Q and review the multiplication and division facts for the 5s and 10s.

Homework

Assign the Homework section in the *Student Guide.*

Assessment

Use the *Making Money* Assessment Pages as a quiz.

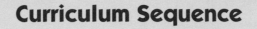

Curriculum Sequence

Base-Ten Number System

Students used base-ten pieces in Grades 2–4 to develop their understanding of the base-ten number system and methods for addition, subtraction, and multiplication. Lesson 3 reviews this material.

Multiplication

In Units 7 and 11 of fourth grade, students learned two paper-and-pencil procedures for one-digit by four-digit multiplication: the all-partials and the compact methods. The all-partials was extended to two-digit by two-digit multiplication. They developed strategies for multiplying numbers with ending zeros and estimating products. Students also may have completed an optional lesson in fourth grade where two-digit by two-digit compact multiplication was introduced. See the Background for this unit and the TIMS Tutor: *Arithmetic* for an example using the all-partials method of multiplication and general information on teaching computation using *Math Trailblazers*.

Multiplication

Students will often use multiplication to solve problems in activities and labs in later units. Practice will be distributed throughout the Daily Practice and Problems and the Home Practice. See DPP items T–Y and BB and the Home Practice in this unit for examples.

In Unit 4, students will use base-ten pieces to explore division.

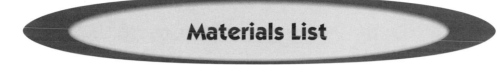

Materials List

Supplies and Copies

Student	Teacher
Supplies for Each Student Group • 1 set of base-ten pieces	**Supplies** • overhead base-ten pieces, optional
Copies • 1 copy of *Making Money* per student (*Unit Resource Guide* Pages 147–149) • 1 table from *Multiplication Table* per student (*Unit Resource Guide* Page 146) • 1 copy of *Base-Ten Board Part 1* and *2* per student, optional (*Unit Resource Guide* Pages 84–85) • 1 copy of *Recording Sheet* per student, optional (*Unit Resource Guide* Page 86)	**Copies/Transparencies** • 1 transparency of *Base-Ten Board Part 1,* optional (*Unit Resource Guide* Page 84) • 1 transparency of *Recording Sheet,* optional (*Unit Resource Guide* Page 86)

All blackline masters including assessment, transparency, and DPP masters are also on the Teacher Resource CD.

Student Books

Multiplication (*Student Guide* Pages 46–55)

Daily Practice and Problems and Home Practice

DPP items K–T (*Unit Resource Guide* Pages 23–27)
Home Practice Part 3 (*Discovery Assignment Book* Page 11)

Note: Classrooms whose pacing differs significantly from the suggested pacing of the units should use the Math Facts Calendar in Section 4 of the *Facts Resource Guide* to ensure students receive the complete math facts program.

Daily Practice and Problems

Suggestions for using the DPPs are on pages 143–144.

K. Bit: Rounding (URG p. 23) [N]

1. Round the following to the nearest hundred:

   A. 381　　　B. 829　　　C. 705

   D. 2323　　E. 4881　　F. 8975

2. Round the following to the nearest thousand:

   A. 2323　　B. 4881　　C. 8975

   D. 4097　　E. 1446　　F. 19,488

L. Task: Big Numbers (URG p. 23) [N]

1. Write the following numbers in order from smallest to largest.

2. Then, write the numbers in words.

   6,549,920　　　4,954,020

   　945,209　　　　456,299

M. Bit: More Multiplication and Division Sentences (URG p. 23) [5×7]

There are 20 students in gym class. They divide into pairs to practice sit-ups. How many pairs of students will practice sit-ups?

A. Draw a picture to illustrate this problem.

B. Write a multiplication sentence and a division sentence to describe this problem.

N. Challenge: Using the Chinese Abacus (URG p. 24) [N] [※]

Explore multiplication on the Chinese abacus. Explain how you can solve the following problems on the abacus. Use pictures of the abacus and label your work.

A. 21 × 5

B. 38 × 10

O. Bit: A Juicy Problem (URG p. 25) [5×7] [※] [N]

Two shipments of fruit were delivered to the school cafeteria. One shipment contained 8 sacks of oranges, 50 pounds to a sack. In the other shipment, there were 7 sacks, also 50 pounds to a sack. How many pounds of fruit were delivered to the cafeteria in all?

P. Challenge: Place Value and Product Size (URG p. 25) [N]

Copy the following diagram onto your paper:

☐ ☐ ☐

× ☐ ☐
―――――――

Choose any 5 digits 1 through 9 to solve these problems. (You can use the same digit more than once.) Use the same 5 digits to answer Questions 1–3.

1. Arrange the digits to produce the largest product possible.

2. Arrange the digits to produce the smallest product possible.

3. How many different products are possible using your 5 digits?

4. Choose 5 new digits and answer the questions again.

Daily Practice and Problems

Suggestions for using the DPPs are on pages 143–144.

Q. Bit: Facts for 5s and 10s (URG p. 26) $\boxed{\begin{smallmatrix}5\\ \times 7\end{smallmatrix}}$

A. $10 \times 3 =$ B. $35 \div 5 =$
C. $80 \div 10 =$ D. $9 \times 5 =$
E. $5 \times 10 =$ F. $25 \div 5 =$
G. $10 \times 10 =$

S. Bit: Changing Numbers (URG p. 26) $\boxed{\text{N}}$

Always begin with the number: 7,382,491.
Change it to:

A. 3 hundred more

B. 9 thousand more

C. 12 million more

D. 70 thousand less

R. Task: Partial Products (URG p. 26) $\boxed{\text{N}}$ $\boxed{\times}$

Irma solved a multiplication problem using the all-partials method of multiplication. Look carefully at her work below. What multiplication problem did she solve?

$$
\begin{array}{r}
\times \quad\quad \\
\hline
27 = 3 \times 9 \\
60 = 3 \times 20 \\
720 = 80 \times 9 \\
\underline{1600} = 80 \times 20 \\
2407
\end{array}
$$

T. Task: Multiplication Practice $\boxed{\times}$ $\boxed{\text{N}}$
   (URG p. 27)

Solve the following problems using paper and pencil. Estimate to make sure your answer makes sense.

A. $516 \times 7 =$

B. $7083 \times 3 =$

C. $97 \times 33 =$

D. $72 \times 8 =$

E. $20 \times 47 =$

F. $23,488 \times 5 =$

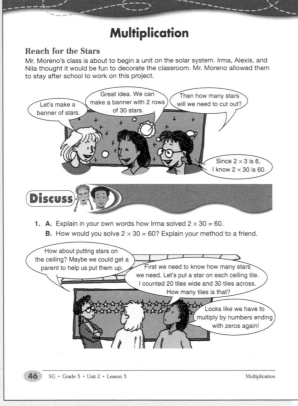

Student Guide - page 46 (Answers on p. 150)

2. Irma learned to look for patterns when multiplying numbers that end in zeros. Find the following products. Use a calculator if needed. Describe the patterns you see.
   A. $2 \times 3 =$
   B. $2 \times 30 =$
   C. $20 \times 3 =$
   D. $20 \times 30 =$
   E. $200 \times 300 =$
   F. $200 \times 30 =$
   G. $20 \times 300 =$

3. How many stars do the students need to cut out to put a star on each ceiling tile?

4. Discuss other ways to compute 20×30.

5. Find the following pairs of products in your head. Check your work on a calculator if needed.

   A. 80   80
      ×2   ×20

   B. 20   20
      ×4   ×40

   C. 50   50
      ×7   ×70

   D. 90   90
      ×7   ×70

   E. 70   70
      ×1   ×10

   F. 30   30
      ×6   ×60

   G. $90 \times 20 =$
      $90 \times 2 =$

   H. $40 \times 50 =$
      $4 \times 50 =$

   I. $60 \times 40 =$
      $6 \times 40 =$

6. Irma, Alexis, and Nila get a package of construction paper. The package contains 20 sheets each of red, blue, yellow, green, and black paper.
   A. How many sheets of construction paper are in the package?
   B. There are 20 packages of construction paper in a box. How many sheets of construction paper are in a box?
   C. If Bessie Coleman School orders 50 boxes of construction paper, how many sheets of construction paper will the school receive?

Multiplication   SG • Grade 5 • Unit 2 • Lesson 5   **47**

Student Guide - page 47 (Answers on p. 150)

Before the Activity

The second part of the activity assumes that students have previously experienced the base-ten pieces to model arithmetic operations. If your students have not, complete the appropriate sections of Lesson 3 as needed. Lesson 3 is optional, introducing the base-ten pieces and using them to review regrouping, addition, and subtraction.

So students can concentrate on learning the procedures for multiplying multidigit numbers, they should have a multiplication table available to help them with their facts. Four small multiplication tables are printed on the *Multiplication Table* Activity Page in the *Unit Resource Guide*. They can be cut out and taped to each student's desk.

Teaching the Activity

Part 1 **Reach for the Stars: Multiplying by Multiples of Ten**

Begin by reading together the opening vignette, Reach for the Stars, on the *Multiplication* Activity Pages in the *Student Guide*. Discuss various ways to think about 2×30 in *Question 1.* Students may remember that to multiply 2×30, they need only multiply 2×3 and append an extra zero. Other students may explain this as taking 2 groups of 30 or doubling 30 to get 60.

Continue with *Questions 2–12* in the *Student Guide*. Allow students to work on problems with calculators either individually or in groups. Ask students whether they can do these problems quickly without a calculator. Help students clearly describe the patterns that will help them multiply numbers with ending zeros. For every zero in both factors, there is a zero in the product. Sometimes, an extra zero is formed from multiplying the nonzero digits. For example, in *Question 12* make sure students realize that 60×500 is 30,000. There are 4 zeros because an extra zero was formed from $6 \times 5 = 30$.

Do more problems together as a class on the board or the overhead projector. For example, find products such as:

70×10	70×20	40×50
70×100	70×200	40×500
70×1000	70×2000	40×5000
etc.	etc.	etc.

Encourage students to predict the products before checking their work on calculators. *Questions 13–16* ask students to find a missing factor. Students can solve these problems by solving a related fact and adding the same number of zeros as are in the product. For example, the related fact for *Question 13* is 5 × 4 = 20. The actual problem is $n \times 40 = 200$. There is one zero in the 40 and 2 zeros in the 200. But, 5 × 4 yields a zero. So, the missing factor is 5.

Assign homework *Questions 1–19.* You can assign half the problems one night and the other half another night.

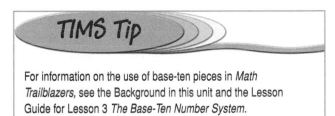

TIMS Tip

For information on the use of base-ten pieces in *Math Trailblazers*, see the Background in this unit and the Lesson Guide for Lesson 3 *The Base-Ten Number System.*

Part 2 **The Solar System: Reviewing Multiplication**

Distribute the base-ten pieces and review the value of the pieces. If you did not complete Lesson 3, model some addition and subtraction problems, especially those that involve regrouping. Remind students that to solve problems on the *Base-Ten Board,* they first recorded their work on the *Recording Sheet.* Later, they learned shortcut methods for doing addition, subtraction, and multiplication problems.

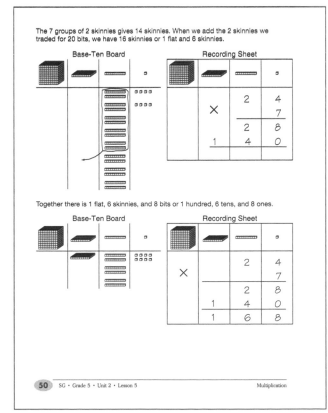

Find the following products with your calculator. Look for patterns.

7. 4 × 7 =
40 × 7 =
4 × 70 =
40 × 70 =
400 × 70 =
40 × 700 =
400 × 700 =

8. 6 × 7 =
60 × 7 =
6 × 70 =
60 × 70 =
600 × 70 =
60 × 700 =
600 × 700 =

9. 8 × 5 =
80 × 5 =
8 × 50 =
80 × 50 =
800 × 50 =
80 × 500 =
800 × 500 =

10. Nila says she can multiply 40 × 40 in her head easily. What method do you think Nila is using? What is 40 × 40?

11. Nila saw that for every zero in the factors, there is a zero in the product. Do you agree? Explain.

12. Alexis says multiplying 60 × 500 is tricky. What is 60 × 500? Why is it tricky?

Find the value of *n* in Questions 13–16.

13. $n \times 40 = 200$

14. $n \times 50 = 2000$

15. $n \times 10 = 2000$

16. $n \times 80 = 4000$

The Solar System

Mr. Moreno's class learned that our solar system includes eight planets: Mercury, Venus, Earth, Mars, Jupiter, Saturn, Uranus, and Neptune.

Earth makes a complete rotation about its axis in about 24 hours. (One rotation of the earth is like one rotation of a basketball on a finger.)

One Earth rotation is what we call a day. To find the number of hours in a week, we multiply 7 days × 24 hours. One way to model this multiplication is to use the base-ten pieces.

Remember, the **base-ten pieces** can be used to model our number system: The **bit** can represent 1:

Since 10 bits make a **skinny,** a skinny can represent 10:

48 SG • Grade 5 • Unit 2 • Lesson 5   Multiplication

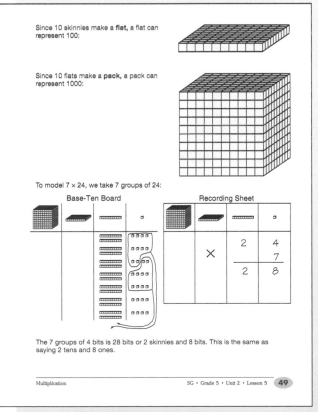

Since 10 skinnies make a **flat,** a flat can represent 100:

Since 10 flats make a **pack,** a pack can represent 1000:

To model 7 × 24, we take 7 groups of 24:

The 7 groups of 4 bits is 28 bits or 2 skinnies and 8 bits. This is the same as saying 2 tens and 8 ones.

Multiplication   SG • Grade 5 • Unit 2 • Lesson 5 **49**

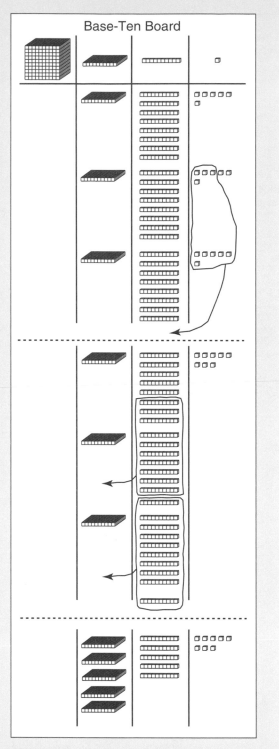

Base-Ten Board

Figure 30: *Using the base-ten pieces to model 186 + 186 + 186 or 186 × 3.*

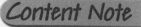
Content Note

You may interchange the words bits, skinnies, flats, and packs for the base-ten words ones, tens, hundreds, and thousands to remind them of the meaning of the pieces. However, when studying decimals, we will assign other values to the pieces. For example, to help students understand decimals, the flat can be the unit, then the skinny is .1 (one-tenth) and the bit is .01 (one-hundredth).

Perhaps students invented their own methods. Invite them to share their methods. When students are familiar with the pieces, pose the following situation:

The bullet trains are some of the fastest trains in the world. One bullet train travels 186 miles per hour. How far can this train travel in 3 hours?

Give children time to work on this problem. Most will recognize this as a multiplication situation. Since the base-ten pieces are on their desks, they may use them to model the situation or use a multiplication algorithm to solve the problem. Others may see this as repeated addition. Make sure everyone can model the problem using the base-ten pieces (or base-ten shorthand).

Use this question to assess whether students understand the values of the pieces and how the pieces can be used to find a solution. Remind them to think about whether their solutions seem reasonable.

Model the problem using the base-ten pieces as shown in Figure 30 or use base-ten shorthand to sketch the problem on the overhead or board. Use the *Recording Sheet* if children would benefit from seeing the column markings. Note to students that you have 3 groups of 6 bits or 18 bits. Ten of these bits can be exchanged to form 1 skinny with 8 bits left over. The 3 groups of 8 skinnies give 24 skinnies plus the extra skinny makes 25 skinnies. From the 25 skinnies we can form 2 flats with

Model Questions 17–20 using the base-ten pieces, or sketch the problems using base-ten shorthand. Then solve the problem.

17. 43	18. 314	19. 502	20. 1023
×4	×3	×5	×3

The table *Our Solar System* gives some information about our solar system. Use it to help you solve the problems on the next few pages. (*Note:* One rotation of any planet is a day on the planet. The fourth column of the table gives the number of Earth hours it takes each planet to make one rotation. One Earth year is equal to the number of Earth days it takes the earth to make one revolution about the sun. The third column in the table gives the number of Earth days it takes each planet to revolve around the sun.)

Our Solar System

Planet	Average distance from the sun in miles (approx.)	Revolution around the sun in Earth days (approx.)	Rotation in Earth hours (approx.)	Diameter at equator (miles) (approx.)
Mercury	36,000,000	88	59	3031
Venus	67,000,000	225	5832	7519
Earth	94,000,000	365	24	7926
Mars	141,000,000	687	25	4221
Jupiter	483,000,000	4332	9	88,734
Saturn	885,000,000	10,760	11	71,000
Uranus	1,779,000,000	30,684	17	32,000
Neptune	2,788,000,000	60,188	16	30,540

Student Guide - page 51 *(Answers on p. 152)*

5 skinnies left. This exchange gives us a total of 5 flats. The total number of pieces is 5 flats, 5 skinnies, and 8 bits. Thus, the train travels 558 miles in 3 hours.

The **all-partials method of multiplication** was introduced in earlier grades as a pencil-and-paper method for solving multiplication problems. Remind students that each product is written on a separate line. While this method takes up more space, it helps children focus on the meaning of multiplication and the value of each place. It also corresponds with the base-ten pieces. Do the problem 186 × 3 by the all-partials algorithm and then by the **compact method.** Figure 31 shows examples of both.

All-partials method   Compact method

$$
\begin{array}{r}
186 \\
\times\,3 \\
\hline
18 \\
240 \\
300 \\
\hline
558
\end{array}
\qquad
\begin{array}{r}
2\,1 \\
186 \\
\times\,3 \\
\hline
558
\end{array}
$$

Figure 31: *186 × 3 done using all-partials algorithm and a standard algorithm*

Review with students the meaning of each step in both methods. Ask questions to remind students that in the all-partials method, every multiplication is written out. For example, when we multiply 3 × 8 in the figure above, we are really multiplying 3 × 80 which gives the **partial product** 240. This corresponds to taking 3 groups of 8 skinnies which is 24 skinnies or 240 bits. Similarly, 3 groups of 1 flat gives 3 flats or 300 bits. Remind students that the compact method shortens the steps because we do not record all the numbers. Since 3 × 6 = 18, we write the 8 in the ones' column but write the 1 above the problem to remind us of the extra ten. Ask such questions as, *"What does the little 2 above the problem mean?"*

Do several more problems involving one-digit times multidigit numbers. If students are having difficulties conceptually, have them model the problems with the base-ten pieces or base-ten shorthand. Here are some example problems:

2 × 274   7 × 306   6 × 78

9 × 1709   4 × 567   6 × 2314

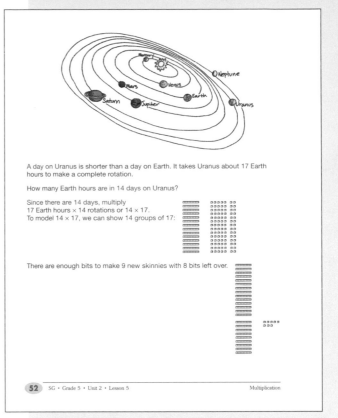

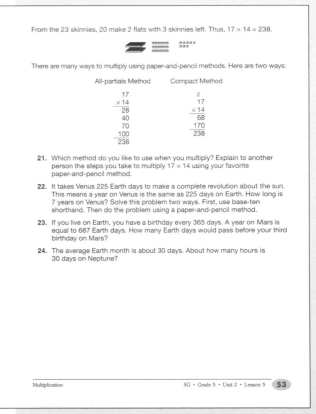

In the second problem listed above, 7×306, note to students that there are only two partial products because we need not record multiplying by 0. When computing this problem using the compact method, 7×6 gives 42, a carry of 4 tens. Then 7×0 tens is 0 plus 4 tens gives a 4 in the tens' place of the product.

$$
\begin{array}{r}
306 \\
\times 7 \\
\hline
42 \\
2100 \\
\hline
2142
\end{array}
\qquad
\begin{array}{r}
{}^{4} \\
306 \\
\times 7 \\
\hline
2142
\end{array}
$$

The following problem reviews two-digit by two-digit multiplication. Use the base-ten pieces or base-ten shorthand to model it.

Mr. Moreno lives 16 miles from school. There were 6 school days in June. How many miles did Mr. Moreno drive going to and from work in June?

Discuss that this problem could be modeled as 16×12 or 12×16 since multiplication is **commutative.** Remind students that the order in which numbers in multiplication and addition problems are written does not matter. Multiplication and addition are both commutative operations. Discuss the fact that subtraction and division are not commutative. That is, $6 \div 3 \neq 3 \div 6$.

Since modeling 12 groups of 16 is easier with the base-ten pieces, we use 12×16. The problem is shown in Figure 32 using base-ten shorthand and is tied to the all-partials method of multiplication.

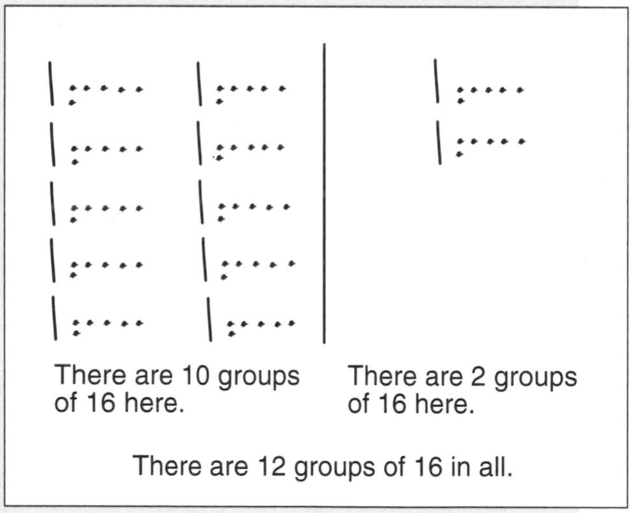

Remind students that we can break 12×16 into $10 \times 16 + 2 \times 16$, which corresponds to the paper-and-pencil computations. Beginning on the right (2×16) we take 2 groups of 6 bits, which gives 12 bits (or 1 skinny and 2 bits).

$$
\begin{array}{r}
16 \\
\times 12 \\
\hline
12
\end{array}
$$

2 times 1 skinny gives 2 skinnies or 20 bits.

$$
\begin{array}{r}
16 \\
\times 12 \\
\hline
12 \\
20
\end{array}
$$

There are 10 groups of 16 here.

There are 2 groups of 16 here.

There are 12 groups of 16 in all.

Figure 32: *Modeling 12×16 with base-ten shorthand*

Look at the left side of Figure 32, which models
10 × 16; 10 groups of 6 bits is 60 bits or 6 skinnies.

$$
\begin{array}{r}
16 \\
\times\,12 \\
\hline
12 \\
20 \\
60 \\
\end{array}
$$

Finally, 10 times 1 skinny gives 10 skinnies or 1 flat.

$$
\begin{array}{r}
16 \\
\times\,12 \\
\hline
12 \\
20 \\
60 \\
100 \\
\hline
192 \\
\end{array}
$$

Together we have 1 flat, 9 skinnies, and 2 bits.
Thus, Mr. Moreno drove 192 miles to school and
back in June.

Note: The two-digit by two-digit compact method
can be explored here. This section is optional. If your
students are not ready or do not need to learn to do
two-digit by two-digit compact multiplication, then
skip this part.

Discuss solving 12 × 16 using the compact method
as shown below. Remind students that the compact
method is similar to the all-partials method but not
all the computations are written out completely.
First multiply 2 × 6 to get 12. This is 2 ones and
1 ten. Write the 2 in the ones' column and place a 1
above the problem (the **carry**) to remind you that
there is an extra ten to take care of. There are more
tens coming from 2 × 10.

$$
\begin{array}{r}
1 \\
16 \\
\times\,12 \\
\hline
2 \\
\end{array}
$$

Then 2 × 10 gives 2 tens plus the extra ten gives
3 tens.

$$
\begin{array}{r}
1 \\
16 \\
\times\,12 \\
\hline
32 \\
\end{array}
$$

Then multiply 10×6 ones, which gives 60 ones or 6 tens. Write a 6 in the tens' column and a 0 in the ones' column so the columns stay lined up.

$$\begin{array}{r} {\scriptstyle 1} \\ 16 \\ \times\,12 \\ \hline 32 \\ 60 \end{array}$$

Finally, 10×10 gives us 1 hundred. Write a 1 in the hundreds' column. Summing the partial products gives a final product of 192.

$$\begin{array}{r} {\scriptstyle 1} \\ 16 \\ \times\,12 \\ \hline 32 \\ 160 \\ \hline 192 \end{array}$$

Practice some more problems together as a class. Here are some examples.

23×34 56×73 17×67 28×45

In a problem such as 28×45, note to students that the carries for the second line of partial products are traditionally begun above the tens' column, even though the carry should be in the hundreds' column as shown in Figure 33.

$$\begin{array}{r} {\scriptstyle 1\;} \\ {\scriptstyle 4\;} \\ 45 \\ \times\,28 \\ \hline 360 \\ 900 \\ \hline 1260 \end{array}$$

Figure 33: *Computing 28 × 45 using the compact method*

In groups or individually, students should read and complete The Solar System section on the *Multiplication* Activity Pages in the *Student Guide.* You can assign homework ***Questions 20–38.*** There are enough questions for a few nights of homework. You may wish to discuss the columns in the solar system chart. Make sure students realize that the second column refers to a revolution around the sun (i.e., a year). The third column refers to the length of a day on each planet measured in Earth hours.

Content Note

Orbits. The average distance between two planets is actually the average distance between their orbits. Thus, the distance between two planets can vary greatly from the average, depending on where they are in their orbits.

DPP items M, O, and Q continue to review the multiplication and division facts for the 5s and 10s.

Homework and Practice

- You can assign **Questions 1–19** in the *Student Guide* Homework section after completing the Reach for the Stars section of the *Multiplication* Activity Pages. After completing The Solar System section, students should do **Questions 20–38.** There are enough problems for several nights of homework.

- DPP items K, L, R, S, and T review rounding and place value concepts. Item T provides multiplication practice.

- You can assign Part 3 of the Home Practice as well.

Answers for Part 3 of the Home Practice are in the Answer Key at the end of this lesson and at the end of this unit.

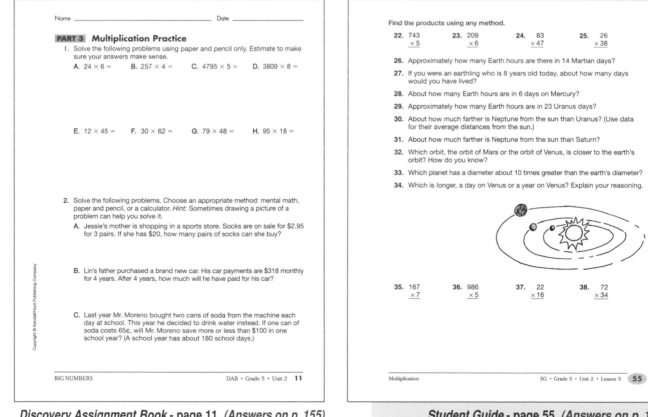

Student Guide - page 54 *(Answers on p. 154)*

Discovery Assignment Book - page 11 *(Answers on p. 155)*

Student Guide - page 55 *(Answers on p. 154)*

Journal Prompt

Explain how to multiply 7 × 325 using any method.

Assessment

- You can have students do **Question 21** in the Homework section in groups and use it to assess their progress.
- Use the *Making Money* Assessment Pages to assess students' understanding of big numbers and multiplication.

Extension

Assign DPP Challenges N and P. Item N requires knowledge of the abacus from Lesson 4.

Software Connection

Math Munchers Deluxe provides practice with facts.

Math Facts and Daily Practice and Problems

Assign items K–T and review the multiplication and division facts for the 5s and 10s.

Part 1. Reach for the Stars: Multiplying by Multiples of Ten

1. Read the opening vignette in the Reach for the Stars section of the *Multiplication* Activity Pages in the *Student Guide*, which introduces the problem 2×30.
2. Discuss various methods of solving 2×30.
3. Discuss patterns when multiplying by multiples of 10.
4. Students complete the *Multiplication* Activity Pages in the *Student Guide* through **Question 16.**

Part 2. The Solar System: Reviewing Multiplication

1. Review working with base-ten pieces.
2. Give the class a three-digit times one-digit multiplication problem and discuss various ways to model and solve.
3. Discuss the all-partials method and compact method for multiplication.
4. Give the class a 2-digit times 2-digit multiplication problem and discuss various ways to model and solve.
5. Discuss multiplying 2-digit times 2-digit numbers using the all-partials method. Discuss the compact method if students are familiar with it.
6. Do the Solar System section of the *Multiplication* Activity Pages in the *Student Guide* in groups. **(Questions 17–24)**

Homework

Assign the Homework section in the *Student Guide*.

Assessment

Use the *Making Money* Assessment Pages as a quiz.

Extension

Assign DPP Challenges N and P.

Connection

Use *Math Munchers Deluxe* to practice facts.

Answer Key is on pages 150–156.

Notes:

Name _____   Date _____

Multiplication Table

×	0	1	2	3	4	5	6	7	8	9	10
0	0	0	0	0	0	0	0	0	0	0	0
1	0	1	2	3	4	5	6	7	8	9	10
2	0	2	4	6	8	10	12	14	16	18	20
3	0	3	6	9	12	15	18	21	24	27	30
4	0	4	8	12	16	20	24	28	32	36	40
5	0	5	10	15	20	25	30	35	40	45	50
6	0	6	12	18	24	30	36	42	48	54	60
7	0	7	14	21	28	35	42	49	56	63	70
8	0	8	16	24	32	40	48	56	64	72	80
9	0	9	18	27	36	45	54	63	72	81	90
10	0	10	20	30	40	50	60	70	80	90	100

×	0	1	2	3	4	5	6	7	8	9	10
0	0	0	0	0	0	0	0	0	0	0	0
1	0	1	2	3	4	5	6	7	8	9	10
2	0	2	4	6	8	10	12	14	16	18	20
3	0	3	6	9	12	15	18	21	24	27	30
4	0	4	8	12	16	20	24	28	32	36	40
5	0	5	10	15	20	25	30	35	40	45	50
6	0	6	12	18	24	30	36	42	48	54	60
7	0	7	14	21	28	35	42	49	56	63	70
8	0	8	16	24	32	40	48	56	64	72	80
9	0	9	18	27	36	45	54	63	72	81	90
10	0	10	20	30	40	50	60	70	80	90	100

×	0	1	2	3	4	5	6	7	8	9	10
0	0	0	0	0	0	0	0	0	0	0	0
1	0	1	2	3	4	5	6	7	8	9	10
2	0	2	4	6	8	10	12	14	16	18	20
3	0	3	6	9	12	15	18	21	24	27	30
4	0	4	8	12	16	20	24	28	32	36	40
5	0	5	10	15	20	25	30	35	40	45	50
6	0	6	12	18	24	30	36	42	48	54	60
7	0	7	14	21	28	35	42	49	56	63	70
8	0	8	16	24	32	40	48	56	64	72	80
9	0	9	18	27	36	45	54	63	72	81	90
10	0	10	20	30	40	50	60	70	80	90	100

×	0	1	2	3	4	5	6	7	8	9	10
0	0	0	0	0	0	0	0	0	0	0	0
1	0	1	2	3	4	5	6	7	8	9	10
2	0	2	4	6	8	10	12	14	16	18	20
3	0	3	6	9	12	15	18	21	24	27	30
4	0	4	8	12	16	20	24	28	32	36	40
5	0	5	10	15	20	25	30	35	40	45	50
6	0	6	12	18	24	30	36	42	48	54	60
7	0	7	14	21	28	35	42	49	56	63	70
8	0	8	16	24	32	40	48	56	64	72	80
9	0	9	18	27	36	45	54	63	72	81	90
10	0	10	20	30	40	50	60	70	80	90	100

Making Money

In March 1994, the United States Treasury Department reported that the total amount of paper money in circulation was more than $350 billion.

The following chart shows the number of bills in circulation for each type of bill. Use this data to answer each question without a calculator. Show all your work.

Denomination (Type of Bill)	Amount of Money in Circulation	Number of Bills in Circulation
$1 bills	$5,674,996,280	5,674,996,280
$2 bills	$972,910,720	486,955,360
$5 bills	$6,672,449,500	1,334,489,900
$10 bills	$13,205,056,280	1,320,505,628
$20 bills	$75,061,576,480	3,753,078,824
$50 bills	?	820,922,986
$100 bills	$207,539,210,500	2,075,392,105

1. Order the numbers in the third column of the chart from the smallest number to the largest number.

2. Write the number of $100 bills in circulation in word form.

3. A. Which type of bill is the most common?

   B. Which type of bill is the least common?

   C. Which two types have about the same number of bills in circulation?

4. If all you knew was the number of $10 bills in circulation, how could you find the amount of money in circulation (the second column) in $10 bills?

5. Estimate the amount of money in circulation for $50 bills.

6. About how many bills were in circulation as of March 1994?

7. After a fund-raiser the Bessie Coleman Parent Teacher Committee counted 17 $20 bills, 24 $10 bills, 16 $5 bills, and 32 $1 bills. How much money did they take in?

8. Advance tickets to the fund-raiser cost $14 for adults. If they sold 37 tickets, how much money did they earn from advance ticket sales?

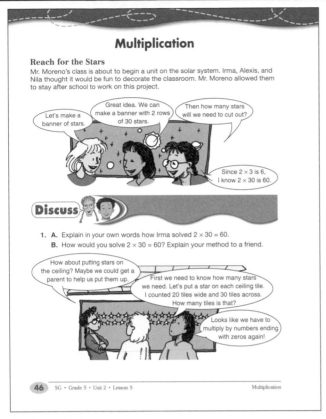

Student Guide - page 46

Student Guide (p. 46)

1.* **A.** Multiply 2 × 3 is 6. Then, add on a zero—60.

   B. Answers will vary.

Student Guide (p. 47)

2. **A.** 6*   **B.** 60

   C. 60   **D.** 600

   E. 6000   **F.** 6000

   G. 60,000

3. 600 stars

4. Answers will vary; 20 × 10 is 200; 200 × 3 = 600

5. **A.** 160; 1600   **B.** 80; 800

   C. 350; 3500   **D.** 630; 6300

   E. 70; 700   **F.** 180; 1800

   G. 1800; 180   **H.** 2000; 200

   I. 2400; 240

6. **A.** 100 sheets

   B. 2000 sheets

   C. 100,000 sheets

Student Guide - page 47

*Answers and/or discussion are included in the Lesson Guide.

Student Guide (pp. 48–50)

7. 28; 280; 280; 2800; 28,000; 28,000; 280,000

8. 42; 420; 420; 4200; 42,000; 42,000; 420,000

9. 40; 400; 400; 4000; 40,000; 40,000; 400,000

10. Multiply the 4 × 4 to get 16. Then add on two zeros—1600.

11. Yes, however, multiplying the two nonzero numbers may result in additional zeros.

12. 30,000. There are 3 zeros in the factors. Multiplying 6 × 5 results in a fourth zero.*

13. 5*

14. 40

15. 200

16. 50

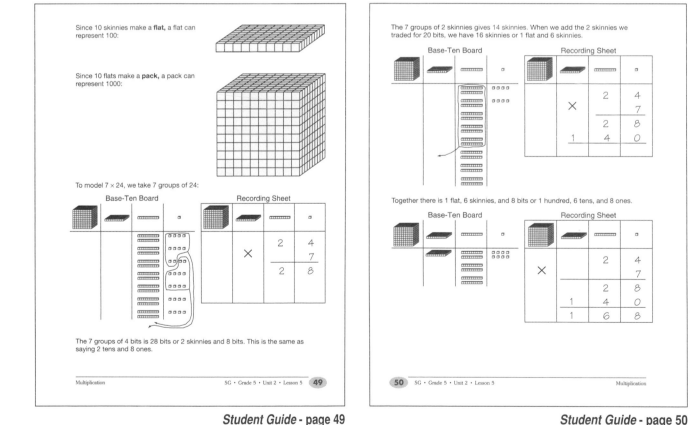

Student Guide - page 48

Student Guide - page 49

Student Guide - page 50

*Answers and/or discussion are included in the Lesson Guide.

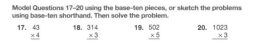

Model Questions 17–20 using the base-ten pieces, or sketch the problems using base-ten shorthand. Then solve the problem.

17.	43	18.	314	19.	502	20.	1023
	×4		×3		×5		×3

The table *Our Solar System* gives some information about our solar system. Use it to help you solve the problems on the next few pages. (*Note:* One rotation of any planet is a day on the planet. The fourth column of the table gives the number of Earth hours it takes each planet to make one rotation. One Earth year is equal to the number of Earth days it takes the earth to make one revolution about the sun. The third column in the table gives the number of Earth days it takes each planet to revolve around the sun.)

Our Solar System

Planet	Average distance from the sun in miles (approx.)	Revolution around the sun in Earth days (approx.)	Rotation in Earth hours (approx.)	Diameter at equator (miles) (approx.)
Mercury	36,000,000	88	59	3031
Venus	67,000,000	225	5832	7519
Earth	94,000,000	365	24	7926
Mars	141,000,000	687	25	4221
Jupiter	483,000,000	4332	9	88,734
Saturn	885,000,000	10,760	11	71,000
Uranus	1,779,000,000	30,684	17	32,000
Neptune	2,788,000,000	60,188	16	30,540

Student Guide - page 51

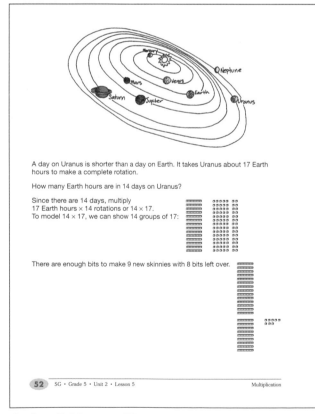

A day on Uranus is shorter than a day on Earth. It takes Uranus about 17 Earth hours to make a complete rotation.

How many Earth hours are in 14 days on Uranus?

Since there are 14 days, multiply 17 Earth hours × 14 rotations or 14 × 17. To model 14 × 17, we can show 14 groups of 17:

There are enough bits to make 9 new skinnies with 8 bits left over.

Student Guide - page 52

17. 172

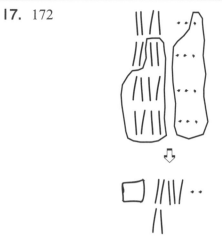

18. 942

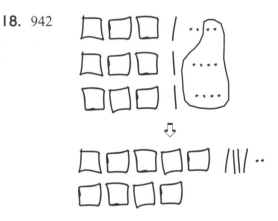

19. 2510

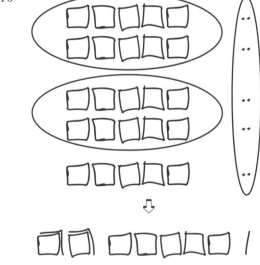

20. 3069

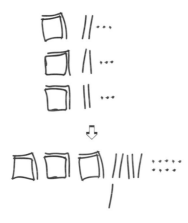

Student Guide (p. 53)

21. Answers will vary.

22. 1575 Earth days

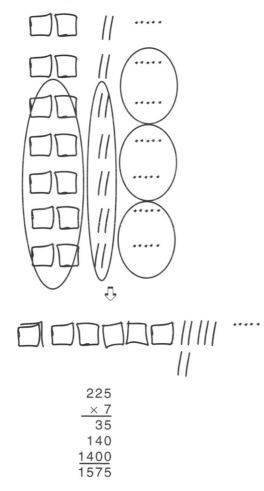

$$
\begin{array}{r}
225 \\
\times\ 7 \\
\hline
35 \\
140 \\
1400 \\
\hline
1575
\end{array}
$$

23. $687 \times 3 = 2061$ days

24. Estimates will vary; 16×30 is between 300 (10×300) and 600 (20×30). A good estimate is about 450 hours.

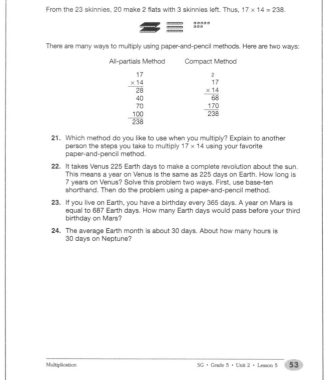

From the 23 skinnies, 20 make 2 flats with 3 skinnies left. Thus, $17 \times 14 = 238$.

There are many ways to multiply using paper-and-pencil methods. Here are two ways:

All-partials Method   Compact Method

$$
\begin{array}{r}
17 \\
\times\ 14 \\
\hline
28 \\
40 \\
70 \\
100 \\
\hline
238
\end{array}
\qquad
\begin{array}{r}
2 \\
17 \\
\times\ 14 \\
\hline
68 \\
170 \\
\hline
238
\end{array}
$$

21. Which method do you like to use when you multiply? Explain to another person the steps you take to multiply 17×14 using your favorite paper-and-pencil method.

22. It takes Venus 225 Earth days to make a complete revolution about the sun. This means a year on Venus is the same as 225 days on Earth. How long is 7 years on Venus? Solve this problem two ways. First, use base-ten shorthand. Then do the problem using a paper-and-pencil method.

23. If you live on Earth, you have a birthday every 365 days. A year on Mars is equal to 687 Earth days. How many Earth days would pass before your third birthday on Mars?

24. The average Earth month is about 30 days. About how many hours is 30 days on Neptune?

Multiplication   SG • Grade 5 • Unit 2 • Lesson 5   **53**

Student Guide - page 53

Homework

Find the products using mental computation.

1. 40 ×70	2. 60 ×60	3. 500 ×60	4. 800 ×30	5. 300 ×30
6. 100 ×100	7. 600 ×40	8. 400 ×200	9. 2000 ×800	10. 6000 ×700

11. Explain how to multiply two numbers that end in zeros.

Find the value of *n* in Questions 12–19.

12. $200 \times n = 1400$
13. $3000 \times 40 = n$
14. $60 \times n = 42,000$
15. $90 \times 90 = n$
16. $n \times 800 = 64,000$
17. $50 \times n = 100$
18. $n \times 50 = 250,000$
19. $n \times 100 = 10,000$

20. The problem below was computed using the all-partials method.

```
    32
  × 76
    12
   180
   140
  2100
  2432
```

A. What numbers were multiplied to get the partial product 12?
B. What numbers were multiplied to get the partial product 180?
C. What numbers were multiplied to get the partial product 140?
D. What numbers were multiplied to get the partial product 2100?

21. A. What multiplication problem are the base-ten pieces modeling?

B. Find the solution to the multiplication problem.

54   SG • Grade 5 • Unit 2 • Lesson 5   Multiplication

Student Guide - page 54

Student Guide (p. 54)

Homework

1. 2800
2. 3600
3. 30,000
4. 24,000
5. 9000
6. 10,000
7. 24,000
8. 80,000
9. 1,600,000
10. 4,200,000

11. Multiply the nonzero numbers in the two factors. Write down their product. Then count up the number of zeros in the factors and add that many zeros to the product.

12. 7
13. 120,000
14. 700
15. 8100
16. 80
17. 2
18. 5000
19. 100

20. A. 6×2 B. 6×30
    C. 70×2 D. 70×30

21. A. 408×3
    B. 1224

Find the products using any method.

22. 743 ×5	23. 209 ×6	24. 83 ×47	25. 26 ×38

26. Approximately how many Earth hours are there in 14 Martian days?
27. If you were an earthling who is 8 years old today, about how many days would you have lived?
28. About how many Earth hours are in 6 days on Mercury?
29. Approximately how many Earth hours are in 23 Uranus days?
30. About how much farther is Neptune from the sun than Uranus? (Use data for their average distances from the sun.)
31. About how much farther is Neptune from the sun than Saturn?
32. Which orbit, the orbit of Mars or the orbit of Venus, is closer to the earth's orbit? How do you know?
33. Which planet has a diameter about 10 times greater than the earth's diameter?
34. Which is longer, a day on Venus or a year on Venus? Explain your reasoning.

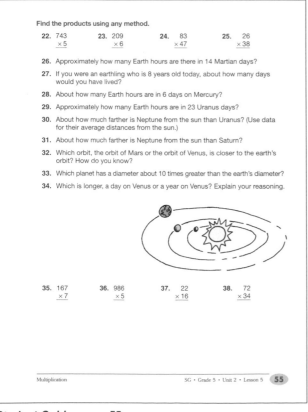

35. 167 ×7	36. 986 ×5	37. 22 ×16	38. 72 ×34

Multiplication   SG • Grade 5 • Unit 2 • Lesson 5   55

Student Guide - page 55

Student Guide (p. 55)

22. 3715
23. 1254
24. 3901
25. 988

26. Estimates will vary; 25×14 is more than 25×10 or 250 and less than 25×20 or 500. About 375 days.

27. Estimates will vary; 8×365 is less than 8×400 or 3200 days and more than 8×300 or 2400. A good estimate is 2800 days.

28. Estimates will vary; 6×59 is about $6 \times 60 = 360$.

29. Estimates will vary; 17×23 is about 400 (20×20) hours.

30. About 1 billion miles

31. About 2 billion miles

32. Venus' orbit; Mars is about 50 billion miles farther from the sun than the Earth, whereas Venus is about 30 billion miles closer to the sun than the Earth.

33. Saturn
34. a Venusian day
35. 1169
36. 4930
37. 352
38. 2448

Discovery Assignment Book (p. 11)

Home Practice*

Part 3. Multiplication Practice

1. **A.** 144   **B.** 1028
   C. 23,975   **D.** 30,472
   E. 540   **F.** 1860
   G. 3792   **H.** 1710

2. **A.** 18 pairs

   B. $15,264

   C. More than $100. Estimates will vary. He would save about $1.20 a day; $1.20 × 180 is about $1 × 200 or $200.

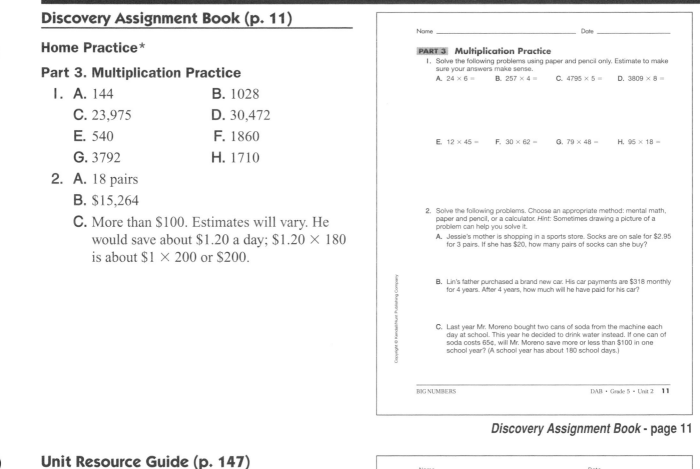

Discovery Assignment Book - page 11

Unit Resource Guide (p. 147)

Making Money

1. 486,955,360; 820,922,986; 1,320,505,628; 1,334,489,900; 2,075,392,105; 3,753,078,824; 5,674,996,280

Name _____ **Date** _____

Making Money

In March 1994, the United States Treasury Department reported that the total amount of paper money in circulation was more than $350 billion.

The following chart shows the number of bills in circulation for each type of bill. Use this data to answer each question without a calculator. Show all your work.

Denomination (Type of Bill)	Amount of Money in Circulation	Number of Bills in Circulation
$1 bills	$5,674,996,280	5,674,996,280
$2 bills	$972,910,720	486,955,360
$5 bills	$6,672,449,500	1,334,489,900
$10 bills	$13,205,056,280	1,320,505,628
$20 bills	$75,061,576,480	3,753,078,824
$50 bills	?	820,922,986
$100 bills	$207,539,210,500	2,075,392,105

1. Order the numbers in the third column of the chart from the smallest number to the largest number.

Assessment Blackline Master   URG • Grade 5 • Unit 2 • Lesson 5   147

Unit Resource Guide - page 147

*Answers for all the Home Practice in the *Discovery Assignment Book* are at the end of the unit.

Name _____ Date _____

2. Write the number of $100 bills in circulation in word form.

3. A. Which type of bill is the most common?

   B. Which type of bill is the least common?

   C. Which two types have about the same number of bills in circulation?

4. If all you knew was the number of $10 bills in circulation, how could you find the amount of money in circulation (the second column) in $10 bills?

5. Estimate the amount of money in circulation for $50 bills.

Copyright © Kendall/Hunt Publishing Company

Unit Resource Guide - page 148

Unit Resource Guide (p. 148)

2. two billion, seventy-five million, three hundred ninety-two thousand, one hundred five
3. **A.** $1 bills
   B. $2 bills
   C. $5 and $10 bills
4. Multiply the number by 10 or add a zero onto the number.
5. Estimates will vary. About 41 billion; 820,000,000 × $100 is 82,000,000,000; 82,000,000,000 ÷ 2 = 41,000,000,000

Name _____ Date _____

6. About how many bills were in circulation as of March 1994?

7. After a fund-raiser the Bessie Coleman Parent Teacher Committee counted 17 $20 bills, 24 $10 bills, 16 $5 bills, and 32 $1 bills. How much money did they take in?

8. Advance tickets to the fund-raiser cost $14 for adults. If they sold 37 tickets, how much money did they earn from advance ticket sales?

Copyright © Kendall/Hunt Publishing Company

Unit Resource Guide - page 149

Unit Resource Guide (p. 149)

6. Answers will vary; 15 billion bills.
7. $692
8. $518

Lesson 6 — Estimating Products

Estimated Class Sessions
1-2

Lesson Overview

Computational estimation is explored. Students find numbers that are convenient to use in estimating products.

Key Content

- Estimating products.
- Using convenient numbers for estimating.
- Multiplying numbers with ending zeros.

Key Vocabulary

- convenient number
- estimate

Math Facts

Assign item U and continue reviewing the multiplication and division facts for the 5s and 10s.

Homework

1. Assign *Questions 1–20* in the Homework section of the *Student Guide*.
2. Assign Part 4 of the Home Practice.

Assessment

1. Use some of the homework problems as assessments.
2. Use DPP item V to assess fluency with paper-and-pencil multiplication.

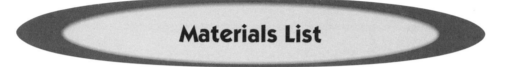

Curriculum Sequence

Before This Unit

Computational estimation was discussed in Grade 4 Units 3, 6, 7, 11, and 13. See Grade 4 Unit 6 Lessons 6 and 7 and Unit 7 Lessons 6 and 7 for specific examples.

After This Unit

Students build and practice estimation skills throughout the curriculum.

Materials List

Supplies and Copies

Student	Teacher
Supplies for Each Student	**Supplies**
Copies • 1 table from *Multiplication Table* per student (*Unit Resource Guide* Page 146)	**Copies/Transparencies**

All blackline masters including assessment, transparency, and DPP masters are also on the Teacher Resource CD.

Student Books

Estimating Products (*Student Guide* Pages 56–59)

Daily Practice and Problems and Home Practice

DPP items U–V (*Unit Resource Guide* Pages 27–28)
Home Practice Part 4 (*Discovery Assignment Book* Page 12)

Note: Classrooms whose pacing differs significantly from the suggested pacing of the units should use the Math Facts Calendar in Section 4 of the *Facts Resource Guide* to ensure students receive the complete math facts program.

Daily Practice and Problems

Suggestions for using the DPPs are on page 163.

U. Bit: Patterns with Zeros (URG p. 27) $\boxed{\begin{smallmatrix}5\\\times7\end{smallmatrix}}$ $\boxed{N}$

Do these problems in your head.

A. $5 \times 3 =$

B. $5 \times 30 =$

C. $5 \times 300 =$

D. $5 \times 3000 =$

E. $5 \times 30,000 =$

What is the pattern when you multiply numbers that end in zero?

V. Task: Multiplication Practice $\boxed{N}$
(URG p. 28)

Solve the following problems using paper and pencil. Estimate to make sure your answer makes sense.

A. $46 \times 7 =$

B. $77 \times 16 =$

C. $54 \times 35 =$

D. $38 \times 30 =$

E. $62 \times 40 =$

F. $7134 \times 5 =$

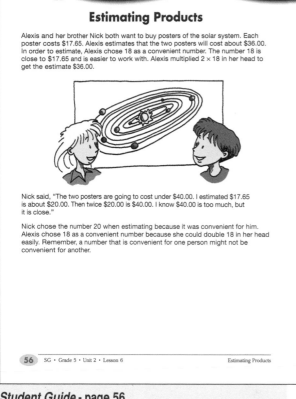

Estimating Products

Alexis and her brother Nick both want to buy posters of the solar system. Each poster costs $17.65. Alexis estimates that the two posters will cost about $36.00. In order to estimate, Alexis chose 18 as a convenient number. The number 18 is close to $17.65 and is easier to work with. Alexis multiplied 2 × 18 in her head to get the estimate $36.00.

Nick said, "The two posters are going to cost under $40.00. I estimated $17.65 is about $20.00. Then twice $20.00 is $40.00. I know $40.00 is too much, but it is close."

Nick chose the number 20 when estimating because it was convenient for him. Alexis chose 18 as a convenient number because she could double 18 in her head easily. Remember, a number that is convenient for one person might not be convenient for another.

Student Guide - page 56

We find estimates when we need to have a good idea about how big or small a number is, but we do not need to know exactly. Sometimes it is impossible to know an exact answer. We use estimates in many different situations.

For example:
You can estimate how far you live from school.
You can estimate how many people are watching a concert.
You can estimate how much you will pay for a full cart of groceries.

When we **estimate,** we find a number or answer that is reasonably close to the actual number. It may be bigger or smaller than the actual number, depending on the problem. To make an estimate we sometimes need to do some number operations in our heads. To make these computations easy to do, we often choose **convenient numbers** to make our estimates. Convenient numbers are really estimates as well.

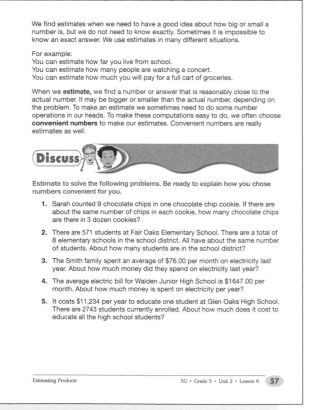

Estimate to solve the following problems. Be ready to explain how you chose numbers convenient for you.

1. Sarah counted 9 chocolate chips in one chocolate chip cookie. If there are about the same number of chips in each cookie, how many chocolate chips are there in 3 dozen cookies?

2. There are 571 students at Fair Oaks Elementary School. There are a total of 8 elementary schools in the school district. All have about the same number of students. About how many students are in the school district?

3. The Smith family spent an average of $76.00 per month on electricity last year. About how much money did they spend on electricity last year?

4. The average electric bill for Walden Junior High School is $1647.00 per month. About how much money is spent on electricity per year?

5. It costs $11,234 per year to educate one student at Glen Oaks High School. There are 2743 students currently enrolled. About how much does it cost to educate all the high school students?

Student Guide - page 57 *(Answers on p. 165)*

Teaching the Activity

As students combine estimation and multiplication skills in this lesson, encourage them to do mental computations and to use calculators only to check their work.

Begin with a discussion about estimating. Explain that we often cannot or do not need to find exact answers—an estimate is good enough. Remind students that **estimate** means "to find about how many" (as a verb) or the "approximate number" (as a noun). We "estimate" the number of people at a ball game to get an "estimate" of the attendance.

Pose the following questions. (These problems will not consider sales tax.)

A. *If 1 apple costs 18¢, about how much do 3 apples cost?*

We can round 18¢ to 20¢. Then, 3×20¢ = 60¢. Students may also round to 15¢. Since 3×15¢ = 45¢, we know that the cost is between 45¢ and 60¢.

B. *Shirts cost $19.50. If you buy 4 shirts, about how much money will you spend?*

C. *A bag of cat litter is $3.67. How much will 2 bags cost?*

Answers will vary. Accept any reasonable answers. Students may round to $3.50, $3.70, $3.75, or $4.00 before multiplying by 2. Students may notice that knowing number facts helps in estimating. For example, if you know the answer to 36 + 36, the estimate of $7.20 for this question comes quickly.

Discuss the necessity of choosing **convenient numbers** that are close enough to give a good estimate but also easy to use in mental computations.

Ask students to read and discuss the *Estimating Products* Activity Pages in the *Student Guide.* Allow students time to complete *Questions 1–5* in groups. Then discuss each problem as a class.

In *Question 1* students estimate the number of chocolate chips in 3 dozen cookies, given there are 9 chocolate chips in one sample cookie. Remind students that there are 12 cookies in 1 dozen. Most students will use 10 as a convenient number for 9 chips. One reasonable estimate is to multiply $10 \times 36 = 360$. Another reasonable convenient number to use is 40 (for 36 cookies in 3 dozen). $9 \times 40 = 360$. Ask students what numbers were convenient for them.

Question 2 asks students to estimate the total number of students in 8 schools of approximately equal enrollment, given there are 571 students at one of the schools. Ask students what convenient numbers they chose. One estimate is $8 \times 600 = 4800$. Another student may refine the estimate by computing $8 \times 500 = 4000$ and choosing a number between 4000 and 4800 such as 4500. Discuss other estimates as well. Encourage students to choose convenient numbers with 1 or 2 nonzero digits so they can multiply in their heads.

Remind students that one way of finding a convenient number is to truncate after the first number, for example, 123 becomes 100 (front-end estimation). Another strategy is to find the closest benchmark number (rounding).

In *Question 3* students estimate the Smith family's yearly electric bill, given they spend $76.00 a month on average. Students may suggest several ways of estimating. One way is to say $76 is close to $75. Another person may find 80 to be a convenient number. Your students may have other suggestions. Impress upon them that there may be several ways to get good estimates. Encourage them to find numbers that are convenient for them.

Question 4 asks students to estimate the yearly electric bill of a junior high school whose average bill is $1647.00 per month. Discuss when and where estimates are appropriate. In this example, the exact amount is necessary to pay the bill. However, only an estimate is needed to set aside (or budget) for next year. Discuss factors that might influence next year's bill. A rise in electric costs, using the school after hours, installation of air conditioners, or a particularly hot summer are all factors that may be considered.

There are several ways to estimate the product. One person might say $1647 is close to $1600 and then compute with paper and pencil—$1600 \times 12 = $19,200. Another may say 1600 is close to 2000 so $2000 \times 12 = 24,000$. To get a better estimate mentally, they might find $1000 \times 12 = 12,000$. Using these two estimates together, they might reason that the number is a bit more than halfway between 12,000 and 24,000, or more than $18,000. Have students describe other ways they approached this problem.

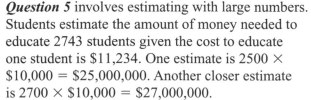

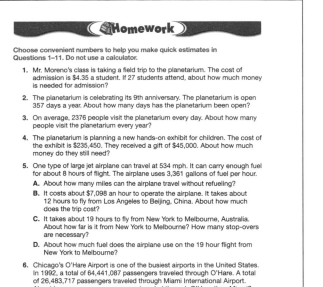

Student Guide - page 58 *(Answers on p. 165)*

Student Guide - page 59 *(Answers on p. 166)*

Question 5 involves estimating with large numbers. Students estimate the amount of money needed to educate 2743 students given the cost to educate one student is $11,234. One estimate is 2500 × $10,000 = $25,000,000. Another closer estimate is 2700 × $10,000 = $27,000,000.

You may wish to practice with several more large number examples in class. Ask students to find numbers convenient for them to work with so they do not need to use a calculator. They may need to use paper and pencil to keep track of all the zeros.

For example, estimate the following products mentally or use paper and pencil to record the zeros.

$23 \times 24,601$

$458 \times 15,349$

$2596 \times 45,321$

$7198 \times 4,215,987$

$2034 \times 1,345,312,654$

Math Facts

DPP item U explores patterns when multiplying with zeros. Continue reviewing the multiplication and division facts for the 5s and 10s.

Homework and Practice

- Students use convenient numbers to estimate the answers to **Questions 1–20** in the Homework section of the *Student Guide.* (If students solve the problems on a calculator, they may run into scientific notation. Discuss these problems after completing Lesson 8 *Exponents and Large Numbers.*)

- Assign Part 4 of the Home Practice that involves problem solving.

Answers for Part 4 of the Home Practice are in the Answer Key at the end of this lesson and at the end of this unit.

Assessment

- Choose several homework problems to use as assessment.

- Assign DPP Task V as an assessment of paper-and-pencil multiplication covered in Lesson 5.

Name _____ Date _____

PART 4 Solving Problems
Solve the following problems. Choose an appropriate method for each: mental math, paper and pencil, or a calculator. Explain your solutions.

1. A mouse can have a litter of as many as 16 pups. A mouse can have up to 6 litters each year. About how many mice, at most, can one mouse produce in 6 years?

2. The U.S. government recommends that girls between the ages of 11 and 14 consume 2400 calories of food a day. Boys of the same age should consume 2800 calories.
   A. A boy follows these guidelines. Will he consume more or less than 25,000 calories in one week?

   B. In one week, how many more calories should a boy eat than a girl?

3. One of the longest running Broadway musical plays ran for about 15 years. On average, there were 409 performances each year.
   A. About how many performances were there in all over the 15 years?

   B. About how many performances were there each month?

12 DAB • Grade 5 • Unit 2   BIG NUMBERS

Discovery Assignment Book - page 12 *(Answers on p. 166)*

At a Glance

Math Facts and Daily Practice and Problems

Assign items U–V and continue reviewing the multiplication and division facts for the 5s and 10s.

Teaching the Activity

1. Do several problems as a group that involve estimating with money. Examples are provided in the Lesson Guide.
2. Use *Questions 1–5* in the *Student Guide* to discuss finding convenient numbers for computing estimates.

Homework

1. Assign *Questions 1–20* in the Homework section of the *Student Guide*.
2. Assign Part 4 of the Home Practice.

Assessment

1. Use some of the homework problems as assessments.
2. Use DPP item V to assess fluency with paper-and-pencil multiplication.

Answer Key is on pages 165–166.

Notes:

Student Guide (p. 57)

Estimates will vary. One reasonable estimate is given for each below.

1. 360 chips (36 × 10)*
2. 5710 students (571 × 10)*
3. $800 (80 × 10)*
4. 17,000 (1700 × 10)*
5. $30,000,000 (10,000 × 3000)*

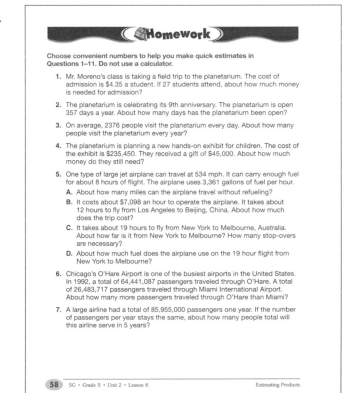

We find estimates when we need to have a good idea about how big or small a number is, but we do not need to know exactly. Sometimes it is impossible to know an exact answer. We use estimates in many different situations.

For example:
You can estimate how far you live from school.
You can estimate how many people are watching a concert.
You can estimate how much you will pay for a full cart of groceries.

When we **estimate**, we find a number or answer that is reasonably close to the actual number. It may be bigger or smaller than the actual number, depending on the problem. To make an estimate we sometimes need to do some number operations in our heads. To make these computations easy to do, we often choose **convenient numbers** to make our estimates. Convenient numbers are really estimates as well.

 **Discuss**

Estimate to solve the following problems. Be ready to explain how you chose numbers convenient for you.

1. Sarah counted 9 chocolate chips in one chocolate chip cookie. If there are about the same number of chips in each cookie, how many chocolate chips are there in 3 dozen cookies?

2. There are 571 students at Fair Oaks Elementary School. There are a total of 8 elementary schools in the school district. All have about the same number of students. About how many students are in the school district?

3. The Smith family spent an average of $76.00 per month on electricity last year. About how much money did they spend on electricity last year?

4. The average electric bill for Walden Junior High School is $1647.00 per month. About how much money is spent on electricity per year?

5. It costs $11,234 per year to educate one student at Glen Oaks High School. There are 2743 students currently enrolled. About how much does it cost to educate all the high school students?

Estimating Products   SG • Grade 5 • Unit 2 • Lesson 6   **57**

Student Guide - page 57

Student Guide (p. 58)

Homework

Estimates will vary. One reasonable estimate is given for each below.

1. $5.00 × 30 = $150
2. 357 × 10 = 3570 days
3. 2500 × 300 = 750,000 people
4. $235,000 − $45,000 = $190,000
5. **A.** 8 × 500 = 4000 miles
   B. $7000 × 10 = $70,000
   C. 20 × 500 = 10,000 miles; about 3 stop-overs
   D. 20 × 3300 = 66,000 gallons
6. 60 million − 20 million = 40 million
7. 90 million × 5 = 450 million passengers

Homework

Choose convenient numbers to help you make quick estimates in Questions 1–11. Do not use a calculator.

1. Mr. Moreno's class is taking a field trip to the planetarium. The cost of admission is $4.35 a student. If 27 students attend, about how much money is needed for admission?

2. The planetarium is celebrating its 9th anniversary. The planetarium is open 357 days a year. About how many days has the planetarium been open?

3. On average, 2376 people visit the planetarium every day. About how many people visit the planetarium every year?

4. The planetarium is planning a new hands-on exhibit for children. The cost of the exhibit is $235,450. They received a gift of $45,000. About how much money do they still need?

5. One type of large jet airplane can travel at 534 mph. It can carry enough fuel for about 8 hours of flight. The airplane uses 3,361 gallons of fuel per hour.
   A. About how many miles can the airplane travel without refueling?
   B. It costs about $7,098 an hour to operate the airplane. It takes about 12 hours to fly from Los Angeles to Beijing, China. About how much does the trip cost?
   C. It takes about 19 hours to fly from New York to Melbourne, Australia. About how far is it from New York to Melbourne? How many stop-overs are necessary?
   D. About how much fuel does the airplane use on the 19 hour flight from New York to Melbourne?

6. Chicago's O'Hare Airport is one of the busiest airports in the United States. In 1992, a total of 64,441,087 passengers traveled through O'Hare. A total of 26,483,717 passengers traveled through Miami International Airport. About how many more passengers traveled through O'Hare than Miami?

7. A large airline had a total of 85,955,000 passengers one year. If the number of passengers per year stays the same, about how many people total will this airline serve in 5 years?

58   SG • Grade 5 • Unit 2 • Lesson 6   Estimating Products

Student Guide - page 58

*Answers and/or discussion are included in the Lesson Guide.

Use the Solar System Chart in Lesson 5 to answer the following questions.

8. Is Uranus's year about 3 times longer than Saturn's year? Explain how you know.

9. If I were a three-year-old Neptunian, about how many Earth days would I have lived?

10. The diameter of the sun is 864,000 miles. About how many Jupiters would need to be lined up to approximate the diameter of the sun?

11. Pluto was once considered to be a planet. At its closest, Pluto is about 2,663,000,000 miles from the earth. About how many round trips would it take to log 1 trillion miles traveling from Earth to Pluto and back?

Estimate the products. First choose numbers that are convenient.

12. 229,476 × 27	**13.** 356,234,045 × 9023	**14.** 1,029,576,123 × 4329
15. 1349 × 267	**16.** 421,467 × 38	**17.** 12,976 × 343
18. 2,794,271 × 679	**19.** 111,111 × 1111	**20.** 343,217 × 999

Estimating Products   SG • Grade 5 • Unit 2 • Lesson 6   **59**

Student Guide - page 59

Student Guide (p. 59)

8. yes, 30,684 is about $3 \times 10,760$ days

9. $60,000 \times 3 = 180,000$ days

10. About 10 Jupiters

11. About 200 round trips; 1 round trip is about 5 billion miles; $5,000,000,000 \times 200 = 1,000,000,000,000$

12. $200,000 \times 30 = 6,000,000$

13. $360,000,000 \times 10,000 = 3,600,000,000,000$

14. 1 billion $\times 4300 = 4,300,000,000,000$

15. $1300 \times 300 = 390,000$

16. $400,000 \times 40 = 16,000,000$

17. $13,000 \times 300 = 3,900,000$

18. $3,000,000 \times 700 = 2,100,000,000$

19. $100,000 \times 1000 = 100,000,000$

20. $300,000 \times 1000 = 300,000,000$

Name _____ Date _____

PART 4 Solving Problems

Solve the following problems. Choose an appropriate method for each: mental math, paper and pencil, or a calculator. Explain your solutions.

1. A mouse can have a litter of as many as 16 pups. A mouse can have up to 6 litters each year. About how many mice, at most, can one mouse produce in 6 years?

2. The U.S. government recommends that girls between the ages of 11 and 14 consume 2400 calories of food a day. Boys of the same age should consume 2800 calories.
   A. A boy follows these guidelines. Will he consume more or less than 25,000 calories in one week?

   B. In one week, how many more calories should a boy eat than a girl?

3. One of the longest running Broadway musical plays ran for about 15 years. On average, there were 409 performances each year.
   A. About how many performances were there in all over the 15 years?

   B. About how many performances were there each month?

12 DAB • Grade 5 • Unit 2   BIG NUMBERS

Discovery Assignment Book - page 12

Discovery Assignment Book (p. 12)

Home Practice*

Part 4. Solving Problems

1. Estimates will vary; 10 pups × 36 litters = 360 pups; 20 pups × 36 litters = 720 pups; Between 360 and 720. About 500 pups.

2. **A.** Less than 25,000; $3000 \times 7 = 21,000$
   B. 400 per day more × 7 = 2800 calories

3. **A.** Estimates will vary. Between $10 \times 400 = 4000$ and $20 \times 400 = 8000$—6000 performances is a reasonable estimate.
   B. 15 years × 12 months in a year = 180 months; $6000 \div 180 =$ about 33 performances a month

*Answers for all the Home Practice in the *Discovery Assignment Book* are at the end of the unit.

Lesson 7

Sand Reckoning

Lesson Overview

Estimated Class Sessions

1

The Adventure Book, *Sand Reckoning,* serves as an introduction to Lessons 8–9, *Exponents and Large Numbers* and *Stack Up. Sand Reckoning* tells the story of Archimedes' estimate for the number of grains of sand it would take to fill the universe.

Key Content

- Using exponents to read large numbers.
- Developing number sense for large numbers.
- Connecting mathematics and science to real-world events.

Key Vocabulary

- googol
- googolplex
- infinite

Math Facts

Assign DPP items W and X for more practice with the multiplication and division facts for the 5s and 10s.

Materials List

Supplies and Copies

Student	Teacher
Supplies for Each Student	**Supplies**
Copies	**Copies/Transparencies**

All blackline masters including assessment, transparency, and DPP masters are also on the Teacher Resource CD.

Student Books

Sand Reckoning (*Adventure Book* Pages 13–20)

Daily Practice and Problems and Home Practice

DPP items W–X (*Unit Resource Guide* Pages 28–29)

Note: Classrooms whose pacing differs significantly from the suggested pacing of the units should use the Math Facts Calendar in Section 4 of the *Facts Resource Guide* to ensure students receive the complete math facts program.

Daily Practice and Problems

Suggestions for using the DPPs are on page 171.

W. Bit: Multiplying by Numbers Ending in Zeros (URG p. 28)

A. $50 \times 7 =$

B. $600 \times 50 =$

C. $60 \times 10 =$

D. $800 \times 100 =$

E. $500 \times 9 =$

F. $200 \times 5000 =$

X. Task: Related Facts (URG p. 29)

Solve each problem. Then name a related division sentence for each.

A. $500 \times 5 = ?$

B. $10 \times 30 = ?$

C. $1000 \times 5 = ?$

D. $400 \times 50 = ?$

Teaching the Activity

This is the story of Ellen, a fifth-grade girl who is raking the leaves in her yard. She tells her father that there must be a "zillion" or at least a billion leaves. He says there are nowhere near that number. A neighbor is strolling by and stops to chat with Ellen. The neighbor, Mrs. Patel, is a scientist who works with very large numbers. She tells Ellen about the way very large numbers are written and about the **googol** (1 with 100 zeros after it—10^{100}) and the **googolplex** (1 with a googol of zeros after it). Mrs. Patel also shares with Ellen the story of Archimedes' attempt to estimate the number of grains of sand in the universe.

Ask students to read the book through, just to enjoy the story. Then choose some of the discussion prompts to bring out the mathematics in the story in a class discussion.

Discussion Prompts

Page 14

- *Describe a method for making a good estimate of the number of leaves in a yard.*

Count samples of leaves from a small area in the yard. Use the sample data to calculate an estimate for the number of leaves in the whole yard.

- *How much area do you think a billion leaves would cover?*

If each leaf were about three square inches, a billion leaves would cover almost $\frac{3}{4}$ of a square mile, about 925 football fields, or about 50 city blocks.

- *Do you really think there are a billion leaves on Ellen's lawn? Is Ellen's estimate high or low?*

Unless Ellen's yard is almost $\frac{3}{4}$ of a square mile, it is unlikely that there are a billion leaves in her yard. There are probably many fewer leaves in her yard.

Page 15

- *How many leaves do you think are in your town? More or less than a million, billion, or a trillion?*

If all the ground in a town with an area of 3 square miles were covered with one layer of leaves, there would be about 4 billion leaves in town.

Sand Reckoning

It's a fine October morning in Oak Park. The sun is shining, but there is a cloud over a certain young Oak Parker: Ellen Novy has to rake the leaves on her lawn.

"There must be a zillion leaves here, Dad," complained Ellen. "It'll take me forever to rake them all."

"There is no such number as a 'zillion,' Ellen," replied Mr. Novy. "If you work hard I'll bet you can be finished in less than one hour."

"Maybe there's not a zillion leaves here, but there must be at least a billion," said Ellen. "A billion leaves to rake and bag! I'll be old and gray before I'm done. Why don't we recycle the leaves right on the lawn? That'd be more ecological, wouldn't it, Dad?"

Adventure Book - page 14

Sand Reckoning

"There are certainly fewer than a billion or even a million leaves on that lawn, Ellen. The sooner you get started, the sooner you'll be done."

"How do you know there are fewer than a million leaves, Dad?" asked Ellen.

"Look, our lawn is about 50 feet across and 30 feet from front to back. That's about 1500 square feet. If there were 100 leaves on each square foot—and actually there aren't nearly that many—there would only be 150,000 leaves, which is a lot less than a million. Now, rake!"

Mr. Novy left Ellen to rake. As she raked, she thought about the other girls and boys in her class. Are they playing right now and having a good time? Or are they raking too? Do they have more or fewer leaves to rake? How many leaves need to be raked in Oak Park right now?

Just then, Mrs. Patel, Ellen's neighbor, happened by. "Hello, Ellen," said Mrs. Patel. "Why such a faraway look?"

"Oh, hi, Mrs. Patel," replied Ellen. "I was just wondering how many leaves there are right now on all the lawns in Oak Park. Do you suppose there are more than a trillion?"

"Let's see. A trillion. That's a million millions, right? A 1 followed by twelve 0s. Hmmm. In my work, we'd call that ten to the twelfth," answered Mrs. Patel. "I'd guess there are far fewer than a trillion, Ellen."

1 trillion is 10^{12}.
Read "ten to the twelfth."
1,000,000,000,000

Adventure Book - page 15

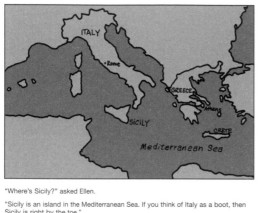

Adventure Book - page 16

Adventure Book - page 17

Page 16

- *Find Sicily on a world map or a globe.*

Page 17

- *What's a quick way to multiply 40 × 40 × 40 and 64,000 × 10,000?*

$4 \times 4 \times 4 = 16 \times 4$ or 64. Then add on the zeros to get 64,000. To multiply $64,000 \times 10,000$, multiply 64×1, then add on 7 zeros to get 640,000,000 or six hundred forty million.

Content Note

Modern physicists and astronomers define a matter-universe roughly as an expanding sphere containing all matter. The boundary of this sphere is considered the edge of the matter-universe. This could be imagined as an ever-expanding balloon with all existing matter inside. Archimedes' view of the universe is less clear but his calculations were remarkable for his time and the tools at his disposal.

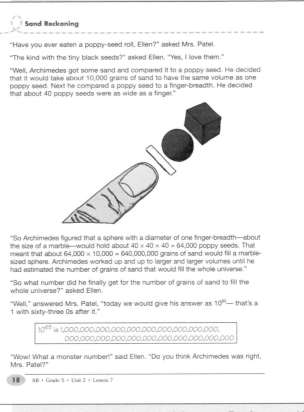

Discussion Prompts

Page 18

- *What does infinite mean? Why do you suppose some people might think that the number of grains needed to fill the universe is an infinite number?*

Infinite means never ending, immeasurably great, or unlimited.

Test Archimedes' approximation. Gather some poppy seeds and line them up. Do you get 40 to be the width of your finger? Is your finger about the same width as a marble? Do you think your approximation for the number of grains of sand in the universe is bigger or smaller than that of Archimedes based on your experiment?

Page 19

- *Write a googol.*

Have a student go to the board and show what a googol looks like. A googol is a 1 with 100 zeros after it.

- *How do you know there is a number larger than a googolplex?*

You can have a googolplex plus one. You can always add one to a number.

Journal Prompt

What do you think about Archimedes' plan to estimate the number of grains of sand in the universe? Why would someone want to know this?

Math Facts

Assign DPP items W and X for more practice with the multiplication and division facts for the 5s and 10s.

Adventure Book - page 18

Sand Reckoning

"Have you ever eaten a poppy-seed roll, Ellen?" asked Mrs. Patel.

"The kind with the tiny black seeds?" asked Ellen. "Yes, I love them."

"Well, Archimedes got some sand and compared it to a poppy seed. He decided that it would take about 10,000 grains of sand to have the same volume as one poppy seed. Next he compared a poppy seed to a finger-breadth. He decided that about 40 poppy seeds were as wide as a finger."

"So Archimedes figured that a sphere with a diameter of one finger-breadth—about the size of a marble—would hold about $40 \times 40 \times 40 = 64,000$ poppy seeds. That meant that about $64,000 \times 10,000 = 640,000,000$ grains of sand would fill a marble-sized sphere. Archimedes worked up and up to larger and larger volumes until he had estimated the number of grains of sand that would fill the whole universe."

"So what number did he finally get for the number of grains of sand to fill the whole universe?" asked Ellen.

"Well," answered Mrs. Patel, "today we would give his answer as 10^{63}— that's a 1 with sixty-three 0s after it."

10^{63} is 1,000,000,000,000,000,000,000,000,000,000, 000,000,000,000,000,000,000,000,000,000,000

"Wow! What a monster number!" said Ellen. "Do you think Archimedes was right, Mrs. Patel?"

18   AB • Grade 5 • Unit 2 • Lesson 7

Adventure Book - page 18

Sand Reckoning

"Well, Ellen," answered Mrs. Patel, "he did very well for his time, but he underestimated the size of the universe by a good bit. Using a modern idea of the size of the universe, we might get about 10^{90} grains of sand."

10^{90} is 1,000,000,000,000,000,000,000,000,000,000, 000,000,000,000,000,000,000,000,000,000, 000,000,000,000,000,000,000,000,000,000

"That must be the biggest number there is!" said Ellen.

"Not at all, Ellen," replied Mrs. Patel. "There's a number called a googol that is even bigger. A googol is a 1 with one hundred 0s after it, 10^{100}."

10^{100} is 10,000,000,000,000,000,000,000,000,000,000, 000,000,000,000,000,000,000,000,000,000, 000,000,000,000,000,000,000,000,000,000, 000,000,000

"A googol! What a silly name." "Who thought of that?" asked Ellen.

"The nine-year-old nephew of Dr. Edward Kasner, a mathematician from New York, thought of it."

"It's fun to think about such big numbers," said Ellen. "Is there an even bigger one?"

"There is always a bigger number, Ellen," answered Mrs. Patel. "The biggest I know of that has a name is a googolplex. A googolplex is a 1 with a googol of 0s after it. If we tried to write a googolplex by writing a 1 and putting a googol of 0s after it, we'd need a piece of paper that would stretch past the farthest star. But even though a googolplex is a huge number, there are still others bigger."

"You mean the numbers keep going on and on forever and ever?" asked Ellen.

"That's right," answered Mrs. Patel.

AB • Grade 5 • Unit 2 • Lesson 7   19

Adventure Book - page 19

Lesson 8

Exponents and Large Numbers

Lesson Overview

Students review the use of exponents. Scientific notation is introduced so students can read, write, and say numbers displayed in scientific notation on a calculator. For example, in Lesson 9 *Stack Up,* students can use their calculators to estimate the number of pennies in a stack that will reach the moon. This number may be displayed on the calculator in scientific notation.

Key Content

- Using exponents.
- Representing large numbers with exponents.
- Multiplying large numbers with ending zeros.
- Reading scientific notation.

Key Vocabulary

- base
- estimate
- exponent
- power
- scientific notation
- standard form

Math Facts

Assign item Y.

Homework

1. Assign *Questions 1–20* in the Homework section of the *Student Guide.*
2. Assign DPP Task Z.

Assessment

Use the open-ended assessment problem in Lesson 9 *Stack Up.*

Curriculum Sequence

Before This Unit

Exponents were introduced in Units 4 and 6 of fourth grade.

Students studied decimals in Unit 15 *Decimal Investigations* in third grade and Unit 10 *Using Decimals* in fourth grade.

After This Unit

Students will work with exponents again in Unit 11 *Number Patterns, Primes, and Fractions.*

Students continue to solve problems involving large numbers, which may appear on calculators in scientific notation. They will study decimals in greater depth in Unit 7.

Materials List

Supplies and Copies

Student	Teacher
Supplies for Each Student • calculator	**Supplies**
Copies	**Copies/Transparencies**

All blackline masters including assessment, transparency, and DPP masters are also on the Teacher Resource CD.

Student Books

Exponents and Large Numbers (*Student Guide* Pages 60–63)

Daily Practice and Problems and Home Practice

DPP items Y–Z (*Unit Resource Guide* Pages 29–30)

Note: Classrooms whose pacing differs significantly from the suggested pacing of the units should use the Math Facts Calendar in Section 4 of the *Facts Resource Guide* to ensure students receive the complete math facts program.

Daily Practice and Problems

Suggestions for using the DPPs are on page 178.

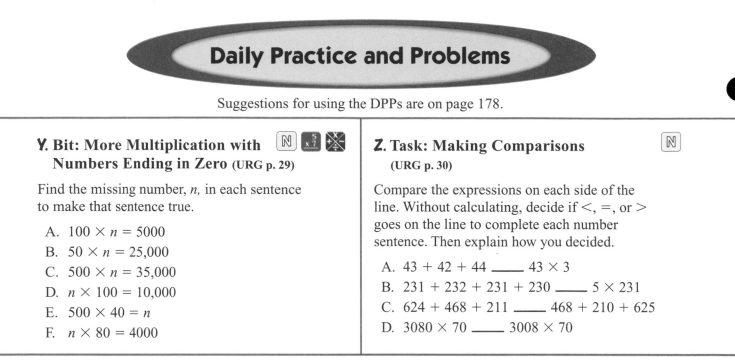

Y. Bit: More Multiplication with Numbers Ending in Zero (URG p. 29)

Find the missing number, n, in each sentence to make that sentence true.

A. $100 \times n = 5000$

B. $50 \times n = 25{,}000$

C. $500 \times n = 35{,}000$

D. $n \times 100 = 10{,}000$

E. $500 \times 40 = n$

F. $n \times 80 = 4000$

Z. Task: Making Comparisons (URG p. 30)

Compare the expressions on each side of the line. Without calculating, decide if $<$, $=$, or $>$ goes on the line to complete each number sentence. Then explain how you decided.

A. $43 + 42 + 44$ _____ 43×3

B. $231 + 232 + 231 + 230$ _____ 5×231

C. $624 + 468 + 211$ _____ $468 + 210 + 625$

D. 3080×70 _____ 3008×70

Have students bring in newspaper articles containing numbers in the millions or billions. Ask them to look specifically for numbers that are written with words and numbers, for example, 2.3 million.

Part 1 Exponents

The *Student Guide* pages for this lesson begin with an overview of exponents that builds on the earlier discussion in the *Adventure Book* in Lesson 7. When exponents are used, the number being multiplied is called the **base.** In the examples below, the base is five. The number of times the base is multiplied is called the **power** or **exponent.** In Example A the exponent (or power) is 4; in Example B the exponent is 3.

A. 5^4 means $5 \times 5 \times 5 \times 5 = 625$
B. 5^3 means $5 \times 5 \times 5 = 125$
C. 5^2 means $5 \times 5 = 25$
D. 5^1 means 5

Encourage students to use the examples above, the examples in the *Student Guide,* and their calculators to answer the following:

- *What does 2^5 mean?* (2^5 means $2 \times 2 \times 2 \times 2 \times 2 = 32$. Encourage students to use correct language in their replies. For example: "Two to the fifth means two times two times two times two times two. That equals 32.")
- *What does 6^3 mean?* (6^3 means $6 \times 6 \times 6 = 216$.)
- *What does 7^2 mean?* (7^2 means $7 \times 7 = 49$. Point out that 7^2 can be read "seven to the second power" or "seven squared.")
- *What does 8^1 mean? What does 9^1 mean? What does 247^1 mean?* (8 to the first power means 8. 9^1 means 9. 247^1 means 247.)

Use **Questions 1–6** in the *Student Guide* to review exponents with students. In particular, ask them to work in groups on **Questions 3–5.** After completing these questions, they should be able to describe the pattern in Figure 34.

$10^1 = 10$	The number of zeros
$10^2 = 100$	in any power of ten
$10^3 = 1000$	written in standard
$10^4 = 10,000$	form is equal to
	the exponent.

Figure 34: *Patterns with powers of ten*

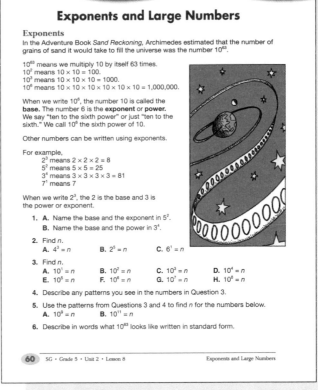

Exponents and Large Numbers

Exponents

In the Adventure Book *Sand Reckoning*, Archimedes estimated that the number of grains of sand it would take to fill the universe was the number 10^{63}.

10^{63} means we multiply 10 by itself 63 times.
10^2 means $10 \times 10 = 100$.
10^3 means $10 \times 10 \times 10 = 1000$.
10^6 means $10 \times 10 \times 10 \times 10 \times 10 \times 10 = 1,000,000$.

When we write 10^6, the number 10 is called the **base.** The number 6 is the **exponent** or **power.** We say "ten to the sixth power" or just "ten to the sixth." We call 10^6 the sixth power of 10.

Other numbers can be written using exponents.

For example,
   2^3 means $2 \times 2 \times 2 = 8$
   5^2 means $5 \times 5 = 25$
   3^4 means $3 \times 3 \times 3 \times 3 = 81$
   7^1 means 7

When we write 2^3, the 2 is the base and 3 is the power or exponent.

1. **A.** Name the base and the exponent in 5^2.
   B. Name the base and the power in 3^4.

2. Find n.
   A. $4^3 = n$ **B.** $2^5 = n$ **C.** $6^1 = n$

3. Find n.
   A. $10^1 = n$ **B.** $10^2 = n$ **C.** $10^3 = n$ **D.** $10^4 = n$
   E. $10^5 = n$ **F.** $10^6 = n$ **G.** $10^7 = n$ **H.** $10^8 = n$

4. Describe any patterns you see in the numbers in Question 3.

5. Use the patterns from Questions 3 and 4 to find n for the numbers below.
   A. $10^9 = n$ **B.** $10^{11} = n$

6. Describe in words what 10^{63} looks like written in standard form.

Student Guide - page 60 (Answers on p. 180)

Content Note

Calculators and Exponents. Different types of scientific calculators use different notation for exponents. Some scientific calculators use a caret (^) to denote exponents. Others use notation such as x^y. Encourage students to follow the manufacturer's directions in using the exponent key on their scientific calculators.

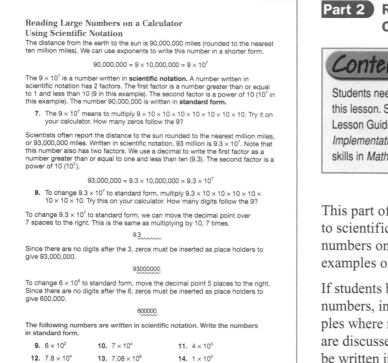

Student Guide - page 61 *(Answers on p. 180)*

Student Guide - page 62 *(Answers on p. 181)*

Content Note

Students need only a familiarity with decimals to complete Part 2 of this lesson. See the Curriculum Sequence at the beginning of the Lesson Guide and the Scope and Sequence in the *Teacher Implementation Guide* for the location of decimal concepts and skills in *Math Trailblazers*.

This part of the lesson provides a gentle introduction to scientific notation so students can read large numbers on calculators. Discuss the definition and examples of scientific notation in the *Student Guide*.

If students brought in newspaper articles with large numbers, include them in the discussion. Find examples where numbers such as 30 million or 5.1 million are discussed. Show students that these numbers can be written in scientific notation using what we know about powers of 10. One million = 1,000,000 = 10^6. So 5.1 million can be written in **scientific notation** as 5.1×10^6. Following the definition and examples in the *Student Guide*, 5.1×10^6 has two factors. The first factor is a number greater than or equal to one and less than ten (5.1 in this example) and the second factor is a power of 10 (10^6 in this example).

5.1 million = $5.1 \times 10^6 = 5.1 \times 10 \times 10 \times 10 \times 10 \times 10 \times 10 = 5,100,000$

Encourage students to experiment with their calculators as they work on this section. *Questions 7* and *8* ask students to multiply expressions like the one above using their calculators. These explorations help students understand how to change numbers written in scientific notation to standard form as in *Questions 9–14.* Check to see that students can correctly write these numbers in standard form. For example, for *Question 10* students change 7×10^4 to standard form. They can multiply $7 \times 10 \times 10 \times 10 \times 10 = 70,000$, which is the same as adding four zeros as shown below.

7
70,000

Question 12 is similar but involves a decimal.

$7.8 \times 10^4 = 7.8 \times 10 \times 10 \times 10 \times 10 = 78,000.$

This is the same as moving the decimal four places to the right as shown here.

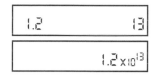

78,000

Questions 15 and *16* ask students to multiply large numbers with ending zeros first mentally or with paper and pencil. Then they use their calculators to find the product of the two numbers. On most scientific calculators the product will be displayed in scientific notation. Two common calculator displays are shown in Figure 35 for the answer to *Question 16.*

1.2	13

$$1.2 \times 10^{13}$$

Figure 35: *400,000 × 30,000,000 in scientific notation on 2 scientific calculators*

Ask students to compare their two answers. By hand, the solution is 12,000,000,000,000 or twelve trillion. Remind students that the product is $4 \times 3 = 12$, followed by 12 zeros. Explain to students that calculators display large numbers in scientific notation. The 13 on the calculator display tells us to multiply by 10, 13 times or $1.2 \times 10 \times 10 \times 10 \times 10 \times 10 \times 10 \times 10 \times 10 \times 10 \times 10 \times 10 \times 10 \times 10$. As noted before, this multiplication can be achieved by moving the decimal point 13 places to the right. We append 12 zeros to give us 12,000,000,000,000. To convince students, have them multiply 1.2 by 10, 13 times together out loud as you write the results on the board: $1.2 \times 10 = 120$; $120 \times 10 = 1200$; $1200 \times 10 = 12,000$, etc.

1.2

12000000000000.

12,000,000,000,000

Figure 36: *Multiplying 1.2 by 10, thirteen times*

Practice more problems as needed. Some are provided below. Ask students to first compute each problem on paper or mentally. Then have them use their calculators and compare the answers.

80,000 × 5,000,000   20,000 × 3,200,000

400,000 × 500,000   30,000 × 800,000,000

For example, 80,000 × 5,000,000 gives 4 followed by an 11 on the calculator. This means multiply 4 by 10, 11 times or move the decimal point 11 places to the right. *Questions 17–24* in the *Student Guide* provide more practice.

At some point, as larger and larger numbers are entered into the calculator, the number becomes too large for the calculator to handle. An error message is given. An interesting challenge is to find the largest number your calculator can handle.

Math Facts

Bit Y from the Daily Practice and Problems provides practice with the 5s and 10s and practice solving problems with ending zeros.

Homework and Practice

- Assign Homework *Questions 1–20* in the *Student Guide.*
- Assign Task Z from the Daily Practice and Problems to practice estimation skills.

Assessment

Use the assessment problem *Stack Up* in Lesson 9 to assess students' abilities to solve problems involving large numbers.

Literature Connection

Schwartz, David M. *How Much Is a Million?* Scholastic Inc., New York, 1985.

A magician illustrates for his friends the magnitude of large numbers by presenting 1 million through four interesting and imaginative questions. One question that is discussed is how many pages in the book are needed to show one million stars.

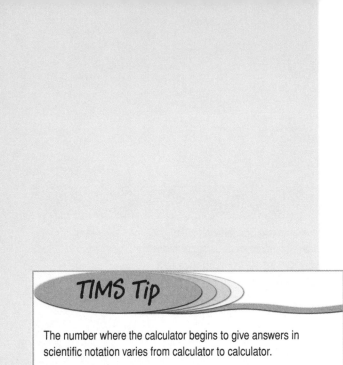

TIMS Tip

The number where the calculator begins to give answers in scientific notation varies from calculator to calculator.

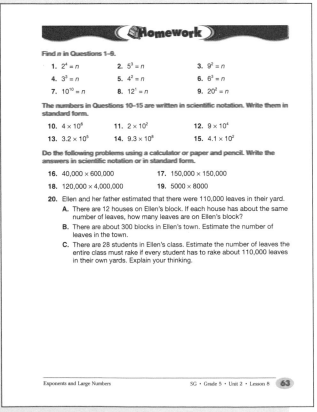

Homework

Find n in Questions 1–9.

1. $2^4 = n$ 2. $5^3 = n$ 3. $9^2 = n$

4. $3^3 = n$ 5. $4^2 = n$ 6. $6^3 = n$

7. $10^{10} = n$ 8. $12^1 = n$ 9. $20^2 = n$

The numbers in Questions 10–15 are written in scientific notation. Write them in standard form.

10. 4×10^6 11. 2×10^2 12. 9×10^4

13. 3.2×10^5 14. 9.3×10^8 15. 4.1×10^2

Do the following problems using a calculator or paper and pencil. Write the answers in scientific notation or in standard form.

16. 40,000 × 600,000   17. 150,000 × 150,000

18. 120,000 × 4,000,000   19. 5000 × 8000

20. Ellen and her father estimated that there were 110,000 leaves in their yard.

  A. There are 12 houses on Ellen's block. If each house has about the same number of leaves, how many leaves are on Ellen's block?

  B. There are about 300 blocks in Ellen's town. Estimate the number of leaves in the town.

  C. There are 28 students in Ellen's class. Estimate the number of leaves the entire class must rake if every student has to rake about 110,000 leaves in their own yards. Explain your thinking.

Exponents and Large Numbers   SG • Grade 5 • Unit 2 • Lesson 8   63

Student Guide - page 63 *(Answers on p. 181)*

At a Glance

Math Facts and Daily Practice and Problems

Assign items Y and Z.

Part 1. Exponents

Discuss the terms base, power, and exponents using the discussion prompts in Part 1 of the Lesson Guide and *Questions 1–6* in the *Student Guide.*

Part 2. Reading Large Numbers on a Calculator Using Scientific Notation

1. Introduce students to scientific notation using *Questions 7–16* of the *Student Guide.*
2. Students practice reading scientific notation using *Questions 17–24.*

Homework

1. Assign *Questions 1–20* in the Homework section of the *Student Guide.*
2. Assign DPP Task Z.

Assessment

Use the open-ended assessment problem in Lesson 9 *Stack Up.*

Connection

Read and discuss *How Much Is a Million?* by David Schwartz.

Answer Key is on pages 180–181.

Notes:

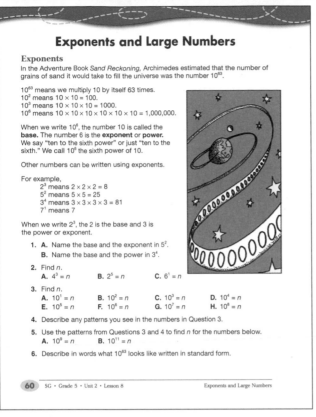

Student Guide - page 60

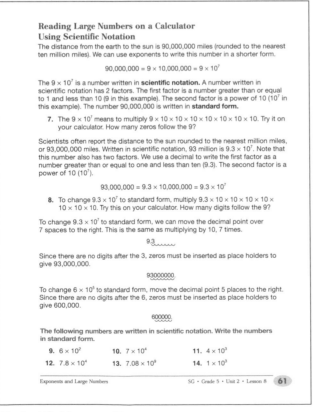

Student Guide - page 61

*Answers and/or discussion are included in the Lesson Guide.

Student Guide (pp. 60–61)

1. **A.** base: 5; exponent: 2
   B. base: 3; power: 4

2. **A.** 64
   B. 32
   C. 6

3. **A.** 10
   B. 100
   C. 1000
   D. 10,000
   E. 100,000
   F. 1,000,000
   G. 10,000,000
   H. 100,000,000

4. Each power of ten can be written as 1 followed by the same number of zeros as the exponent.

5. **A.** 1,000,000,000
   B. 100,000,000,000

6. 1 followed by 63 zeros

7. 90,000,000. There are seven zeros after the 9.

8. 93,000,000. There are seven digits following the 9.

9. 600

10. 70,000*

11. 4000

12. 78,000*

13. 7,080,000,000

14. 1000

Student Guide (pp. 62–63)

15. A. 600,000,000,000,000

    B. 14 zeros

    C. 6×10^{14}

16. A. 12,000,000,000,000

    B. 13 digits

    C. 1.2×10^{13}

17. 1,600,000,000,000; 1.6×10^{12}

18. 100,000,000,000; 1×10^{11}

19. 720,000,000,000; 7.2×10^{11}

20. 490,000,000,000,000; 4.9×10^{14}

21. 12,100,000,000; 1.21×10^{10}

22. 750,000,000,000; 7.5×10^{11}

23. A. 93,000,000

    B. Estimates will vary. About 2,700,000,000 miles ($90,000,000 \times 30$)

24. A. three million, five hundred seventy-three thousand

    B. Estimates will vary. About 28,000,000,000 miles ($4,000,000 \times 7,000$)

Homework

1. 16
2. 125
3. 81
4. 27
5. 16
6. 216
7. 10,000,000,000
8. 12
9. 400
10. 4,000,000
11. 200
12. 90,000
13. 320,000
14. 930,000,000
15. 410

16. 2.4×10^{10}; 24,000,000,000

17. 2.25×10^{10}; 22,500,000,000

18. 4.8×10^{11}; 480,000,000,000

19. 4×10^{7}; 40,000,000

20. A. 1,320,000 leaves ($110,000 \times 12$)

    B. Estimates will vary. One reasonable estimate is 390,000,000 leaves ($300 \times 1,300,000$).

    C. Estimates will vary. One reasonable estimate is 110,000 leaves $\times$ 30 students or 3,300,000 leaves.

---

15. A. Multiply $20,000,000 \times 30,000,000$ without your calculator.
    B. How many zeros follow the 6?
    C. Multiply $20,000,000 \times 30,000,000$ on your calculator.

Calculators automatically put large numbers into scientific notation.

Some calculators show scientific notation like this:

> $6. \times 10^{14}$

Some calculators show 6×10^{14} something like this:

> 6   14

These calculators display the power of 10 in the right corner. They do not show the 10.

16. A. Multiply $400,000 \times 30,000,000$ without your calculator.
    B. How many digits follow the 1?
    C. Multiply $400,000 \times 30,000,000$ with your calculator.

Do the following problems using a calculator. Write the answers in scientific notation and in standard form.

17. $20,000 \times 80,000,000$
18. $2000 \times 50,000,000$
19. $600,000 \times 1,200,000$
20. $7,000,000 \times 70,000,000$
21. $110,000 \times 110,000$
22. $2,500,000 \times 300,000$

23. Earth is about 93 million miles from the sun. Neptune is about 30 times farther from the sun than Earth.
    A. Write the number 93 million in standard form.
    B. About how far is Neptune from the sun?

24. Scientists have found that there are other star systems beyond our own. The very nearest star system is Alpha Centauri. Alpha Centauri is about 7000 times farther from us than Pluto. Pluto is about 3,573,000 miles from Earth.
    A. Write the number 3,573,000 in words.
    B. About how far are we from Alpha Centauri? Explain your thinking.

62 SG • Grade 5 • Unit 2 • Lesson 8   Exponents and Large Numbers

Student Guide - page 62

Homework

Find n in Questions 1–9.

1. $2^4 = n$
2. $5^3 = n$
3. $9^2 = n$
4. $3^3 = n$
5. $4^2 = n$
6. $6^3 = n$
7. $10^{10} = n$
8. $12^1 = n$
9. $20^2 = n$

The numbers in Questions 10–15 are written in scientific notation. Write them in standard form.

10. 4×10^6
11. 2×10^2
12. 9×10^4
13. 3.2×10^5
14. 9.3×10^8
15. 4.1×10^2

Do the following problems using a calculator or paper and pencil. Write the answers in scientific notation or in standard form.

16. $40,000 \times 600,000$
17. $150,000 \times 150,000$
18. $120,000 \times 4,000,000$
19. 5000×8000

20. Ellen and her father estimated that there were 110,000 leaves in their yard.
    A. There are 12 houses on Ellen's block. If each house has about the same number of leaves, how many leaves are on Ellen's block?
    B. There are about 300 blocks in Ellen's town. Estimate the number of leaves in the town.
    C. There are 28 students in Ellen's class. Estimate the number of leaves the entire class must rake if every student has to rake about 110,000 leaves in their own yards. Explain your thinking.

Exponents and Large Numbers   SG • Grade 5 • Unit 2 • Lesson 8 63

Student Guide - page 63

Lesson 9

Stack Up

Estimated Class Sessions
1-2

Lesson Overview

This assessment lesson is an open-ended problem designed to give baseline data on students' abilities to solve problems and communicate solution strategies. Students work in groups to find the number of pennies needed to build a stack tall enough to reach the moon. They may use tools they use in class, including graph paper, calculators, and rulers. Students use the Student Rubrics: *Telling* and *Solving* to develop their problem-solving strategies, explain their solutions in writing, and revise their work. Students place their work on this lesson in their collection folders. By adding this piece to their portfolios, they can compare results on this problem to their work on similar problems during the rest of the school year.

Key Content

- Developing number sense for large numbers.
- Collecting and using data to solve problems.
- Solving extended-response problems and communicating solution strategies.
- Measuring length in centimeters.
- Reading scientific notation.
- Solving problems involving multiplication and division.
- Using the *Solving* and *Telling* Rubrics to self-assess problem-solving skills.

Math Facts

Complete DPP item AA and continue reviewing the multiplication and division facts for the 5s and 10s.

Curriculum Sequence

Before This Unit

Establishing a Baseline

In Unit 1, students used the Student Rubric: *Knowing* as a guide for exemplary work as they completed the lab *Searching the Forest* in Lesson 1. Students included the lab in their collection folders.

After This Unit

Documenting Mathematical Growth

Students will solve similar problems, write about their solution strategies, and include their work in their portfolios so that improvements in their problem-solving abilities can be documented. In particular, students' work with this activity will be compared to open-ended problems in Unit 8 at midyear and Unit 16 at the end of the year.

Materials List

Supplies and Copies

Student	Teacher
Supplies for Each Student • calculator • ruler **Supplies for Each Student Group** • 20 pennies	**Supplies**
Copies • 1 copy of *Stack Up* per student (*Unit Resource Guide* Pages 195–196) • 1 copy of *Centimeter Graph Paper* per student, optional (*Unit Resource Guide* Page 197)	**Copies/Transparencies** • 1 copy of *TIMS Multidimensional Rubric* (*Teacher Implementation Guide*, Assessment section) • 1 transparency or poster of Student Rubrics: *Solving* and *Telling*, optional (*Teacher Implementation Guide*, Assessment section)

All blackline masters including assessment, transparency, and DPP masters are also on the Teacher Resource CD.

Student Books

Student Rubric: *Solving* (*Student Guide* Appendix B and Inside Back Cover)
Student Rubric: *Telling* (*Student Guide* Appendix C and Inside Back Cover)

Daily Practice and Problems and Home Practice

DPP items AA–BB (*Unit Resource Guide* Page 30)

Note: Classrooms whose pacing differs significantly from the suggested pacing of the units should use the Math Facts Calendar in Section 4 of the *Facts Resource Guide* to ensure students receive the complete math facts program.

Assessment Tools

TIMS Multidimensional Rubric (*Teacher Implementation Guide*, Assessment section)

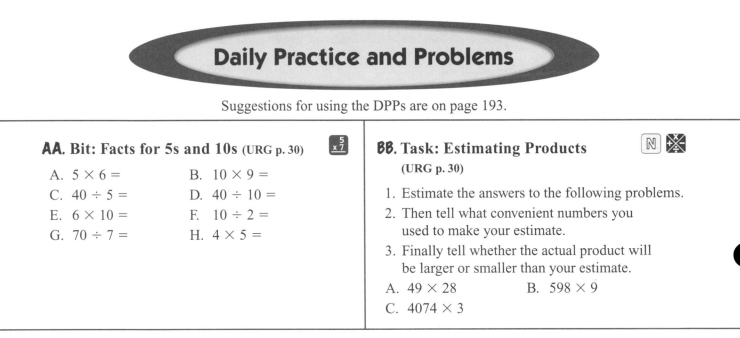

Daily Practice and Problems

Suggestions for using the DPPs are on page 193.

AA. Bit: Facts for 5s and 10s (URG p. 30)

A. $5 \times 6 =$	B. $10 \times 9 =$
C. $40 \div 5 =$	D. $40 \div 10 =$
E. $6 \times 10 =$	F. $10 \div 2 =$
G. $70 \div 7 =$	H. $4 \times 5 =$

BB. Task: Estimating Products (URG p. 30)

1. Estimate the answers to the following problems.
2. Then tell what convenient numbers you used to make your estimate.
3. Finally tell whether the actual product will be larger or smaller than your estimate.

A. 49×28 B. 598×9
C. 4074×3

To begin this activity, read **Question 3** on the *Stack Up* Assessment Pages. Explain to students that they will work together to solve this problem, but first they will need to collect information about pennies. They collect this data by completing **Questions 1–2** on the *Stack Up* Assessment Pages. Groups of two or three students work well for collecting this data. Students should work without consulting you unless they need clarification of a question. Encourage students to use tools available in the classroom such as calculators and rulers.

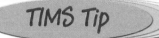

TIMS Tip

As students measure stacks of pennies, ask them to look at their rulers. Is there a small gap between the first centimeter and the end of the ruler? If so, encourage students to develop a strategy that results in accurate measurements.

Since this problem involves very large numbers, calculators are an appropriate tool for solving this problem. Scientific calculators will display the answer in scientific notation. (See Written work from Student C in Figure 39 for a solution from a student who used a scientific calculator.) Although many four-function calculators will not be able to display the final result, students can use them or paper-and-pencil procedures with a strategy similar to the following:

If a stack of 35 pennies measures 5 centimeters, then there will be 70 pennies in a stack that measures 10 cm. Since there are 100 cm in a meter, then there will be 10×70 or 700 pennies in a one-meter stack.

Since there are 1000 meters in a kilometer, there will be 1000×700 pennies or 700,000 pennies in a one-kilometer stack.

The moon is 384,400 kilometers from Earth. So, the number of pennies needed to reach the moon is 384,400 km $\times$ 700,000 pennies. Students can first multiply 3844×7 using paper and pencil or any calculator.

$$\begin{array}{r} 3844 \\ \times \quad 7 \\ \hline 26{,}908 \end{array}$$

Then they complete the calculation using what they know about multiplying with ending zeros. Since there are two zeros at the end of 384,400

and five zeros at the end of 700,000, they add $2 + 5$ or 7 zeros to 26,908. So, it takes about

384,400 km $\times$ 700,000 pennies = 269,080,000,000 pennies to reach the moon.

After student groups complete **Questions 1–2,** they begin work on **Question 3.** You may want students to continue this work in their small groups or have them work independently. Students should use information from **Questions 1–2** to help them find their solution. Note those students who require extra support to complete this task successfully so you can include this information in evaluating their work. Once a solution is reached, students should write a clear explanation of their problem-solving process. Each student should write his or her explanation independently.

Before students begin to write, review the student rubrics (*Solving* and *Telling*), advising them that you will score their work using these rubrics. This will help students more clearly understand your expectations. Encourage students to describe each step in their procedures, including how they gathered data. They should explain how they found each number in any intermediate steps. Give them an opportunity to revise their written explanations based on your comments. For example, you may need to ask a student to explain his or her process more clearly. Or, you may need to remind a student to include units or labels in an explanation.

To assist you in scoring your students' work, questions specific to this activity are listed below:

Solving

- Did students use the data gathered in **Questions 1–2** effectively?
- Are the strategies complete and efficient? For example, do they include gathering data on the number of pennies needed to make a stack 1 meter tall?
- Did students organize their data? For example, did they use a table or graph?
- Did students relate this problem to previously encountered mathematics such as the use of scientific notation on the calculator?
- Did students stick to the problem until they collected enough data and arrived at a solution?
- Did they try to solve the problem a second way to check their solution?
- Did they look back at the problem to see if their data was accurate and the results of their calculations were reasonable?

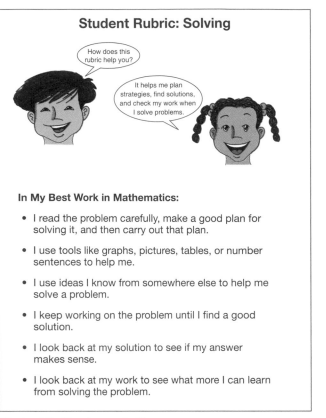

Student Rubric: Solving

How does this rubric help you?

It helps me plan strategies, find solutions, and check my work when I solve problems.

In My Best Work in Mathematics:

• I read the problem carefully, make a good plan for solving it, and then carry out that plan.

• I use tools like graphs, pictures, tables, or number sentences to help me.

• I use ideas I know from somewhere else to help me solve a problem.

• I keep working on the problem until I find a good solution.

• I look back at my solution to see if my answer makes sense.

• I look back at my work to see what more I can learn from solving the problem.

Student Guide - Appendix B

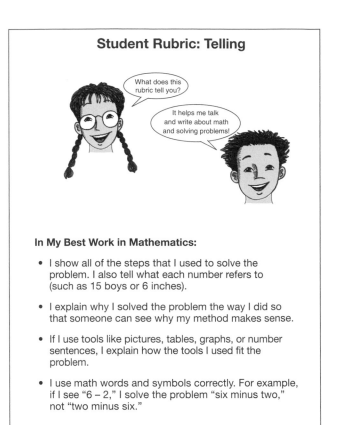

Student Rubric: Telling

What does this rubric tell you?

It helps me talk and write about math and solving problems!

In My Best Work in Mathematics:

• I show all of the steps that I used to solve the problem. I also tell what each number refers to (such as 15 boys or 6 inches).

• I explain why I solved the problem the way I did so that someone can see why my method makes sense.

• If I use tools like pictures, tables, graphs, or number sentences, I explain how the tools I used fit the problem.

• I use math words and symbols correctly. For example, if I see "6 – 2," I solve the problem "six minus two," not "two minus six."

Student Guide - Appendix C

Telling

• Did students explain their procedures?

• Did they describe their data collection?

• Did students clearly describe all their strategies?

• Did they explain how and why they used the numbers in each operation performed?

• Did they use appropriate number sentences and other symbolic representations? For example, did they explain how they converted scientific notation to standard notation?

• Did students label their work, using correct units when appropriate?

Students should add this assessment activity to their collection folders in preparing to begin their portfolios in the following lesson. The purpose of the assessment is to provide a record of each student's problem-solving abilities at the beginning of the year, not to test mastery of concepts taught in this unit. Many students, especially those who are new to *Math Trailblazers,* may not be proficient problem solvers or good communicators at this time. However, students will have many opportunities to enhance their skills in later units. By including a record of students' current abilities in their portfolios, improvements will be clearly evident.

You can score ***Question 3*** using the Telling and Solving dimensions of this rubric. Three examples of student work are scored here using these dimensions of the *TIMS Multidimensional Rubric.* You may also wish to score students' work using the Knowing dimension. By scoring work using more than one dimension, students and parents get a broader view of students' progress. In the examples shown, Student B's solution is incorrect and she earns a low score on the Solving dimension. (She would also earn a low score on the Knowing dimension.) However, a higher score (3) on the Telling dimension tells her that she can communicate well.

Content Note

Different calculators display scientific notation in different ways. The calculator used by Students A, B, and C displays scientific notation as shown here:

```
2.6139      11
```

This display means 2.6139×10^{11} or 261,390,000,000.

Written work from Student A:

700 × 1000 = 700,000. pennies in a km

Then we multipluied 700,000×384,400

It would take 2,690,800,000,000 pennies to reach the moon

2.6908 11

Check this #. (Teacher notes)

The first thing we wanted to find out was how many pennies are in a km. we multiplied 700×1000=700,000 pennies in a km. Then we multiplied 700,000× 384,400=2.6908 then we moved the decimal over eleven times We found out that it would take 2,690,800,000 pennies to reach the moon.

Teacher notes { Check this # - you said you moved the decimal 11 places - did you really do that?

Solving	Level 4	Level 3	Level 2	Level 1
Identifies the elements of the problem and their relationships to one another	All major elements identified	Most elements identified	Some, but shows little understanding of relationships	Few or none
Uses problem-solving strategies which are…	Systematic, complete, efficient, and possibly elegant	Systematic and nearly complete, but not efficient	Incomplete or unsystematic ✗	Not evident or inappropriate
Organizes relevant information…	Systematically and efficiently	Systematically, with minor errors	Unsystematically ✗	Not at all
Relates the problem and solution to previously encountered mathematics and makes connections that are…	At length, elegant, and meaningful	Evident	Brief or logically unsound ✗	Not evident
Persists in the problem-solving process…	At length	Until a solution is reached	Briefly ✗	Not at all
Looks back to examine the reasonableness of the solution and draws conclusions that are…	Insightful and comprehensive	Correct	Incorrect or logically unsound	Not present ✗

Telling	Level 4	Level 3	Level 2	Level 1
Includes response with an explanation and/or description which is…	Complete and clear	Fairly complete and clear	Perhaps ambiguous or unclear	Totally unclear or irrelevant
Presents supporting arguments which are…	Strong and sound	Logically sound, but may contain minor gaps	Incomplete or logically unsound	Not present
Uses pictures, symbols, tables, and graphs which are…	Correct and clearly relevant	Present with minor errors or some-what irrelevant	Present with errors and/or irrelevant	Not present or completely inappropriate
Uses terminology…	Clearly and precisely	With minor errors	With major errors	Not at all

Figure 37: *Student A's work and scores on the rubrics*

Solving: 2

Student A found the number of pennies needed to build a stack tall enough to reach the moon. However, this student needed considerable teacher support while devising his plan. In anecdotal notes, the teacher recorded that student A was unable to use the data gathered in *Questions 1–2* effectively without direction. There is no evidence that Student A looked back at his work to check the reasonableness of his results.

Telling: 2

Student A's written explanation partially explains the procedure he used to arrive at his solution. He did not, however, explain how he arrived at the numbers he used in his calculations. For example, he did not tell us why he multiplied 700 × 1000 to find the number of pennies in a kilometer. It is unclear how the number 700 was obtained. Though the teacher assumed he used the number 1000 because there are 1000 meters in a kilometer, the student did not state this in his explanation.

Written work from Student B:

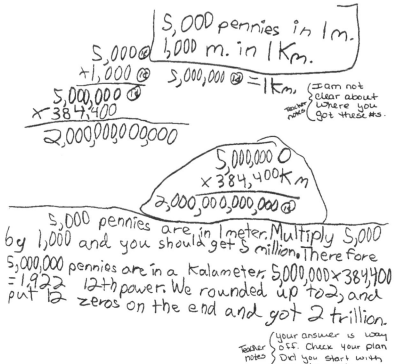

5,000 pennies in 1m.
1,000 m. in 1 Km.

5,000 @
+1,000 @   5,000,000 @ = 1Km.   *(Teacher notes)* I am not clear about where you got these #s.
5,000,000 @
× 384,400
2,000,000,000,000

5,000,000 0
× 384,400 Km
2,000,000,000,000 @

5,000 pennies are in 1meter. Multiply 5,000 by 1,000 and you should get 5 million. Therefore 5,000,000 pennies are in a Kalameter. 5,000,000×384,400 = 1,922 12th power. We rounded up to 2, and put 12 zeros on the end and got 2 trillion.

(Teacher notes) Your answer is way off. Check your plan. Did you start with the right #'s.

Solving	Level 4	Level 3	Level 2	Level 1
Identifies the elements of the problem and their relationships to one another	All major elements identified	Most elements identified	Some, but shows little understanding of relationships ✗	Few or none
Uses problem-solving strategies which are…	Systematic, complete, efficient, and possibly elegant	Systematic and nearly complete, but not efficient	Incomplete or unsystematic ✗	Not evident or inappropriate
Organizes relevant information…	Systematically and efficiently	Systematically, with minor errors ✗	Unsystematically	Not at all
Relates the problem and solution to previously encountered mathematics and makes connections that are…	At length, elegant, and meaningful	Evident	Brief or logically unsound ✗	Not evident
Persists in the problem-solving process…	At length	Until a solution is reached	Briefly ✗	Not at all
Looks back to examine the reasonableness of the solution and draws conclusions that are…	Insightful and comprehensive	Correct	Incorrect or logically unsound	Not present ✗

Telling	Level 4	Level 3	Level 2	Level 1
Includes response with an explanation and/or description which is…	Complete and clear	Fairly complete and clear	Perhaps ambiguous or unclear	Totally unclear or irrelevant
Presents supporting arguments which are…	Strong and sound	Logically sound, but may contain minor gaps	Incomplete or logically unsound	Not present
Uses pictures, symbols, tables, and graphs which are…	Correct and clearly relevant	Present with minor errors or somewhat irrelevant	Present with errors and/or irrelevant	Not present or completely inappropriate
Uses terminology…	Clearly and precisely	With minor errors	With major errors	Not at all

Figure 38: *Student B's work and scores on the rubrics*

Solving: 2

Student B was unable to devise an appropriate plan for solving this problem. The teacher noted that even after verbal prompts, this student was unable to pull the correct data needed from *Questions 1–2*. This student found that a stack of 5000 pennies equals 1 meter. This number is not reasonable given the data that the student collected. The student did not check back and therefore based her plan on incorrect numbers. While Student B showed her work in a somewhat organized way, she was not able to tell the teacher how she arrived at the numbers she used. There is no evidence that Student B looked back at her work to check if her solution was reasonable.

Telling: 3

Though Student B arrived at an incorrect solution to this problem, her explanation of her procedure was fairly complete and clear. She supported her work in a logical manner. Student B did not label her work correctly or use correct units consistently in her explanation.

Written work from Student C:

I took the number 680 because 680 pennies =: 1 meter. Then I x's it by 1000, because 1000 m make 1 km. I got the # 680,000. 680,000 is how many pennies it takes to make 1 km. After that I x's it by 384,400, which is the average of how far away the moon is. When I finished, I got my answer, it takes 261,390,000,000. pennies to reach the moon.

* My calculator did not look like this 261,390,000,000. It looked like this 2.6139 11. I got the number 261,390,000,000 by moving the decimal down 11 spaces and adding 0's to the blank spaces.

(Teacher notes) Did your calculator look like this? How did you get from your calculator display to this #?

Solving	Level 4	Level 3	Level 2	Level 1
Identifies the elements of the problem and their relationships to one another	All major elements identified ✗	Most elements identified	Some, but shows little understanding of relationships	Few or none
Uses problem-solving strategies which are…	Systematic, complete, efficient, and possibly elegant ✗	Systematic and nearly complete, but not efficient	Incomplete or unsystematic	Not evident or inappropriate
Organizes relevant information…	Systematically and efficiently ✗	Systematically, with minor errors	Unsystematically	Not at all
Relates the problem and solution to previously encountered mathematics and makes connections that are…	At length, elegant, and meaningful	Evident ✗	Brief or logically unsound	Not evident
Persists in the problem-solving process…	At length	Until a solution is reached ✗	Briefly	Not at all
Looks back to examine the reasonableness of the solution and draws conclusions that are…	Insightful and comprehensive	Correct	Incorrect or logically unsound	Not present ✗

Telling	Level 4	Level 3	Level 2	Level 1
Includes response with an explanation and/or description which is...	Complete and clear	Fairly complete and clear	Perhaps ambiguous or unclear	Totally unclear or irrelevant
Presents supporting arguments which are...	Strong and sound	Logically sound, but may contain minor gaps	Incomplete or logically unsound	Not present
Uses pictures, symbols, tables, and graphs which are...	Correct and clearly relevant	Present with minor errors or some-what irrelevant	Present with errors and/or irrelevant	Not present or completely inappropriate
Uses terminology...	Clearly and precisely	With minor errors	With major errors	Not at all

Figure 39: *Student C's work and scores on the rubrics*

Solving: 3

Student C devised a plan that incorporated all relevant data from *Questions 1–2.* She used strategies that were efficient and complete. Student C organized her work carefully. However, there is no evidence that Student C looked back at her work to see if her results were reasonable.

Telling: 4

Student C's written explanation was complete and clear. She clearly explained her procedure, telling why she chose the steps that she took. While Student C did not use number sentences to show her work, she did write out her calculations using correct labels and units.

Journal Prompt

Explain how your group worked on this problem together. What role did each group member take? How did your group solve disagreements?

Math Facts

DPP item AA reviews the multiplication and division facts for the 5s and 10s.

Homework and Practice

Assign DPP Task BB, which provides practice estimating products.

Literature Connection

- Cole, Joanna. *The Magic School Bus: Lost in the Solar System.* Scholastic Inc., New York, 1990.

  This book describes a field trip taken by Mrs. Frizzle's class on its magic school bus. Students travel throughout the solar system, visiting the sun, the moon, and the planets. While the story is fiction, many interesting facts are presented. This story can be shared as a read-aloud, but for students to get all the information the book contains, it should also be available for students to read in small groups or independently.

- Schwartz, David M. *If You Made a Million.* Scholastic Inc., New York, 1989.

  In this story, students learn about money by exploring how many pennies, nickels, dimes, or quarters you need to equal 1 dollar, 10 dollars, 100 dollars, and so on up to 1 million dollars. Students are told that a stack of 10,000 pennies ($100) would be 50 feet tall, and a stack of 100 million pennies ($1 million) would be 95 miles tall. Use this book as a discussion starter before starting this assessment activity or as an extension after completing the task.

At a Glance

Math Facts and Daily Practice and Problems

Complete DPP items AA–BB and continue reviewing the multiplication and division facts for the 5s and 10s.

Teaching the Activity

1. Divide students into groups of two or three.

2. Read through *Question 3* on the *Stack Up* Assessment Pages together. Review the Student Rubrics: *Telling* and *Solving*.

3. Students complete *Questions 1–2* in small groups. They may use classroom tools, including calculators, rulers, and graph paper.

4. Make anecdotal records indicating those students who need extra support to solve problems.

5. Students complete *Question 3.* Students can work independently or in small groups to find their solution. However, they write their explanations independently.

6. Review written responses and make suggestions for revision using the student rubrics as guides.

7. Students revise work based on written comments.

8. Score student work using the *TIMS Multidimensional Rubric.*

9. Students place the assessment in their collection folders.

Connection

Read and discuss *The Magic School Bus: Lost in the Solar System* or *If You Made a Million.*

Answer Key is on page 198.

Notes:

Stack Up

Work with a small group to collect data using pennies. Each group will need 20 pennies. You may use any tools that you use in class, including graph paper, a ruler, and a calculator.

1. **A.** Predict how many pennies you will need to build a stack of pennies with a height of 5 cm.

    B. Check your prediction. How many pennies did you need?

    How accurate was your prediction?

2. **A.** How many pennies would you need to build a stack 1 meter tall? (100 cm = 1 m)

    B. Explain how you found your answer.

3. The moon moves around the Earth in an orbit. Its average distance from the Earth is 384,400 km. (1 km = 1000 m) How many pennies would you need to build a stack to reach the moon? Show all your work. Write a paragraph to justify your solution.

Name _____ Date _____

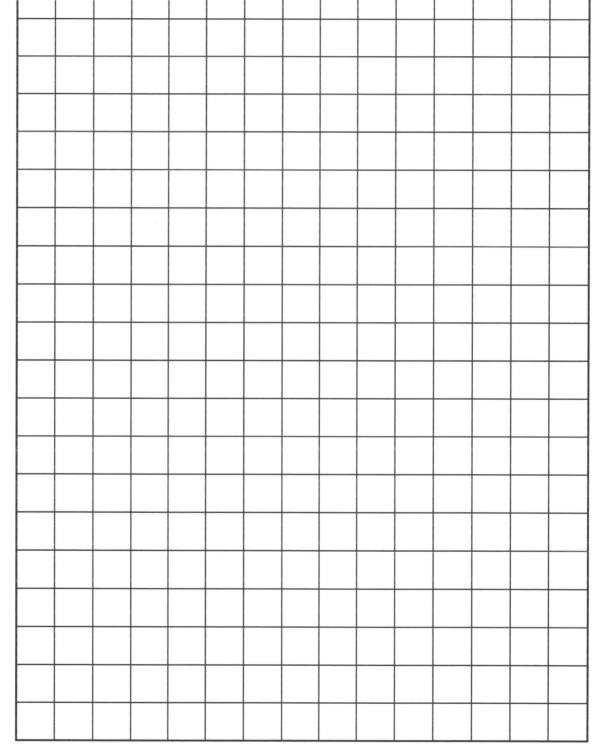

Centimeter Graph Paper, Blackline Master

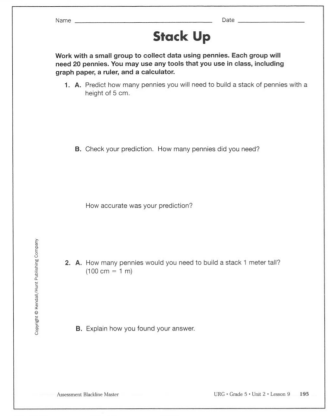

Unit Resource Guide - page 195

Unit Resource Guide (pp. 195–196)

Stack Up*

See Lesson Guide 9 for sample student work graded using the *TIMS Multidimensional Rubric.*

Name _____ Date _____

3. The moon moves around the Earth in an orbit. Its average distance from the Earth is 384,400 km. (1 km = 1000 m) How many pennies would you need to build a stack to reach the moon? Show all your work. Write a paragraph to justify your solution.

196   URG • Grade 5 • Unit 2 • Lesson 9   Assessment Blackline Master

Unit Resource Guide - page 196

*Answers and/or discussion are included in the Lesson Guide.

Lesson 10 Portfolios

Estimated Class Sessions

I

Students begin collecting their work for possible inclusion in their portfolios.

Key Content

- Using portfolios.
- Reflecting on one's work.

Key Vocabulary

- portfolio

Math Facts

Complete DPP item CC.

Assessment

1. Begin student portfolios as a selection of best work.
2. Transfer appropriate documentation of the Unit 2 *Observational Assessment Record* to students' *Individual Assessment Record Sheets*.

Curriculum Sequence

Before This Unit

In Unit 1, students put completed activities and labs in collection folders in anticipation of choosing work to include in a more formal portfolio.

After This Unit

Students will continue to add to their collection folders. Periodically, they will choose pieces to place in their portfolios to document growth over time.

Materials List

Supplies and Copies

Student	Teacher
Supplies for Each Student • folder	**Supplies** • hanging rack or box for storing folders
Copies	**Copies/Transparencies**

All blackline masters including assessment, transparency, and DPP masters are also on the Teacher Resource CD.

Student Books

Portfolios (*Student Guide* Pages 64–65)

Daily Practice and Problems and Home Practice

DPP items CC–DD (*Unit Resource Guide* Page 31)

Note: Classrooms whose pacing differs significantly from the suggested pacing of the units should use the Math Facts Calendar in Section 4 of the *Facts Resource Guide* to ensure students receive the complete math facts program.

Assessment Tools

Observational Assessment Record (*Unit Resource Guide* Pages 15–16)
Individual Assessment Record Sheet (*Teacher Implementation Guide,* Assessment section)

Daily Practice and Problems

Suggestions for using the DPPs are on page 203.

CC. Bit: Quiz: 5s and 10s (URG p. 31) $\boxed{\frac{5}{\times 7}}$

A. $7 \times 5 =$ B. $40 \div 4 =$

C. $10 \div 2 =$ D. $8 \times 10 =$

E. $9 \times 5 =$ F. $6 \times 10 =$

G. $30 \div 6 =$ H. $10 \times 2 =$

I. $15 \div 5 =$ J. $70 \div 10 =$

K. $40 \div 8 =$ L. $5 \times 10 =$

M. $10 \times 3 =$ N. $25 \div 5 =$

O. $90 \div 9 =$ P. $4 \times 5 =$

Q. $10 \times 10 =$

DD. Task: Scientific Notation [N] ✖
(URG p. 31)

1. Explain how to multiply $29{,}000{,}000 \times 600$ without a calculator. What do you get for an answer?

2. Now use your calculator. What does the calculator window show? What do the symbols on the display mean?

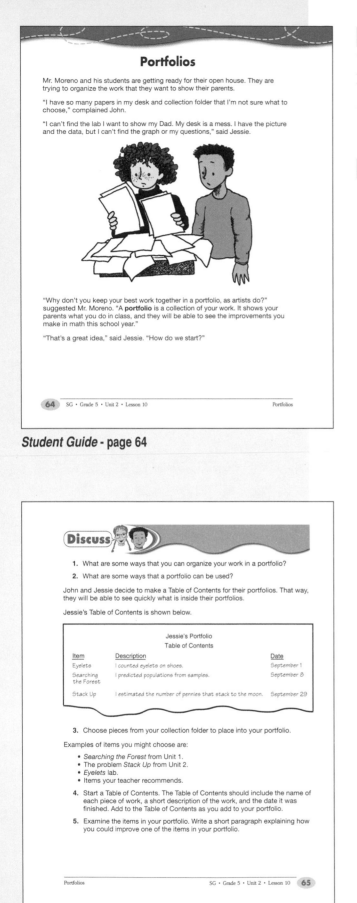

Student Guide - page 64

Student Guide - page 65 (Answers on p. 206)

There are many different approaches to setting up portfolios. We address one procedure in this lesson guide. You may choose a way that is better suited to your classroom. The TIMS Tutor: *Portfolios* offers several tips on organizing portfolios.

Teaching the Activity

Read the *Portfolios* Activity Pages to begin discussion. In addition to the questions posed in the *Student Guide,* you may also ask the following questions:

- *What is a **portfolio?*** (a collection of an artist's work; the case in which an artist carries his or her work; a term investors use in the business community; a collection of student work that shows how a student's skills, attitudes, and knowledge grow over time)

- *Who might use a portfolio?* (artists, business investors, students)

Pass out a folder to each student. Ask them to label it "Portfolio." Explain that they will be using portfolios in math as a way to collect and share their work throughout the school year.

Discuss the intent of the portfolio with your class. You can focus the portfolios on a specific area, such as measurement or graphing, or you may want to focus on communication. Let students know what types of work will be put into the portfolios, who will read them, and what will become of them at the end of each semester (or school year). You should decide approximately how many pieces you will include in the portfolio each semester. While students should select most pieces that will be part of the portfolio, you may insist on including certain pieces. An example might be an assessment activity.

As students complete an activity, they should date it and place it in their collection folders. Every two to three weeks, students should review the contents of their collection folders and choose one or two pieces to include in their portfolios. They may keep the other pieces in the collection folder or take them home.

As students begin to add pieces to their portfolio folders, they should start a table of contents. The table of contents will include the name and date of each entry and a brief description of the activity. Students can also write why they choose to add it to their portfolio. This writing encourages reflection and self-assessment. As part of the process, have students select one piece and write how they might improve it.

Throughout the semester, whole-class and peer consultations will help students review their portfolio work or help in selecting work to include in the portfolio.

Math Facts

DPP item CC is a quiz on the multiplication and division facts for the 5s and 10s. After taking the quiz, students update their *Facts I Know* charts.

Homework and Practice

DPP Task DD provides practice with scientific notation.

Assessment

You should not feel that you must assess the portfolios. The work included in them has most likely already been graded, and the collection itself is a direct indicator of achievement and attitude. If you intend to grade the portfolios, let students know your expectations in advance. Your expectations may include standards for organization, reflective writing, selection of items, and neatness.

For more information about portfolios and assessment, see the TIMS Tutor: *Portfolios* and the Assessment section in the *Teacher Implementation Guide*.

Transfer appropriate documentation from Unit 2 *Observational Assessment Record* to students' *Individual Assessment Record Sheets*.

Extension

Have students design covers for their portfolios.

Literature Connection

Read the poem *Arithmetic* by Carl Sandburg to students. Discuss the difference between mathematics and arithmetic. Students can write about:

- What they think the differences are between mathematics and arithmetic.
- Which line of the poem they think best describes arithmetic.
- A line of the poem that they disagree with.

Other possibilities:

- Draw a picture to illustrate the line of the poem they think best describes arithmetic and tell why they picked that line.
- Write a poem called "Mathematics" similar to Carl Sandburg's poem.
- Write a line for a poem called "Mathematics" and draw a picture to illustrate that line. You can create a class poem by putting students' lines together.

Use Carl Sandburg's poem to assess students' attitudes toward mathematics at the start of the year. Place students' work on this poem in their portfolios. Then at the end of the school year, read and discuss the poem again to see how students' attitudes have changed.

This poem can be found in poetry anthologies or other works such as:

- Sandburg, Carl. *Complete Poems*. Harcourt, Brace, Jovanovich, New York, 1970.

At a Glance

Math Facts and Daily Practice and Problems

Complete DPP items CC and DD.

Teaching the Activity

1. Define portfolios with your class by reading and discussing *Questions 1–2* on the *Portfolios* Activity Pages in the *Student Guide.*
2. Pass out folders and have them label the folders as portfolios.
3. Define the purpose of portfolios for your classroom.
4. Define the type of work to be collected and who will be responsible for collecting it.
5. Students select work from their collection folders to include in their portfolios.
6. Students begin a Table of Contents following the example in the *Student Guide.*
7. Students design covers for portfolios. (optional)

Assessment

1. Begin student portfolios as a selection of best work.
2. Transfer appropriate documentation from the Unit 2 *Observational Assessment Record* to students' *Individual Assessment Record Sheets.*

Extension

Have students design covers for their portfolios.

Connection

Read and discuss *Arithmetic* by Carl Sandburg.

Answer Key is on page 206.

Notes:

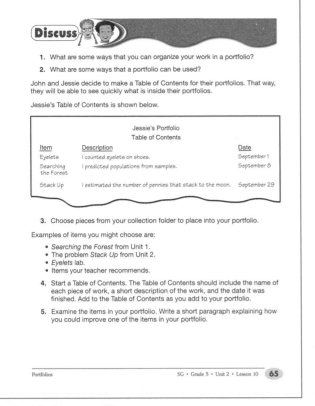

Student Guide - page 65

Student Guide (p. 65)

1. The class may choose to focus on one particular area, such as measurement or graphing, or you may want to focus on communication or problem solving. Decide about how many pieces will be included in the portfolio each semester. Students will keep all their work in a collection folder. Each activity should be dated. As students begin to choose pieces from their collection folders to add to their portfolios, they should start a table of contents. The table of contents will include the name and date of each entry and a brief description of the activity. Students may also write why they choose to add each piece to the portfolio.*

2. The portfolio will show how students' skills and knowledge grow over time. Teachers, parents, and students can review the portfolios.*

3.*

4.*

5.*

*Answers and/or discussion are included in the Lesson Guide.

Discovery Assignment Book (p. 10)

Part 2. Numbers in the Hundreds and Thousands

1.

2. **A.** 3 digits; 512 + 369 is less than 1000; it is about 880.

   B. 2 digits. The difference is less than 100.

   C. 5 digits. Estimating, the sum will be more than 10,000.

   D. $10 \times 65 = 650$, $20 \times 65 = 1300$. The answer is in the middle. Add 300 to 650 and get 950. Subtract 300 from 1300 and get 1000. The number in the middle of 950 and 1000 is 975—3 digits.

   E. 4 digits. The difference is about 4000.

Name _____ **Date** _____

PART 2 Numbers in the Hundreds and Thousands

1. Number the line below from 0 to 10,000. Skip count by 1000s.

|_____|____|____|____|____|____|____|____|____|____|
0

Read each of the facts about the United States below. Then make a tick mark on the number line above to show where each number falls on the line. Label the tick mark with the appropriate letter.

   A. The highest bridge over water in the world—1053 feet—is in Colorado. It is the suspension bridge over the Royal Gorge of the Arkansas River.

   B. Mount Katahdin is the highest spot in Maine—5268 feet. This mountain is the first place in the entire United States to get hit with sunlight when the sun rises in the morning.

   C. The world's tallest living redwood tree on record stands 367 feet tall. Redwood trees are native to California.

2. Without actually finding exact answers to these problems, give the number of digits in the answer. Explain how you know.

   A. 512 + 369

   B. 843 − 776

   C. 2190 + 8756

   D. 15 × 65

   E. 4589 − 637

Discovery Assignment Book - page 10

Discovery Assignment Book (p. 11)

Part 3. Multiplication Practice

1. **A.** 144

   B. 1028

   C. 23,975

   D. 30,472

   E. 540

   F. 1860

   G. 3792

   H. 1710

2. **A.** 18 pairs

   B. $15,264

   C. More than $100. Estimates will vary. He would save about $1.20 a day. $1.20 × 180 is about $1 × 200 or $200.

Name _____ **Date** _____

PART 3 Multiplication Practice

1. Solve the following problems using paper and pencil only. Estimate to make sure your answers make sense.

   A. 24 × 6 =   **B.** 257 × 4 =   **C.** 4795 × 5 =   **D.** 3809 × 8 =

   E. 12 × 45 =   **F.** 30 × 62 =   **G.** 79 × 48 =   **H.** 95 × 18 =

2. Solve the following problems. Choose an appropriate method: mental math, paper and pencil, or a calculator. *Hint:* Sometimes drawing a picture of a problem can help you solve it.

   A. Jessie's mother is shopping in a sports store. Socks are on sale for $2.95 for 3 pairs. If she has $20, how many pairs of socks can she buy?

   B. Lin's father purchased a brand new car. His car payments are $318 monthly for 4 years. After 4 years, how much will he have paid for his car?

   C. Last year Mr. Moreno bought two cans of soda from the machine each day at school. This year he decided to drink water instead. If one can of soda costs 65¢, will Mr. Moreno save more or less than $100 in one school year? (A school year has about 180 school days.)

Discovery Assignment Book - page 11

Name _____ Date _____

PART 4 **Solving Problems**

Solve the following problems. Choose an appropriate method for each:
mental math, paper and pencil, or a calculator. Explain your solutions.

1. A mouse can have a litter of as many as 16 pups. A mouse can have up to 6 litters each year. About how many mice, at most, can one mouse produce in 6 years?

2. The U.S. government recommends that girls between the ages of 11 and 14 consume 2400 calories of food a day. Boys of the same age should consume 2800 calories.
   A. A boy follows these guidelines. Will he consume more or less than 25,000 calories in one week?

   B. In one week, how many more calories should a boy eat than a girl?

3. One of the longest running Broadway musical plays ran for about 15 years. On average, there were 409 performances each year.
   A. About how many performances were there in all over the 15 years?

   B. About how many performances were there each month?

Copyright © Kendall/Hunt Publishing Company

12 DAB • Grade 5 • Unit 2   BIG NUMBERS

Discovery Assignment Book - page 12

Discovery Assignment Book (p. 12)

Part 4. Solving Problems

1. Estimates will vary. 10 pups $\times$ 36 litters $=$ 360 pups; 20 pups $\times$ 36 litters $=$ 720 pups; Between 360 and 720. About 500 pups.

2. **A.** Less than 25,000. 3000 $\times$ 7 $=$ 21,000

   B. 400 per day more $\times$ 7 $=$ 2800 calories

3. **A.** Estimates will vary. Between 10 $\times$ 400 $=$ 4000 and 20 $\times$ 400 $=$ 8000—6000 performances is a reasonable estimate.

   B. 15 years $\times$ 12 months in a year $=$ 180 months; 6000 $\div$ 180 $=$ about 33 performances a month

Glossary

This glossary provides definitions of key vocabulary terms in the Grade 5 lessons. Locations of key vocabulary terms in the curriculum are included with each definition. Components Key: URG = *Unit Resource Guide* and SG = *Student Guide.*

A

Acute Angle (URG Unit 6; SG Unit 6)
An angle that measures less than 90°.

Acute Triangle (URG Unit 6 & Unit 15; SG Unit 6 & Unit 15)
A triangle that has only acute angles.

All-Partials Multiplication Method (URG Unit 2)
A paper-and-pencil method for solving multiplication problems. Each partial product is recorded on a separate line. (*See also* partial product.)

$$\begin{array}{r} 186 \\ \times\ 3 \\ \hline 18 \\ 240 \\ 300 \\ \hline 558 \end{array}$$

Altitude of a Triangle (URG Unit 15; SG Unit 15)
A line segment from a vertex of a triangle perpendicular to the opposite side or to the line extending the opposite side; also, the length of this line. The altitude is also called the height of the triangle.

Angle (URG Unit 6; SG Unit 6)
The amount of turning or the amount of opening between two rays that have the same endpoint.

Arc (URG Unit 14; SG Unit 14)
Part of a circle between two points. (*See also* circle.)

Area (URG Unit 4 & Unit 15; SG Unit 4 & Unit 15)
A measurement of size. The area of a shape is the amount of space it covers, measured in square units.

Average (URG Unit 1 & Unit 4; SG Unit 1 & Unit 4)
A number that can be used to represent a typical value in a set of data. (*See also* mean, median, and mode.)

Axes (URG Unit 10; SG Unit 10)
Reference lines on a graph. In the Cartesian coordinate system, the axes are two perpendicular lines that meet at the origin. The singular of axes is axis.

B

Base of a Triangle (URG Unit 15; SG Unit 15)
One of the sides of a triangle; also, the length of the side. A perpendicular line drawn from the vertex opposite the base is called the height or altitude of the triangle.

Base of an Exponent (URG Unit 2; SG Unit 2)
When exponents are used, the number being multiplied. In $3^4 = 3 \times 3 \times 3 \times 3 = 81$, the 3 is the base and the 4 is the exponent. The 3 is multiplied by itself 4 times.

Base-Ten Pieces (URG Unit 2; SG Unit 2)
A set of manipulatives used to model our number system as shown in the figure below. Note that a skinny is made of 10 bits, a flat is made of 100 bits, and a pack is made of 1000 bits.

Base-Ten Shorthand (URG Unit 2)
A graphical representation of the base-ten pieces as shown below.

Nickname	Picture	Shorthand
bit		•
skinny		/
flat		
pack		

Benchmarks (SG Unit 7)
Numbers convenient for comparing and ordering numbers, e.g., $0, \frac{1}{2}, 1$ are convenient benchmarks for comparing and ordering fractions.

Best-Fit Line (URG Unit 3; SG Unit 3)
The line that comes closest to the points on a point graph.

Binning Data (URG Unit 8; SG Unit 8)
Placing data from a data set with a large number of values or large range into intervals in order to more easily see patterns in the data.

Bit (URG Unit 2; SG Unit 2)
A cube that measures 1 cm on each edge. It is the smallest of the base-ten pieces and is often used to represent 1. (*See also* base-ten pieces.)

C

Cartesian Coordinate System (URG Unit 10; SG Unit 10)
A method of locating points on a flat surface by means of an ordered pair of numbers. This method is named after its originator, René Descartes. (*See also* coordinates.)

Categorical Variable (URG Unit 1; SG Unit 1)
Variables with values that are not numbers. (*See also* variable and value.)

Center of a Circle (URG Unit 14; SG Unit 14)
The point such that every point on a circle is the same distance from it. (*See also* circle.)

Centiwheel (URG Unit 7; SG Unit 7)
A circle divided into 100 equal sections used in exploring fractions, decimals, and percents.

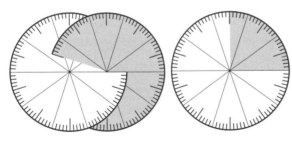

Central Angle (URG Unit 14; SG Unit 14)
An angle whose vertex is at the center of a circle.

Certain Event (URG Unit 7; SG Unit 7)
An event that has a probability of 1 (100%).

Chord (URG Unit 14; SG Unit 14)
A line segment that connects two points on a circle. (*See also* circle.)

Circle (URG Unit 14; SG Unit 14)
A curve that is made up of all the points that are the same distance from one point, the center.

Circumference (URG Unit 14; SG Unit 14)
The distance around a circle.

Common Denominator (URG Unit 5 & Unit 11; SG Unit 5 & Unit 11)
A denominator that is shared by two or more fractions. A common denominator is a common multiple of the denominators of the fractions. 15 is a common denominator of $\frac{2}{3}$ ($= \frac{10}{15}$) and $\frac{4}{5}$ ($= \frac{12}{15}$) since 15 is divisible by both 3 and 5.

Common Fraction (URG Unit 7; SG Unit 7)
Any fraction that is written with a numerator and denominator that are whole numbers. For example, $\frac{3}{4}$ and $\frac{9}{4}$ are both common fractions. (*See also* decimal fraction.)

Commutative Property of Addition (URG Unit 2)
The order of the addends in an addition problem does not matter, e.g., $7 + 3 = 3 + 7$.

Commutative Property of Multiplication (URG Unit 2)
The order of the factors in a multiplication problem does not matter, e.g., $7 \times 3 = 3 \times 7$. (*See also* turn-around facts.)

Compact Method (URG Unit 2)
Another name for what is considered the traditional multiplication algorithm.

$$\begin{array}{r} {}^{2\,1}186 \\ \times\ 3 \\ \hline 558 \end{array}$$

Composite Number (URG Unit 11; SG Unit 11)
A number that has more than two distinct factors. For example, 9 has three factors (1, 3, 9) so it is a composite number.

Concentric Circles (URG Unit 14; SG Unit 14)
Circles that have the same center.

Congruent (URG Unit 6 & Unit 10; SG Unit 6)
Figures that are the same shape and size. Polygons are congruent when corresponding sides have the same length and corresponding angles have the same measure.

Conjecture (URG Unit 11; SG Unit 11)
A statement that has not been proved to be true, nor shown to be false.

Convenient Number (URG Unit 2; SG Unit 2)
A number used in computation that is close enough to give a good estimate, but is also easy to compute with mentally, e.g., 25 and 30 are convenient numbers for 27.

Convex (URG Unit 6)
A shape is convex if for any two points in the shape, the line segment between the points is also inside the shape.

Coordinates (URG Unit 10; SG Unit 10)
An ordered pair of numbers that locates points on a flat surface relative to a pair of coordinate axes. For example, in the ordered pair (4, 5), the first number (coordinate) is the distance from the point to the vertical axis and the second coordinate is the distance from the point to the horizontal axis. (*See also* axes.)

Corresponding Parts (URG Unit 10; SG Unit 10)
Matching parts in two or more figures. In the figure below, Sides AB and A′B′ are corresponding parts.

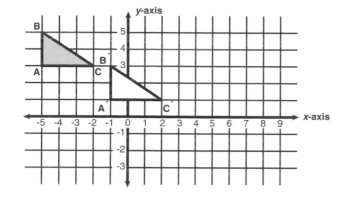

Cryptography (SG Unit 11) The study of secret codes.

Cubic Centimeter (URG Unit 13)
The volume of a cube that is one centimeter long on each edge.

D

Data (SG Unit 1)
Information collected in an experiment or survey.

Decagon (URG Unit 6; SG Unit 6)
A ten-sided, ten-angled polygon.

Decimal (URG Unit 7; SG Unit 7)
1. A number written using the base ten place value system.
2. A number containing a decimal point.

Decimal Fraction (URG Unit 7; SG Unit 7)
A fraction written as a decimal. For example, 0.75 and 0.4 are decimal fractions and $\frac{75}{100}$ and $\frac{4}{10}$ are the equivalent common fractions.

Degree (URG Unit 6; SG Unit 6)
A degree (°) is a unit of measure for angles. There are 360 degrees in a circle.

Denominator (URG Unit 3; SG Unit 3)
The number below the line in a fraction. The denominator indicates the number of equal parts in which the unit whole is divided. For example, the 5 is the denominator in the fraction $\frac{2}{5}$. In this case the unit whole is divided into five equal parts. (*See also* numerator.)

Density (URG Unit 13; SG Unit 13)
The ratio of an object's mass to its volume.

Diagonal (URG Unit 6)
A line segment that connects nonadjacent corners of a polygon.

Diameter (URG Unit 14; SG Unit 14)
1. A line segment that connects two points on a circle and passes through the center.
2. The length of this line segment.

Digit (SG Unit 2)
Any one of the ten symbols 0, 1, 2, 3, 4, 5, 6, 7, 8, 9. The number 37 is made up of the digits 3 and 7.

Dividend (URG Unit 4 & Unit 9; SG Unit 4 & Unit 9)
The number that is divided in a division problem, e.g., 12 is the dividend in 12 ÷ 3 = 4.

Divisor (URG Unit 2, Unit 4, & Unit 9; SG Unit 2, Unit 4, & Unit 9)
In a division problem, the number by which another number is divided. In the problem 12 ÷ 4 = 3, the 4 is the divisor, the 12 is the dividend, and the 3 is the quotient.

Dodecagon (URG Unit 6; SG Unit 6)
A twelve-sided, twelve-angled polygon.

E

Endpoint (URG Unit 6; SG Unit 6)
The point at either end of a line segment or the point at the end of a ray.

Equally Likely (URG Unit 7; SG Unit 7)
When events have the same probability, they are called equally likely.

Equidistant (URG Unit 14)
At the same distance.

Equilateral Triangle (URG Unit 6, Unit 14, & Unit 15)
A triangle that has all three sides equal in length. An equilateral triangle also has three equal angles.

Equivalent Fractions (URG Unit 3; SG Unit 3)
Fractions that have the same value, e.g., $\frac{2}{4} = \frac{1}{2}$.

Estimate (URG Unit 2; SG Unit 2)
1. To find *about* how many (as a verb).
2. A number that is *close to* the desired number (as a noun).

Expanded Form (SG Unit 2)
A way to write numbers that shows the place value of each digit, e.g., 4357 = 4000 + 300 + 50 + 7.

Exponent (URG Unit 2 & Unit 11; SG Unit 2 & Unit 11)
The number of times the base is multiplied by itself. In $3^4 = 3 \times 3 \times 3 \times 3 = 81$, the 3 is the base and the 4 is the exponent. The 3 is multiplied by itself 4 times.

Extrapolation (URG Unit 13; SG Unit 13)
Using patterns in data to make predictions or to estimate values that lie beyond the range of values in the set of data.

F

Fact Families (URG Unit 2; SG Unit 2)
Related math facts, e.g., 3 × 4 = 12, 4 × 3 = 12, 12 ÷ 3 = 4, 12 ÷ 4 = 3.

Factor Tree (URG Unit 11; SG Unit 11)
A diagram that shows the prime factorization of a number.

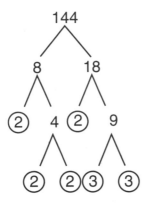

Factors (URG Unit 2 & Unit 11; SG Unit 2 & Unit 11)
1. In a multiplication problem, the numbers that are multiplied together. In the problem $3 \times 4 = 12$, 3 and 4 are the factors.
2. Numbers that divide a number evenly, e.g., 1, 2, 3, 4, 6, and 12 are all the factors of 12.

Fair Game (URG Unit 7; SG Unit 7)
A game in which it is equally likely that any player will win.

Fewest Pieces Rule (URG Unit 2)
Using the least number of base-ten pieces to represent a number. (*See also* base-ten pieces.)

Fixed Variables (URG Unit 4; SG Unit 3 & Unit 4)
Variables in an experiment that are held constant or not changed, in order to find the relationship between the manipulated and responding variables. These variables are often called controlled variables. (*See also* manipulated variable and responding variable.)

Flat (URG Unit 2; SG Unit 2)
A block that measures 1 cm $\times$ 10 cm $\times$ 10 cm. It is one of the base-ten pieces and is often used to represent 100. (*See also* base-ten pieces.)

Flip (URG Unit 10; SG Unit 10)
A motion of the plane in which the plane is reflected over a line so that any point and its image are the same distance from the line.

Forgiving Division Method
(URG Unit 4; SG Unit 4)
A paper-and-pencil method for division in which successive partial quotients are chosen and subtracted from the dividend, until the remainder is less than the divisor. The sum of the partial quotients is the quotient. For example, $644 \div 7$ can be solved as shown at the right.

$$
\begin{array}{r}
92 \\
7\overline{)644} \\
\underline{140} \quad 20 \\
504 \\
\underline{350} \quad 50 \\
154 \\
\underline{140} \quad 20 \\
14 \\
\underline{14} \quad 2 \\
0 \quad 92
\end{array}
$$

Formula (SG Unit 11 & Unit 14)
A number sentence that gives a general rule. A formula for finding the area of a rectangle is Area = length $\times$ width, or $A = l \times w$.

Fraction (URG Unit 7; SG Unit 7)
A number that can be written as a/b where a and b are whole numbers and b is not zero.

G

Googol (URG Unit 2)
A number that is written as a 1 with 100 zeroes after it (10^{100}).

Googolplex (URG Unit 2)
A number that is written as a 1 with a googol of zeroes after it.

H

Height of a Triangle (URG Unit 15; SG Unit 15)
A line segment from a vertex of a triangle perpendicular to the opposite side or to the line extending the opposite side; also, the length of this line. The height is also called the altitude.

Hexagon (URG Unit 6; SG Unit 6)
A six-sided polygon.

Hypotenuse (URG Unit 15; SG Unit 15)
The longest side of a right triangle.

I

Image (URG Unit 10; SG Unit 10)
The result of a transformation, in particular a slide (translation) or a flip (reflection), in a coordinate plane. The new figure after the slide or flip is the image of the old figure.

Impossible Event (URG Unit 7; SG Unit 7)
An event that has a probability of 0 or 0%.

Improper Fraction (URG Unit 3; SG Unit 3)
A fraction in which the numerator is greater than or equal to the denominator. An improper fraction is greater than or equal to one.

Infinite (URG Unit 2)
Never ending, immeasurably great, unlimited.

Interpolation (URG Unit 13; SG Unit 13)
Making predictions or estimating values that lie between data points in a set of data.

Intersect (URG Unit 14)
To meet or cross.

Isosceles Triangle (URG Unit 6 & Unit 15)
A triangle that has at least two sides of equal length.

J

K

L

Lattice Multiplication
(URG Unit 9; SG Unit 9)
A method for multiplying that uses a lattice to arrange the partial products so the digits are correctly placed in the correct place value columns. A lattice for $43 \times 96 = 4128$ is shown at the right.

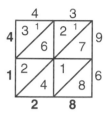

Legs of a Right Triangle (URG Unit 15; SG Unit 15)
The two sides of a right triangle that form the right angle.

Length of a Rectangle (URG Unit 4 & Unit 15; SG Unit 4 & Unit 15)
The distance along one side of a rectangle.

Line
A set of points that form a straight path extending infinitely in two directions.

Line of Reflection (URG Unit 10)
A line that acts as a mirror so that after a shape is flipped over the line, corresponding points are at the same distance (equidistant) from the line.

Line Segment (URG Unit 14)
A part of a line between and including two points, called the endpoints.

Liter (URG Unit 13)
Metric unit used to measure volume. A liter is a little more than a quart.

Lowest Terms (SG Unit 11)
A fraction is in lowest terms if the numerator and denominator have no common factor greater than 1.

M

Manipulated Variable (URG Unit 4; SG Unit 4)
In an experiment, the variable with values known at the beginning of the experiment. The experimenter often chooses these values before data is collected. The manipulated variable is often called the independent variable.

Mass (URG Unit 13)
The amount of matter in an object.

Mean (URG Unit 1 & Unit 4; SG Unit 1 & Unit 4)
An average of a set of numbers that is found by adding the values of the data and dividing by the number of values.

Measurement Division (URG Unit 4)
Division as equal grouping. The total number of objects and the number of objects in each group are known. The number of groups is the unknown. For example, tulip bulbs come in packages of 8. If 216 bulbs are sold, how many packages are sold?

Median (URG Unit 1; SG Unit 1)
For a set with an odd number of data arranged in order, it is the middle number. For an even number of data arranged in order, it is the mean of the two middle numbers.

Meniscus (URG Unit 13)
The curved surface formed when a liquid creeps up the side of a container (for example, a graduated cylinder).

Milliliter (ml) (URG Unit 13)
A measure of capacity in the metric system that is the volume of a cube that is one centimeter long on each side.

Mixed Number (URG Unit 3; SG Unit 3)
A number that is written as a whole number followed by a fraction. It is equal to the sum of the whole number and the fraction.

Mode (URG Unit 1; SG Unit 1)
The most common value in a data set.

Mr. Origin (URG Unit 10; SG Unit 10)
A plastic figure used to represent the origin of a coordinate system and to indicate the directions of the x- and y- axes. (and possibly the z-axis).

N

N-gon (URG Unit 6; SG Unit 6)
A polygon with N sides.

Negative Number (URG Unit 10; SG Unit 10)
A number less than zero; a number to the left of zero on a horizontal number line.

Nonagon (URG Unit 6; SG Unit 6)
A nine-sided polygon.

Numerator (URG Unit 3; SG Unit 3)
The number written above the line in a fraction. For example, the 2 is the numerator in the fraction $\frac{2}{5}$. In this case, we are interested in two of the five parts. (*See also* denominator.)

Numerical Expression (URG Unit 4; SG Unit 4)
A combination of numbers and operations, e.g., $5 + 8 \div 4$.

Numerical Variable (URG Unit 1; SG Unit 1)
Variables with values that are numbers. (*See also* variable and value.)

O

Obtuse Angle (URG Unit 6; SG Unit 6)
An angle that measures more than 90°.

Obtuse Triangle (URG Unit 6 & Unit 15; SG Unit 6 & Unit 15)
A triangle that has an obtuse angle.

Octagon (URG Unit 6; SG Unit 6)
An eight-sided polygon.

Ordered Pair (URG Unit 10; SG Unit 10)
A pair of numbers that gives the coordinates of a point on a grid in relation to the origin. The horizontal coordinate is given first; the vertical coordinate is given second. For example, the ordered pair (5, 3) gives the coordinates of the point that is 5 units to the right of the origin and 3 units up.

Origin (URG Unit 10; SG Unit 10)
The point at which the x- and y-axes intersect on a coordinate plane. The origin is described by the ordered pair (0, 0) and serves as a reference point so that all the points on the plane can be located by ordered pairs.

P

Pack (URG Unit 2; SG Unit 2)
A cube that measures 10 cm on each edge. It is one of the base-ten pieces and is often used to represent 1000. (*See also* base-ten pieces.)

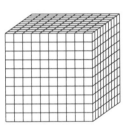

Parallel Lines
(URG Unit 6 & Unit 10)
Lines that are in the same direction. In the plane, parallel lines are lines that do not intersect.

Parallelogram (URG Unit 6)
A quadrilateral with two pairs of parallel sides.

Partial Product (URG Unit 2)
One portion of the multiplication process in the all-partials multiplication method, e.g., in the problem 3×186 there are three partial products: $3 \times 6 = \underline{18}$, $3 \times 80 = \underline{240}$, and $3 \times 100 = \underline{300}$. (*See also* all-partials multiplication method.)

Partitive Division (URG Unit 4)
Division as equal sharing. The total number of objects and the number of groups are known. The number of objects in each group is the unknown. For example, Frank has 144 marbles that he divides equally into 6 groups. How many marbles are in each group?

Pentagon (URG Unit 6; SG Unit 6)
A five-sided polygon.

Percent (URG Unit 7; SG Unit 7)
Per hundred or out of 100. A special ratio that compares a number to 100. For example, 20% (twenty percent) of the jelly beans are yellow means that out of every 100 jelly beans, 20 are yellow.

Perimeter (URG Unit 15; SG Unit 15)
The distance around a two-dimensional shape.

Period (SG Unit 2)
A group of three places in a large number, starting on the right, often separated by commas as shown at the right.

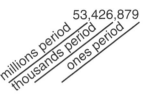

Perpendicular Lines (URG Unit 14 & Unit 15; SG Unit 14)
Lines that meet at right angles.

Pi (π) (URG Unit 14; SG Unit 14)
The ratio of the circumference to diameter of a circle. $\pi = 3.14159265358979.\ldots$ It is a nonterminating, nonrepeating decimal.

Place (SG Unit 2)
The position of a digit in a number.

Place Value (URG Unit 2; SG Unit 2)
The value of a digit in a number. For example, the 5 is in the hundreds place in 4573, so it stands for 500.

Polygon (URG Unit 6; SG Unit 6)
A two-dimensional connected figure made of line segments in which each endpoint of every side meets with an endpoint of exactly one other side.

Population (URG Unit 1 Unit 1)
A collection of persons or things whose properties will be analyzed in a survey or experiment.

Portfolio (URG Unit 2; SG Unit 2)
A collection of student work that show how a student's skills, attitudes, and knowledge change over time.

Positive Number (URG Unit 10; SG Unit 10)
A number greater than zero; a number to the right of zero on a horizontal number line.

Power (URG Unit 2; SG Unit 2)
An exponent. Read 10^4 as, "ten to the fourth power" or "ten to the fourth." We say 10,000 or 10^4 is the fourth power of ten.

Prime Factorization (URG Unit 11; SG Unit 11)
Writing a number as a product of primes. The prime factorization of 100 is $2 \times 2 \times 5 \times 5$.

Prime Number (URG Unit 11; SG Unit 11)
A number that has exactly two factors: itself and 1. For example, 7 has exactly two distinct factors, 1 and 7.

Probability (URG Unit 7; SG Unit 1 & Unit 7)
A number from 0 to 1 (0% to 100%) that describes how likely an event is to happen. The closer that the probability of an event is to one, the more likely the event will happen.

Product (URG Unit 2; SG Unit 2)
The answer to a multiplication problem. In the problem $3 \times 4 = 12$, 12 is the product.

Proper Fraction (URG Unit 3; SG Unit 3)
A fraction in which the numerator is less than the denominator. Proper fractions are less than one.

Proportion (URG Unit 3 & Unit 13; SG Unit 13)
A statement that two ratios are equal.

Protractor (URG Unit 6; SG Unit 6)
A tool for measuring angles.

Q

Quadrants (URG Unit 10; SG Unit 10)
The four sections of a coordinate grid that are separated by the axes.

Quadrilateral (URG Unit 6; SG Unit 6)
A polygon with four sides. (*See also* polygon.)

Quotient (URG Unit 4 & Unit 9; SG Unit 2, Unit 4, & Unit 9)
The answer to a division problem. In the problem $12 \div 3 = 4$, the 4 is the quotient.

R

Radius (URG Unit 14; SG Unit 14)
1. A line segment connecting the center of a circle to any point on the circle.
2. The length of this line segment.

Ratio (URG Unit 3 & Unit 12; SG Unit 3 & Unit 13)
A way to compare two numbers or quantities using division. It is often written as a fraction.

Ray (URG Unit 6; SG Unit 6)
A part of a line with one endpoint that extends indefinitely in one direction.

Rectangle (URG Unit 6; SG Unit 6)
A quadrilateral with four right angles.

Reflection (URG Unit 10)
(*See* flip.)

Regular Polygon (URG Unit 6; SG Unit 6; DAB Unit 6)
A polygon with all sides of equal length and all angles equal.

Remainder (URG Unit 4 & Unit 9; SG Unit 4 & Unit 9)
Something that remains or is left after a division problem. The portion of the dividend that is not evenly divisible by the divisor, e.g., $16 \div 5 = 3$ with 1 as a remainder.

Repeating Decimals (SG Unit 9)
A decimal fraction with one or more digits repeating without end.

Responding Variable (URG Unit 4; SG Unit 4)
The variable whose values result from the experiment. Experimenters find the values of the responding variable by doing the experiment. The responding variable is often called the dependent variable.

Rhombus (URG Unit 6; SG Unit 6)
A quadrilateral with four equal sides.

Right Angle (URG Unit 6; SG Unit 6)
An angle that measures 90°.

Right Triangle (URG Unit 6 & Unit 15; SG Unit 6 & Unit 15)
A triangle that contains a right angle.

Rubric (URG Unit 1)
A scoring guide that can be used to guide or assess student work.

S

Sample (URG Unit 1)
A part or subset of a population.

Scalene Triangle (URG Unit 15)
A triangle that has no sides that are equal in length.

Scientific Notation (URG Unit 2; SG Unit 2)
A way of writing numbers, particularly very large or very small numbers. A number in scientific notation has two factors. The first factor is a number greater than or equal to one and less than ten. The second factor is a power of 10 written with an exponent. For example, 93,000,000 written in scientific notation is 9.3×10^7.

Septagon (URG Unit 6; SG Unit 6)
A seven-sided polygon.

Side-Angle-Side (URG Unit 6 & Unit 14)
A geometric property stating that two triangles having two corresponding sides with the included angle equal are congruent.

Side-Side-Side (URG Unit 6)
A geometric property stating that two triangles having corresponding sides equal are congruent.

Sides of an Angle (URG Unit 6; SG Unit 6)
The sides of an angle are two rays with the same endpoint. (*See also* endpoint and ray.)

Sieve of Eratosthenes (SG Unit 11)
A method for separating prime numbers from nonprime numbers developed by Eratosthenes, an Egyptian librarian, in about 240 BCE.

Similar (URG Unit 6; SG Unit 6)
Similar shapes have the same shape but not necessarily the same size.

Skinny (URG Unit 2; SG Unit 2)
A block that measures 1 cm × 1 cm × 10 cm.
It is one of the base-ten pieces
and is often used to represent 10.
(*See also* base-ten pieces.)

Slide (URG Unit 10; SG Unit 10)
Moving a geometric figure in the plane by moving every point of the figure the same distance in the same direction. Also called translation.

Speed (URG Unit 3 & Unit 5; SG Unit 3 & Unit 5)
The ratio of distance moved to time taken, e.g.,
3 miles/1 hour or 3 mph is a speed.

Square (URG Unit 6 & Unit 14; SG Unit 6)
A quadrilateral with four equal sides and four right angles.

Square Centimeter (URG Unit 4; SG Unit 4)
The area of a square that is 1 cm long on each side.

Square Number (URG Unit 11)
A number that is the product of a whole number multiplied by itself. For example, 25 is a square number since $5 \times 5 = 25$. A square number can be represented by a square array with the same number of rows as columns. A square array for 25 has 5 rows of 5 objects in each row or 25 total objects.

Standard Form (SG Unit 2)
The traditional way to write a number, e.g., standard form for three hundred fifty-seven is 357. (*See also* expanded form and word form.)

Standard Units (URG Unit 4)
Internationally or nationally agreed-upon units used in measuring variables, e.g., centimeters and inches are standard units used to measure length and square centimeters and square inches are used to measure area.

Straight Angle (URG Unit 6; SG Unit 6)
An angle that measures 180°.

T

Ten Percent (URG Unit 4; SG Unit 4)
10 out of every hundred or $\frac{1}{10}$.

Tessellation (URG Unit 6 & Unit 10; SG Unit 6)
A pattern made up of one or more repeated shapes that completely covers a surface without any gaps or overlaps.

Translation
(*See* slide.)

Trapezoid (URG Unit 6)
A quadrilateral with exactly one pair of parallel sides.

Triangle (URG Unit 6; SG Unit 6)
A polygon with three sides.

Triangulating (URG Unit 6; SG Unit 6)
Partitioning a polygon into two or more nonoverlapping triangles by drawing diagonals that do not intersect.

Turn-Around Facts (URG Unit 2)
Multiplication facts that have the same factors but in a different order, e.g., $3 \times 4 = 12$ and $4 \times 3 = 12$. (*See also* commutative property of multiplication.)

Twin Primes (URG Unit 11; SG Unit 11)
A pair of prime numbers whose difference is 2. For example, 3 and 5 are twin primes.

U

Unit Ratio (URG Unit 13; SG Unit 13)
A ratio with a denominator of one.

V

Value (URG Unit 1; SG Unit 1)
The possible outcomes of a variable. For example, red, green, and blue are possible values for the variable *color.* Two meters and 1.65 meters are possible values for the variable *length.*

Variable (URG Unit 1; SG Unit 1)
1. An attribute or quantity that changes or varies. (*See also* categorical variable and numerical variable.)
2. A symbol that can stand for a variable.

Variables in Proportion (URG Unit 13; SG Unit 13)
When the ratio of two variables in an experiment is always the same, the variables are in proportion.

Velocity (URG Unit 5; SG Unit 5)
Speed in a given direction. Speed is the ratio of the distance traveled to time taken.

Vertex (URG Unit 6; SG Unit 6)
A common point of two rays or line segments that form an angle.

Volume (URG Unit 13)
The measure of the amount of space occupied by an object.

W

Whole Number
Any of the numbers 0, 1, 2, 3, 4, 5, 6 and so on.

Width of a Rectangle (URG Unit 4 & Unit 15; SG Unit 4 & Unit 15)
The distance along one side of a rectangle is the length and the distance along an adjacent side is the width.

Word Form (SG Unit 2)
A number expressed in words, e.g., the word form for 123 is "one hundred twenty-three." (*See also* expanded form and standard form.)

X

Y

Z